Health, the Individual, and Integrated Medicine

Health, the Individual, and Integrated Medicine

Revisiting an Aesthetic of Health Care

David Aldridge

Jessica Kingsley Publishers
London and New York

First published in the United Kingdom in 2004
by Jessica Kingsley Publishers Ltd
116 Pentonville Road
London N1 9JB, England
and
29 West 35th Street, 10th fl.
New York, NY 10001-2299, USA
www.jkp.com

Copyright © David Aldridge 2004

Library of Congress Cataloging in Publication Data
Aldridge, David, 1947-
Health, the individual, and integrated medicine : revisiting an aesthetic of health care / David Aldridge.-- 1st American ed.
  p. ; cm.
Includes bibliographical references and index.
ISBN 1-84310-232-3 (pbk.)
 1. Alternative medicine. 2. Integrated delivery of health care. 3. Medical anthropology. 4. Medicine--Research--Philosophy.
 [DNLM: 1. Biomedical Research. 2. Complementary Therapies. 3. Esthetics--psychology. 4. Patient Care--psychology. WB 890 A365h 2004] I. Title.
 R733.A434 2004
 615.5 dc22

2004000479

British Library Cataloguing in Publication Data
A CIP catalogue record for this book is available from the British Library

ISBN 1 84310 232 3

Printed and Bound in Great Britain by
Athenaeum Press, Gateshead, Tyne and Wear

Contents

This book is dedicated to Lucanne Magill who integrates music therapy into palliative care at Memorial Sloan-Kettering Cancer Center, New York and who sings with me daily no matter how far we are apart

Preface

My research career began as an angry response to my own lack of knowledge and to the recalcitrance of modern medicine to the needs of the people that I was counselling. Turning the energy of that emotion into the flame of motivation fuelling the research endeavour has taken some time. Apart from a few burnt fingers over the years, I hope that the heat has generated a little light in the realm of understanding what it is to fall sick and be a part of the process of healing.

The story begins in 1980. I had been working voluntarily for the Samaritans on the night shift. It was the usual Friday night with the regular callers and some new voices requiring comfort during the dark hours of the morning. As the shift closed, a colleague came into the centre from her nursing shift on the ward of the local hospital. There had been five new admissions for attempted suicide in the night. From their ages, and what she knew of them, it was clear that none had called the previous night. Either we were failing in our service to provide adequate counselling or the service itself was missing a group of young people completely. Most of my callers had been older and known to me. I then began a search to find out why we were missing such distress in what was a rural community where it should have been easy to coordinate our initiatives. By asking doctors and psychologists, nurses and social workers, priests and teachers, it was clear that a need was easily recognized, but we were all at a loss about what to do. Then the breakthrough came: 'Why not ask the patients themselves?' This perspective has been at the heart of my research since then. We know it now as qualitative research, but as far as I knew then it just seemed a sensible way of finding out what we needed to know. Ask and people will tell you. What I didn't realize at the time was that this would be seen as a rather unusual stance to take.

At the same time as this personal methodological breakthrough was taking place, I also realized how angry many of us were that we were so helpless in the face of the challenge of suicide. Suicidal behaviour threatened us in a way that made our every effort appear redundant. How easy it was to blame these deviant patients for their non-compliance with our carefully structured and well-meaning interventions. However, when we heard the stories of what was happening, most of us knew how fortunate we were not to have been faced by their difficulties. Yet, in the face of this helplessness, there was an anger at the psychiatric services. Over and over again I was hearing medical practitioners say that suicide was a completely unpredictable phenomenon. Although there was a vast literature about suicide, the act was a result of individual choice and this choice was totally unreasonable and a sign of a disturbed personality. Working with the suicidal revealed a completely different reality. From the patient's perspective, the causal chain of events leading to suicide was very clear. This was no idiosyncratic response by a deviant personality but a final response to hopelessness in a context of unmitigated distress. Knowing that, what was I going to do about it? And what was I going to do with the anger that I felt at a profession?

Academia calls

There was only one way to go and that was to change the world with a PhD study. Now everybody, except doctoral students in the first flush of acceptance, knows that you do not change the world with research. In those heady days of 1982, aged 35 and with a grant from the Open University, the world of academia beckoned seductively. At last, the chance to do something seriously and make some contribution to science. Remember that this motivation was fuelled by an anger aiming to set the world to rights. This motivation is what I seek in my doctoral students today, that small flame that burns to understand, to make sense of the world, to make a contribution. The whole process of researching will attempt to douse that flame. Idealism becomes tempered by the ways of the world, and the arrogance of anger becomes refined in the face of broadened knowledge. That is the process of researching, but the initial flame has to be present – we have to burn.

My research lasted three years and I emerged as a proud doctoral fellow from the Open University with the conviction that this piece of research about suicidal behaviour from an ecosystemic perspective would change the landscape of professional practice (Aldridge 1984a, 1984b, Aldridge and Dallos 1986; Aldridge and Rossiter 1983, 1984, 1985). Wasn't that why I had done research? At last I could begin a job where students would be taught from my perspective, and, as I thought then, the only true perspective. My academic career could really begin – there would surely be an offer to publish and universities would see how audaciously new such ideas were. Out with the old, and redundant, and in with the new, dynamic systems perspective. We have to remember that in the 1980s everything was systems this, systems that. Ripe for holism, we had outgrown both socialism and reductionism. Yet life has a wonderful way of bringing us down to earth – from doctoral student to the ranks of the unemployed in one fell swoop. So much for research as a passport to a golden future.

What was I going to do? When asked, I could only think about doing research. Not only was a fire lit, it wasn't so easily extinguished. However, it was a totally impractical career stance to take as nobody wanted research. Community services were being faced with massive cutbacks, teaching posts were being lopped from university budgets, research was seen as a luxury. Once more I returned to voluntary work. The theme of dying had been a central concept working with the suicidal and during this time I had begun to talk with cancer sufferers and their families. Local church groups were working together to help the dying and there was a growing ecumenical movement around the concept of healing that emphasized a lay involvement (Aldridge 1986, 1987a, 1987b, 1987c, 1987d).

As synchronicity would have it, I made contact with a bishop in the Church of England who was interested in the practice of healing in the Church. While it was difficult enough to get other church members interested in healing, it was even more difficult getting medical researchers interested in the phenomenon. Although there were general practitioners (GPs) interested in healing, who in a university department was going to jeopardize their career in looking at such a concept?

Fortunately, someone without a career to jeopardize could take a look at what was happening and this is what I did. It was the focus of my first book about healing in the Church (Aldridge 1987a). Like the work with suicidal patients, it was concerned with what both practitioners and patients had to say. Both were expert informants. Linking both pieces of work was a concern with dying. The central part of healing ministries was working with the chronically ill and the dying. Just as suicide patients had exhausted the resources of those with whom they had lived, many of the cancer patients and their families had exhausted the resources both of their own bodies and their medical practitioners (Aldridge 1987b, 1987c, 1987d, 1988b). Furthermore, for the suicidal and the dying, all hope had gone. From this perspective, I began to understand the spiritual need being expressed by those in distress. At that time expressing such a need, or saying that you had lost your relationship to your God, was to invite doubts about your psychological condition. Again, that flame of anger burned fiercer: 'Why, in the very hour of our deepest distress, is it not possible to speak openly with our primary caregiver about what distresses us, about what lies heavy in our hearts?'

Anyone with a smattering of psychological knowledge will see that this was an angry young man seeking justification in the world, a rampant narcissism determined to prove others wrong and himself right. All well and true. Yet somehow there was a small truth about the advocacy needs of patients, that they knew best about their lives, that if we openly listened we could indeed bring, with them as partners, a resolution of distress. What I could not understand then, as I fail to understand now, is why medical practitioners, with their claims to being scientists, systematically deny knowledge from the human social sciences of anthropology, psychology and sociology. But even more pronounced was the attitude of the Church and medicine, two bastions of culture, to lay knowledge and understanding. The dismissal of lay approaches effectively divorced the sufferer from his own healing resources (Aldridge 1988c).

The streets of London

During my doctoral work I had made friends with Derek Chase who was a trainee in general medical practice. He knew my family well and we shared similar interests. If you like cricket, you can say that you share similar interests. Eventually, he moved away from the rural town where I was living and made his mark in London. While there he began to write to me about the exciting work he was doing in general practice, the concept of holistic medicine. This was in 1986 and there was a sudden eruption of discourse about medical alternatives and holistic practice, complementary medicine and healing. Suddenly, what had seemed esoteric and confined to the Church was finding a resonance in other initiatives springing up throughout Europe (Aldridge 1989a). We knew already, at least those of us involved with different psychotherapeutic movements, that the humanistic psychology and family therapy movements in the USA had begun to challenge orthodox approaches. For someone who was an undergraduate in the 1960s, these movements weren't strange. We were former hippies growing staid. At one time we would have said that this was our karma, but fortunately the word has fallen out of favour, although, as you can see, it serves its nostalgic purpose.

There was a holistic medicine conference around this time and I was fortunate enough, and probably cheap enough, to make an analysis of a questionnaire enquiry used at the conference. With that money I bought my first computer, an Amstrad word processor, and was set upon the road writing my own papers. For those of us who have struggled with typewriters and two-finger typing, literally cutting copy and pasting it together, the word processor was a boon. With a hot word processor and data from the conference I was able to knit together a little paper for the newsletter of the organization responsible for the conference. It was hardly the *New England Journal of Medicine* but from this modest start I was contacted about working in an innovatory, exciting venture that was being started in the Department of General Practice at St Mary's Hospital Medical School in London, which eventually became known as the Crypt Project.

Our first meeting was in Derek Chase's flat over the ubiquitous pot of English tea, where we wove all sorts of plans for research. I remember being adamant about not wanting to concentrate on clinical controlled trials of alternative medicine because the methodology was alien to the questions and interests that we seemed to have together about health care delivery. A substantial consideration was that I also had no experience of such clinical trials but, lacking any sense of modesty, that consideration failed to dawn upon me at that moment. Throughout the years I have experienced the same problem over and over again; many of us talk about research, and debate actively about which methods to use, without having any real research experience or, perhaps more importantly, any clinical research experience. Clinical practice is a messy laboratory and the purity of academia is often polluted by day-to-day realities. This is not to say that I am against controlled clinical trials. My position is that such trials are one of the research methods that we have in the toolbox of research. There are many valid methods; finding the appropriate method to answer the question that we are asking is the central issue. To force all questions into one method is methodolatry, not methodology. Unfortunately, we have the same problem today with the concept of evidence-based medicine. The concept is sound when it stays within its own borders. When randomized controlled trials become the only evidentiary basis for health care delivery then we have a triumph of a scientific technocracy that ignores the caring and social dimension of health care delivery.

The Crypt Project

Anyway, to return to the Crypt Project. At first I turned the project down. Somehow, it did not sound quite right. However, as my friend pointed out, I was unemployed and where would I ever get the chance again as a social scientist to work in such a prestigious medical project? How true, and how easy it is to succumb to vanity. But it was work and before long I was grateful to have the chance to work in such a project. What it also meant was working away from my home and family in the week. This was both a curse and a blessing and is something that I now take into consideration when planning research projects with colleagues. For protracted projects it is important to consider the personnel management of those involved. We learn how to research, we learn how to do clinical practice, some learn how to manage clinical practice, but how many of us learn how to manage research projects?

Once the project was underway, we began to come up against the difficulties of doing research with a third party budget. Unfortunately, the prime sponsor died and a trust was set up to administer the funds. Their expectations about research were different to those that we had planned initially and the trust administrators themselves suggested a research committee. Things were going rapidly downhill as I was expecting to be in control of the research and now a committee was going to decide on issues of which I had previously been in charge. It is from these experiences that I emphasize the politics of research management. For my then boss, it was even more difficult. He was stuck between a loyalty to me as his researcher and a loyalty to the supervising research committee. That I was a social scientist researcher became a thorn in the medical flesh, so to speak, as I will now illustrate.

We identified chronic asthma as a problem then, as it is today, that challenged conventional health care practice. At the same time, we wanted to introduce acupuncture into general medical practice. From the literature it appeared that acupuncture could provide some relief that we could assess both subjectively, through patient diaries, and objectively, through airway impedance measures. The literature was quite diffuse and varied in its findings. A point of focus was the methodology to be used. The main points were that I thought it important to use the acupuncture sites that the acupuncturist wanted to use, which might vary from patient to patient, and not use prespecified sites. Otherwise, we would have a trial of needling and not acupuncture as I, or my acupuncturist colleague, understood it. I then wrote a paper about the proposal for a clinical trial of acupuncture for the treatment of chronic asthma in adult patients (see Chapter 3). For the project this was a first, submitting a paper about a specific alternative medicine to an established medical journal, and I was excited about the outcome. Once we could break into the mainstream of medical publishing I believed that we would be setting a precedent. At this time, we have to remember, the British Medical Association was criticizing alternative medicine very strongly (Pietroni and Aldridge 1987).

One morning, I was confronted by an irate boss, fresh from a visit to a member of the research committee. A former senior official in the general practice hierarchy, he informed me that such a paper, as the committee member saw it, would never be published. Being directly responsible for the project, he felt terribly let down in the situation as he had relied upon me to give him that research support he needed. Research itself was to lend credibility and validity to what we were attempting to do. The major criticism of the paper was that the paper was too controversial and political to be published. True, I write like that, that is how social scientists are taught to write. In that moment the writing was not just in the paper but on the wall for me. However, all was not gloom and doom.

As the research committee news about the paper was being delivered, the postman was delivering a letter about the very paper itself. *The Journal of the Royal Society of Medicine* had accepted the paper with the commentary from the editor that it was exactly what they needed. The Royal Society of Medicine at that time was active in promoting a sensible debate between alternative medical practitioners and conventional medical approaches through a series of symposia supported by the Prince of Wales. We had, then, the first success that we sought, but this was hollow. I believed myself to be vindicated but, as we all know, there is nothing more annoying than a self-righteous researcher and my days were numbered at the project. My presence was causing conflict for the research committee and I was becoming unhappy about not being able to do the work that I wanted to do.

This is not an isolated incident for researchers. While clinicians work in teams and have support from their colleagues, researchers have often failed to recognize the need for collegial research support. In planning research, it is vital to offer the researcher a clear management structure for support, and supervision when necessary.

Over the sea and far away

Within the Crypt Project, we also had an independent department for music therapy with whom we were attempting to collaborate on research projects. One of my colleagues at that time said that although we were the avant garde in our own eyes, many of our ideas had already been put into practice in Germany. She had worked in the general hospital in Herdecke, a hospital based on anthroposophy principles using the teachings of Rudolf Steiner. The debate about medical alternatives had been a hot one in Germany, particularly concerning the use of herbal medicines, and, coincidentally, I had used the papers from two researchers at this hospital to support my ethical arguments against the sole use of clinical controlled trials in medical practice. So packing up my bags, and without any knowledge of German, I visited the university hospital to see what they were doing. Indeed, they were practising holistic medicine using conventional medical practice with herbal remedies, massage, oils, dietary practices, creative arts therapies, the use of fairy tales in psychiatry, physiotherapy and eurhythmy as they had been for years. Admittedly, the structure was not that of general medical practice in England, but the principle on which German medicine is based is that there was a freer access to the hospital for patients.

The situation was worsening for me in England; there were researchers knocking at the door who could do the job better than I could. Yet, redemption was in sight. Konrad Schily, the President of the University at Witten Herdecke, had heard that I was visiting the university and wanted to speak with me. He and I had the same vision for the way in which medicine and the arts could work together, that both sets of knowledge were necessary for the practice of medicine and, more importantly, for the training of medical practitioners. We both questioned the efficiency of clinical trials when conducted in isolation from other forms of research; we also questioned the purpose for which medical research was being done. In this environment it was also possible to talk about the spiritual dimension of knowledge, about the ramifications of hope and despair for clinical practice and patient recovery, even the process of dying.

Eventually, I was offered a job at the university after a spell as a self-employed research consultant (another term for saying that I would do anything rather then be unemployed). Once in Germany, I could work as I saw fit, being paid a good salary but being given no research budget. Over the following years, everything that we had planned together over Derek Chase's dining table came to pass, although not in the time span that we had hoped, and not in the working configuration either.

The Royal Society of Medicine were adventurous enough to publish a series of speculative papers about music and communication (Aldridge 1989c), decision making in health care (Aldridge 1990a), the delivery of health care alternatives (Aldridge 1990b), music therapy in the treatment of coma patients (Aldridge, Gustorff and Hannich 1990), aesthetics in the practice of medical research (Aldridge 1991a), spiritual considerations in healing (Aldridge 1991c), ethics and education (Aldridge 1992b) and music therapy as assessment and therapy with Alzheimer's patients (Aldridge 1993a). The reader will find these reflected in the following chapters.

My impulse to be a researcher proved to be the right one, though I did need to find the appropriate setting.

Coda

Times have changed. From those early days of championing holistic medicine and wrestling with the British Medical Association about the validity of alternative medicine, and negotiating the validity of the term 'complementary medicine', we now have a situation where we can reasonably talk about integrative medicine and that is evident both in practice and research. The music therapy practice examples in Chapters 8 and 9 were made with Lucanne Magill at the Integrated Medicine Department at Memorial Sloan Kettering in New York.

The delivery of health care is still a contentious issue. The initial assumptions by Beveridge were that the cost of the National Health Service in Britain would fall as therapy brought about reductions in illness. Instead we have a spectrum of redefined health needs that have continually expanded. Health care needs are increasingly medicalized and self-care is becoming a lost cause abandoned to a consumer culture of medical services. What were once called alternative and complementary approaches have been commodified as modern health care. Yet nothing changes; rules governing guidelines for the application of the medical product, misguidedly called a service, are controlled by the recommendations of an increasing medical elite, the purveyors of evidence-based medicine. These guardians of the medical scientific culture have undertaken to engineer the delivery of health care based on a set of rules that are far removed from the everyday practice of clinical medicine and health care delivery. Evidence based medicine can tell us little about suffering and dying, nor about healing. Neither does it celebrate those artisans of clinical practice where tradition and expertise are the daily tools of the trade. Expertise is not evidence but in the healing relationship it is paramount. Medical bureaucracy is establishing an orthodoxy that is impoverishing our healing cultures. By denying recognition of a variety of evidences for healing, then we are denying our communities the right to understand their own healing resources and express their own needs. We may have a statistical basis for successful treatment but suffering will continue.

One thread that runs through the tapestry of the following documents is that of lay involvement in healing. This is sometimes expressed as if we should consult lay advice as an adjunct to our professional opinion. But I would turn this around and argue that we should discover how best our specialist knowledge fits into the ecology of everyday understandings of those whom we serve. We perform our health the majority of the time without doctors and therapists. Health is not simply an integration of medical interventions, it includes care as a cultural and social activity of which we all participate.

Another thread running through the rug of ideas is that of the aesthetic. While we argue for the scientific in medicine, we must not neglect the aesthetic. We have seen this in our work with multiple sclerosis patients. When treated with music therapy over a year, depression was lifted and anxiety alleviated but, above all, self-acceptance was improved. There were no functional changes in terms of improved mobility. However, with a change in self-identity from being stigmatized as a chronically sick, degenerative person (multiple sclerosis is termed a neuro-degenerative disease), to that of being a person with creative abilities, we saw an improvement in well-being. We perform our lives and this performance is assessed not only on functional scales but also in terms of aesthetic criteria.

What have I learned from all this? First, if you want to do research it is a lonely road. It is advisable to organize research supervision and ask for regular research support, even if this is informal. Simply organizing someone to talk with on a regular basis helps, even if they are not a researcher. Research may take you away from your home and family for lengths of time. Time is needed to think, and writing needs seclusion. Both these resources need to be negotiated with a partner.

Second, be clear about who holds and controls the purse strings, and who is going to make the decisions about the research approach and the publication of research results. For some academic researchers, the research supervisor will demand to be a co-author on all papers produced from the project. Some institutions will demand that any paper produced from their institute is submitted for departmental scrutiny before it can be sent to a journal. Research has its own politics based on the control of money, access to being published and the needs of institutions. For the naive researcher, as I was, these politics are easily overlooked. They can be debilitating in the long term if not understood.

As a senior academic, I believe it is important to foster the development of our younger and junior colleagues. That means also giving them the chance to publish alone and develop their own ideas. This is not altruistic; it is only when we are challenged by our former students that we begin to grow. In addition, in the competitive world of research funding, we see young people reaching professorial posts quite quickly. And so they should, although it is still difficult for women. Yet, once some people are in post, they are abandoned to their own isolated projects. The old-fashioned concept of mentoring seems to have fallen by the wayside.

Another aspect of the politics of research is that my research discoveries are not always what others wanted me to find out for them. In one project, some people wanted me to say that a particular approach to holistic medical treatment for cancer in children was better than treatment in comparative conventional hospitals in terms of being humane and acceptable to patients, siblings and the parents of the children. It turned out not to be the case; paediatric medicine has been at the forefront of incorporating new initiatives and there was no difference between an holistic approach and a supposedly conventional approach. In fact, a radical holistic approach can be as hidebound as any other, and conventional medicine approaches in paediatrics already have a built-in flexibility based on sound practice and pragmatic science.

The third lesson I have learned is that there is a real difference between doing academic research for a qualification and working as a researcher in a project. An academic project for a master's qualification or a doctoral thesis focuses on the student and his or her needs. While needing to be academically sound and methodologically rigorous, it is the training of the scientist that is the principal guiding force. When working for a research project, the focus shifts to a group need and to the needs of the target population in clinical research. Both types of work need not exclude each other but for the purposes of supervision it is important to identify and establish whose needs are to be met.

Finally, it really is satisfying to be finding things out. The ramifications of what we discover are not always comfortable for those with whom we may be working. In one study of music therapy, we discovered that music therapy was indeed beneficial. However, that benefit tailed off after ten weekly sessions. This meant that the practice of seeing children over a prolonged period of time, as was the current practice, was questionable in terms of the efficacy it brought. For the therapists who had always worked in the long term, it demanded a major change in their thinking to contemplate a change in practice. To their credit, this has been achieved (Aldridge 1996).

My book about suicide that started the whole process off was eventually published (Aldridge 1998). It is based on material collected 13 years ago for a doctoral thesis. A long ripening period for such ideas perhaps, but the ideas are being put into practice, from what various correspondents tell me, and that is gratifying.

The work started with church groups and described in my first book (Aldridge 1987a) has developed over the years and has culminated in a further volume (Adridge 2000d). This work too has been taken up by varying groups and is used as a textbook in a training course where theologians and medical practitioners study together. Ideas reach their fruition but we cannot determine when that will be.

My anger at the recalcitrance of medical administration has been transformed into a dogged determination. What I have learned is that patience is a virtue not easily achieved but necessary if we are to do any work that is of benefit for the communities to whom we have responsibility. Perhaps a lesson to be learned from these experiences is that we can trust that our work will have its day, ideas will find their niche and our writings do find resonance. The time frame may be other than we, or our employers, may expect. What I still fail to understand is the unwillingness of medical approaches, in terms of health care delivery, to address themselves to what we know from the social sciences and, in particular, medical anthropology. I hope that the reader will find in this book evidence of those attempts to build bridges between differing understandings and forgive me when my abilities are not up to the task. The fire still burns, however.

CHAPTER 1

Making and Taking Health Care Decisions

I want to say a sentence to you and then I want to interpret that sentence in about four different ways, all of which are related to what we are talking about. And the sentence is, 'Each person is his own central metaphor.'

Mary Catherine Bateson (1972, p.285)

The position I want to take in this chapter is that of an anthropologist. The area I wish to talk about is that of the perception and coding of illness behaviour. My premise is that when we make and take health care decisions they are based on multiple perceptions made by intimately related persons based on a shared reality that has been constructed by those persons.

In this way of understanding, 'problems', when presented as illness or disease, are located within what we might call an 'ecology of ideas'. There is no one reality from which we can determine our understandings, only varying ways of fitting behaving and thinking together. This perspective moves away from the notion of an individual reality, 'I', and towards the notion of community and shared reality, 'You and I together.'

Catching a cold

I caught a cold recently. Not that I went out one wet dark night, grabbed a cold and brought it home with me. Yet, in talking about this cold, which at times became my cold, I used a particular description common to our culture which most people understood, which few people questioned and which had little to do with the process of infection. This is not an isolated example. We still talk about the sun rising and setting as if the sun orbited the earth, yet we know theoretically and experientially that the earth orbits the sun.

In addition I had this cold as an object like most of us have refrigerators.

Illness in the context of marriage and the family

My first inklings that something was different followed a weekend decorating the kitchen at home. Not only was I tired, but I developed a sore throat. I mentioned this soreness to my wife, who concluded, quite rightly, that I had had enough of decorating; and, quite wrongly, that the soreness in my throat was a result of 'dust'.

While speaking with my mother in the usual exchange of pleasantries I mentioned the sore throat. This was meant as a subtle hint to curtail the conversation. What it elicited from my mother was a statement that the soreness must be a result of the dust produced in the process of decorating my apartment. Apart from the astonishing incidence of my mother and my wife agreeing on anything it did point to an interesting theoretical point. In making sense of a situation, and in particular 'symptoms', causation is attributed to an agent, i.e. dust, in the context of a temporal event , i.e. decorating.

Later that same day things had taken a turn for the worse. My nose began to run. Given this information my mother's diagnosis would have been quite different. In my family of origin 'colds' are caught as a direct result of negligence. Either one goes out too soon after having a bath, neglects to wear a vest or discards clothing too early in the season. This has recently been tempered by an acceptance that living in centrally heated conditions is bad for you, especially if one goes from heat to cold. That is a sure-fire way of 'catching' a cold. There is certainly no notion of bacterial or viral infection.

Infection, in my original family, is a term used by doctors and medical scientists which has no bearing on real life situations; and given the inability of modern medicine to cure the common cold, is of explanatory rather than practical value. Some concession is made to the notion of 'germs'. These too, like colds, can be caught and exist in the ether like microscopic caterpillars.

The meaning of illness

By now the cold had definitely caught me. Like some monster it had invaded my whole being, and quite literally had me by the 'throat'. After a night of fitful sleep my wife had changed her diagnosis to that of 'summer cold'.

On arrival at work I received the first of a series of 'new' diagnoses. As, by now, my nose was well and truly recalcitrant to any air flow, the initial conditional diagnosis was that of 'hay fever'.

Hayfever and allergies are very big in our office with its emphasis on an holistic approach to medicine and psychoneuroimmunology. It is almost impossible to say psychoneuroimmunology with a head cold. The hayfever diagnosis went by the board quite quickly. Like all provisional hypotheses it was invalidated by further information. However, it did demonstrate an important part of the process of diagnosis. In lay terms the explanation of symptoms is initially dependent on a temporal context, i.e. a running nose in summer is likely to be hayfever.

Once I had croaked further details of the symptoms to my colleagues a firmer, more confident diagnosis was made. The basis for this diagnosis was made on observations of my general demeanour, the sound of my voice, the reported history I gave to my colleagues and the persistent use of tissues during the relating of this account.

Implications for treatment

A number of treatment suggestions followed this diagnosis. The principal injunction for treatment was to consume generous quantities of alcohol, notably whisky. To support this, what I assumed to be palliative, treatment I was encouraged to go home to bed. Presumably going to bed would avoid the iatrogenic problems of the treatment, i.e. falling down from too much alcohol. Not wishing to appear weak or sickly I struggled on at work.

A friend and colleague who is a general practitioner, seeing my plight, laid his hand upon my forehead and pronounced that I was feverish. Now that was the act of a true physician. I was soon to realize the personal, and social, implications of this viral infection. While willing to 'lay on hands' diagnostically he refused to go out for a drink that evening when invited. Obviously the sick as persons are not to be mixed with, and are temporarily not in the set labelled 'friends'. He suggested that I could meditate upon the meaning of the illness. Yet another solution.

Yet another colleague, wishing to discuss a matter of some importance with the author, offered a more holistic comment on my plight. As a psychologist and psychotherapist in the 'humanist' tradition she broached the idea of stress, T-lymphocyte suppression and the possibility that this cold was occurring at a significant point in my life.

I must point out that during this process of escalating symptoms I had become irritable with friends and more and more despondent about the world in general, and, as is usual at such times, was convinced that all my career decisions had been wrong. Those who favour a psychological approach to medicine will already be formulating a model which links depression, the suppression of T lymphocytes, infection and physical symptoms. My perspective might be the other way round; cold (infection) first, depression later. However, as this is a chicken and egg situation, the best we can say is, and this is the point of the story, different explanations exist concurrently according to our own world views, and the 'patient' does not always reflect the epistemological position of the observers.

Beginnings and endings

One other consideration we may wish to make here is that when we talk of events we place them in a particular time frame. Events are, like this sentence, separated from other events by particular markers. Some theorists refer to this process as one of 'punctuation'. When we talk of episodes of illness we punctuate them by using certain markers from the general text of our lives.

First we note a difference. With my cold, you will recall, I first noticed that a sore throat and feelings of lassitude indicated a difference. In retrospect I could have perhaps detected other signs of an impending cold in the days before. To notice a difference, then, we have to have some notion of threshold, i.e. when does soreness become sore enough to become noticeable, when does tiredness become lassitude? At the same time we attribute causality; is tiredness a result of working hard or is it a symptom of infection?

In talking about this cold you will also notice that I am using a description of process. Symptoms escalate, albeit undetected, until they 'become' noticeable. The end of this process is marked by an absence of symptoms, although it seems that generally we have fewer markers for determining the end of a process than the beginning of a process. Stated in another way, I believe that we have developed a language which is refined in ways of talking about becoming ill, yet is impoverished in ways of talking about becoming well.

Meaning and implication: The semantics and politics of illness behaviour

When we talk about illness, whether it is taking the decision that we are 'ill' or making the decision to 'go home', which is a step in managing the illness, then we are making statements about our own beliefs and experiences in the world. The punctuation of an episode from the ceaseless stream of life's events has both semantic and political implications – semantic in the sense that explanations invoke meanings from a given episode; political in the sense that human behaviour is managed, obligations are suspended and actions are taken.

Both the semantic and the political are linked. Fay Fransella (Fransella and Frost 1977) writes:

> As a society we construct the social world according to our interests and beliefs, as individuals we construct our beliefs to make sense of our own particular experience of the world. So shared experiences and beliefs support each other – at least for a good deal of the time. (p.24)

When we offer descriptions of our own behaviour to others, i.e. 'I have a really sore throat and I think I must have a cold', we are entering a realm where our description of a current reality is open to validation by another person. The validation of one person's description by another person is a political act. While this may not have serious overtones in the context of a head cold, in that for me the only suspension of obligation was that I got out of doing the washing-up for 48 hours, there are powerful implications for those persons who wish to have their experience of pain validated when it is not supported by physiological evidence.

In the context of a therapist–patient relationship the patient offers up symptoms or descriptions which they believe entitles them to the legitimate status 'sick' (Parsons 1951). The therapist or doctor may interpret those same symptoms and descriptions as an example of the patient malingering and therefore making an illegitimate claim to the status 'sick'. In this context of consultation the therapist invalidates the patient, nothing is shared and a common legitimate reality is not negotiated.

Life events

Life events have been seen as important precursors of illness. Mechanic (1974) points out the role that life events play in the occurrence of illness behaviour, but is careful to say that life changes, medical history, psychological distress and illness behaviour interact in complex ways. Although life events research has been predominantly orientated towards individuals and pathology (Brown, Harris and Peto 1973; Finlay-Jones and Brown 1981), that research also directs us to consider how individual life changes demand a complex response from the families of the individual (Dohrenwend and Dohrenwend 1974).

Within the literature there is a lack of consensus as to how individuals and families are influenced by life events, but the implication is that the way that life events and life cycle changes are managed is crucial to health. We are left with a number of questions from the life events research:

1. How do some people and not others construe particular times and events in their lives as stressful?

2. How do some families collectively see some life events as indicators of change?

3. How are some adaptations at the level of physiological functioning related to what people think and what their loved ones do?

4. What construings are resident within 'culture' which offer understandings of life events which attribute 'stress', and how do these affect individual and family understandings?

Gregory Bateson (1973) offers an answer to these questions. He sees life events not as causative but as indicative. The recognition of a life event depends upon how individuals and social groups are informed by themselves and their culture as to what events make a difference. There is a process of co-evolution where individuals and social groups inform their culture and culture informs individuals and their groups (Blumer 1962). Other researchers have described this relationship between culture and symptoms, and cultural components in the expression of pain (Schwab and Schwab 1978; Zborowski 1952; Zola 1966).

What counts as illness

If we take an episode of illness, which itself can be seen as a life event, then there are a number of stages in that episode when meanings are offered to others for validation. Making sense of the world is just that, a 'making' of sense. When we make sense it is made in the context of a relationship. Cecil Helman reminds us:

> Consultations between doctors and patients do not take place in a vacuum. Rather, they are embedded in a particular time and place, and in a particular physical, social or cultural setting. That is, each consultation is embedded in a particular context. These contexts are important, because they shape what is said in the consultation, how it is said, how it is interpreted, and how it is acted upon. (1986, p.37)

We can apply the same criteria of time and place to our personal relationships. Helman also goes on to distinguish internal and external contexts.

An internal context is the set of hidden assumptions and responses that each party brings to the relationship. These would include our past experiences of illness, the explanations for the origin of the illness and how symptoms should be treated. As we can see 'my cold' was interpreted according to a number of internal contexts. It must be remembered that these contexts are not fixed but negotiated.

An external context includes the setting in which the event takes place and also includes rules of conduct. In some ways an external context is a form of ritual; it is punctuated as being separate from 'everyday life' and governed by explicit and implicit rules of conduct about how people are to act, speak and dress and what they are to talk about.

At an obvious level we see this in public rituals like weddings and funerals (and conferences!), but we also have ritualized ways of dealing with deference, greetings and leaving (Geertz 1957; Leach 1957).

At a more fundamental level we have our own internal rituals for recognizing 'stress' or 'no stress' which are based upon a highly complex immunological language which is more than a biochemical alphabet. This language can be used to identify what is 'self' and 'not self'. In such a way we are daily constituting ourselves. We make a sense of the world bodily. However, as we all are aware we also make sense of the world psychologically, socially and spiritually.

Sometimes this bodily sense becomes evident in another realm of experience. When we experience pain then a message is being sent from one systemic level (somatic) to another (psychic). This message needs to be interpreted. It is not always immediately discernible what pain a message is about. For instance, in the case of back pain is it about muscular distress, or is it a metaphor about distress in a different systemic context, e.g. having too much to bear or a lack of support? In research into the common cold, the researchers found that people with different representational styles (verbal, visual or enactive) had different ways of being ill (Aylwin, Durand and Wilson 1985). Verbalizers, people who use inner speech, were prone to mouth ulcers. However, visualizers showed no particular propensity for any problems but there was a negative correlation with relaxation and resistance to infection. Somehow literally the way we see the world and represent it to ourselves is a health enhancing activity. Making sense is not only a passive process, but an active process we do to the world.

Rules for the making of sense

A number of authors suggest that 'making sense' is rule based (Bateson 1978; Cushman and Whiting 1972; Harré and Secord 1973; Hoffman 1981). These rules can be separated into two forms (Pearce and Cronen 1980). First, there are rules of constitution. A constitutive rule would be invoked when we say this behaviour (a sore throat) counts as evidence of another state (a cold). Second, there are rules of regulation. A regulative rule would be invoked when we say if this behaviour (a sore throat) counts as evidence of a particular state (having a cold), then do a particular activity (go home to bed).

Constitutive rules, then, are generally concerned with meaning. Regulative rules are concerned with the politics of relationship and the linking of meaning and action.

This corresponds to the interrelated healing functions of the provision of meaning and the control of sickness which Kleinman and Sung (1979) describe. They argue that modern professional health care attends solely to the control of sickness and neglects the understanding of meaning. Furthermore,

> the biomedical education of physicians and other modern health profes-
> sionals, while providing them with the knowledge to control sickness, sys-
> tematically blinds them to the second of these core clinical functions (the
> understanding of meaning), which they learn neither to recognize or to
> treat. (p.8)

If we return to the understanding of life events we could hypothesize that con-stitutive rules exist which identify particular acts as life events. Regulative rules would propose a way of handling such events.

In an episode of illness there will be stages when behaviour is understood in terms of constitution, i.e. meaning, and, in turn, regulation, i.e. control or management. Episodes have critical times when they are seen 'to start' and 'to end'. This is the process of 'punctuation' (Bateson 1979) and is a selective structuring of reality. Punctuation is vital to interaction as it is a means of orga-nizing behavioural events both in terms of meaning and process.

We see this when someone says 'He always starts an argument', or 'Her problems began when her husband died.' While such punctuations may be shared, they may also be the source of conflict. For instance, some of us may recall situations where one person has said 'I was only trying to be helpful and support you', and their partner says 'You were interfering and undermining my ability.' In such an exchange the two punctuations of the same behaviour, 'helpful/interfering', are a characterization of the relationship. This has been described as a 'rule' of the relationship (Jackson 1965).

In our modern Western culture the predominant focus to punctuate the start of an episode of illness appears to be one of recognizing symptoms which are validated in the context of a relationship whether it be familial, filial or fraternal. If we return to my sore throat we can see that in the relational context of marriage and family of origin, and in the temporal context of decorating, then a sore throat was seen as a result of dust and was not evidence of illness. The possibility of my having a cold was not validated.

However, after offering further evidence for validation, i.e. the classical symptoms of a cold and a fitful night's sleep, then I was recognized as having 'a cold'. My personal reality was negotiated and validated in the context of a relationship. Similarly, as my symptoms persisted the various meanings inferred from them by others were used to offer a number of prescriptions for regulating that illness.

In terms of a cold this was quite straightforward as the causative agent was seen as a viral infection and not open to a great deal of debate, and there was a general consensus of opinion that the only recourse was palliative. However, in considering other forms of illness meanings are not so clear cut, or can be pejorative.

Symptoms can be employed as a 'language' within a group of people (Kreitman, Smith and Eng-Seong 1969), and in particular families (Haley 1980; Madanes 1981), where other groups would use less pathological forms of communication. Symptoms become part of a vocabulary of distress. Pain then becomes an indicator not only of physiological distress but also a marker of existential despair, or personal 'hurt' or unwillingness to co-operate.

This medium for communication does not have to be invented, it exists within the sub-culture of the group or family. We see this when someone has a day off work regularly with a headache. If this should occur repeatedly at times when their work is to be scrutinized by a superior then we might infer as a group that the headache is 'caused' by the imminent scrutiny. In this way we can be said to have shared meanings.

This process is reflected in our therapeutic systems, as we heard earlier. We learn a set of shared meanings whereby symptoms located in particular contexts are understood in a particular way; that is, the process of diagnosis. This would correspond to a set of 'constitutive rules'. Acupuncturists will recognize disturbances in ch'i. Neuro-linguistic programmers will recognize maladaptive speech patterns. Structural family therapists will see family coalitions and permeable boundaries. Transactional analysts will hear the child speaking. A priest will recognize the sinner and the sin.

Similarly the process of diagnosis would lead to implications for what to do about those symptoms; that is, the process of treatment. This would correspond to a set of 'regulative rules'. The acupuncturist will endeavour to restore balance, the neuro-linguist will intervene by talking directly to the somatic system responsible for the problem, the family therapist will ask the family to change seats and move closer together, the transactional analyst will encourage the child to speak to the adult, while the priest will confer absolution.

The challenge for the therapist or practitioner is that although the symptoms reported by the patient may fit the practitioner's set of rule-based understandings, those rules and corresponding understandings may be quite different to those of the patient and the patient's family. All too often patient and therapist can be at odds because the important phase of negotiating common or shared meanings is missed out.

The implications for therapy are that we must be concerned with understanding what the symptoms constitute for the patient, and what the patient has previously done to regulate those symptoms. In a similar way, we must be aware that by the time a patient reaches the therapist or practitioner they have been through a process where their symptoms have been negotiated and validated in other contexts which may have far more significance for them as persons.

What I want to propose is that sometimes when we see people with persistent problems then it may well be that their personal meaning system – their sets of constitutive and regulative rules – has been invalidated in other relational contexts, and they too have invalidated the systems of meanings offered by significant others. When such a situation of mutual invalidation occurs and symptoms appear as 'intractable' then we find that the patient is given a label of deviance or described as resistant rather than the therapist having failed to understand the patient. This too would be falling into a trap of blaming one person in the relationship rather than looking at the therapeutic process itself and the relationship between therapist and patient.

Conclusion

Making and taking health care decisions is a process. We become aware of events which make a difference. Some of these are seen as symptoms and are seen as indicative of certain states. These constitutive rules are learned through experience and are validated in the context of families and friends. We rarely have to invoke these rules as they are habitual. In the context of illness behaviour they form a repertoire for the management of distress. Occasionally when we come into contact with other persons and other groups we find that those rules are questioned and that repertoire is inappropriate.

As these rules are learned in families they persist over time, and can be carried over from one generation to the next. In this way some particular forms of illness behaviour such as depression appear to be hereditary. However, we have not as yet identified the gene responsible for depression, and nor are we likely to. It could well be that depression is not hereditary but it does run in families. At certain times and in particular situations, faced with personal failure in a context of relational conflict, there may be constitutive and regulative rules which propose particular behaviours, e.g. become depressed. These behaviours are learned in families and transmitted from one generation to the next.

At which level, then, do we choose to intervene, and at which point in the cycle do we choose to enter? A challenge for us as practitioners and researchers is to elicit those cyclic patterns of behaviour with their underlying rule structures whereby physiological changes occur in response to personal and relational crises. There may well be rules operating which say that in this context (a conference) a particular action (speaking to a group of one's peers) constitutes a threat and that is regulated by a particular behaviour (elevated heart rate, increase in perspiration, suppression of lymphocytes). While this may well be 'normal' behaviour (and the attribution of normality itself is rule dependent), if there were a set of rules which interpreted all situations as threats (to be regulated by an elevated heart rate or a suppression of lymphocytes) then we might speculate that there is an underlying disease or at least a maladaptive coping strategy.

In this sort of description diseases are not fixed or immutable – they are open to change at different levels of intervention, e.g. a change in a constitutive rule would mean that some events would no longer count as crises; a change in regulative rule would mean a change in response. We do this in treatment where some of us look for underlying attitudes and attempt to change these (the process of constitution), whereas some therapists will attempt to provoke changes in response to stimuli (the process of regulation).

This rule making is in a Jungian sense a problem of knowledge:

> But what is recognition or knowledge in this sense? We speak of knowing something when we succeed in linking a new perception to an already established context in such a way that we hold in consciousness not only the new perception but this context as well. 'Knowing' is based, therefore, upon a conscious connection between psychic contents. (Jung 1961, p.112).

My thesis is that these connections are rule based. It is important to remember the notion of rule is used here as a metaphor for what happens, not that there is literally a rule book in the head or the family.

These rules need not necessarily be cognitive. They may act solely at the level of physiology where there are physiological changes occurring in response to biochemical markers in the context of immunological stress. As stated earlier what we need to address ourselves to is the continuing problem of how the threat to a threshold at one level, i.e. the cognitive, brings about a response at another level, i.e. the physiological. A rules-based explanation addresses this by offering a means of description (but not a causal link) of what happens. By understanding the interaction between these levels we can intervene at differing levels.

For instance, in working with patients who had attempted suicide and had seemingly intractable symptoms (Aldridge and Rossiter 1985), which were expressed as chronic pain, there were a number of choices for intervention. First, they could have been given further analgesics. As analgesics were proving to be ineffective there seemed to be little point, and these were rejected by the patient anyway. Second, there were opportunities for changing the personal attitudes to the pain using relaxation exercises, hypnotic techniques, charting techniques and other psychotherapeutic strategies. In this way we could say that there are personal rules of constitution and regulation. Third, as the patients were seen with their spouses or parents, an intervention could be made which addressed the patterns of family interaction surrounding the presenta-tion of the symptoms (Aldridge and Rossiter 1984). These could be formulated as familial rules of constitution and regulation. Lastly, because the patients had a history of repeated contact with medical practitioners, there was a possibility of talking to the medical community about their referral patterns and their approach to patients who 'refused to get better'. These could be broadly cate-gorized as cultural rules of constitution and regulation.

In the end it was a combination of approaches which appeared to work. Each intervention was located within the context of another. The charting techniques were introduced to the person in the presence of their family. This work was also presented to the community of physicians who were referring patients. These physicians saw the cyclical pattern which led to the situation of seemingly 'intractable symptoms'. The personal was located within the familial, which in turn was located within the cultural. We see this reflected in our health care initiatives where we are beginning to see that health care initiatives can be invoked at the personal level of self-care and at the level of changing social con-ditions. What we need to look at is the mediating context of the family, for it may be our spouses, or those with whom we live, who significantly influence what sense we make of our lives and what endeavours we pursue to change that sense. It is they with whom we negotiate our health.

Similarly we must continue to be aware that healers and patients are not independent of the cultural context of clinical care, and the explanatory models we bring to bear on illness and healing are resident within this cultural context. In this way we will begin to understand the meaning of illness and the attendant implications for healing rather than the headlong pursuit into the management of disease. This will change our clinical practice and, more fundamentally, our research endeavours.

However, we must be wary. The way we construct our meanings of problems, particularly when presented by the people who come to see us for therapy, may be a contribution to the way in which the problem is maintained rather than allowing change to happen. The aphorism 'Psychoanalysis is the illness whose cure it considers itself to be' might well be heeded and applied to our own disciplines (Watzlawick 1984).

Finally I want to remind us of an area which I have not addressed directly, and that is the problem of mind and the attendant phenomena of consciousness. Gregory Bateson implies that in every unity where there are conversation-like actions there is an ecology of ideas and the presence of mind. Varela takes this notion further and talks about a mind-like activity beyond our own individual minds where there is a higher order of unity, and which is not readily amenable to consciousness. Apart from sounding remarkably Jungian it does point to a higher order of rules of constitution and regulation whereby we are made sense of and regulated. We are part of a system which accommodates us. We move from isolation to unity. As Varela (1979) writes:

> Thus we do not have…a world of shared regularities that we can alter at whim. In fact the understanding is beyond our will because the autonomy of the social and biological systems we are in goes beyond our skill, because our evolution makes us part of a social aggregate and a natural aggregate which have an autonomy compatible with but not reducible to our autonomy as biological individuals. (p.276)

Consider this world view with that of Jung (1959):

> A more or less superficial layer of the unconscious is undoubtedly personal. I call it the personal unconscious. But this personal unconscious rests upon a deeper layer, which does not derive from personal experience and is not a personal acquisition but is inborn. This deeper layer I call the collective unconscious. I have chosen the term 'collective' because this

part of the unconscious is universal not individual; in contrast to the personal psyche, it has contents and modes of behaviour that are more or less the same everywhere and in all individuals. It is, in other words, identical in all men and thus constitutes a common psychic substrate of a superpersonal nature which is present in every one of us. (p.4)

Perhaps we are living in an age where our understandings gleaned from differing world views are becoming unified. Our decisions in health care are made according to those meanings, and they are taken according to how that sense is made. While not curing the common cold, it does give you something to think about while you are recovering.

CHAPTER 2

Lifestyle, Charismatic Ideology and a Praxis Aesthetic

A pure aesthetic expresses, in rationalized form, the ethos of a cultured elite or, in other words, of the dominated fraction of the dominant class. As such, it is a misrecognized social relationship. 'The denial of lower, coarse, vulgar, venal, servile – in a word, natural – enjoyment, which constitute the sacred sphere of culture, implies an affirmation of the superiority of those who can be satisfied with the sublimated, refined, disinterested, gratuitous, distinguished pleasures forever closed to the profane. That is why art and cultural consumption are predisposed, consciously, and deliberately or not, to fulfil a social function of legitimating social differences.

Pierre Bourdieu (1993, p.25)

The main impulse for this chapter came to me from a variety of sources. These sources were incidents taken from daily life and, although they are anecdotal, indicate the difficulties that we face when we talk about health and the practices that are used to maintain and promote health. Indeed, one of the significant points of this chapter will be that health is heterogeneous and that such ideas come out of the practice of daily living rather than being homogeneous and based upon a rationalist unified theory. Such a demand for consistency may be misleading (Kirmayer 1994) and hide the discrepancies between varying forms of knowledge. While the above quote is made with regard to art and literature as cultural processes, I shall be arguing that health too is a cultural process and can be similarly subjected to an aesthetic critique.

I want to use a few introductory anecdotes for two reasons. First, we see how health is a complex set of ideas and, second, that we need to consider the day-to-day narratives of individuals as they talk about health. This latter point is not new in terms of health care research and qualitative methods (Milburn 1996; Radley and Billig 1996), but what I will also be suggesting is that most research makes an assumption that health and illness are opposing poles of a continuum. My proposal is that health and illness may be so constructed by health care professionals trained to think in such a way, but such an ideology may not be reflected in the everyday lives of other people. Perhaps the realms of health and illness are quite separate in practice? Rather than being oppositional they are competing discourses (McRobbie 1996) relevant for making sense of particular situations.

The first incident is one that occurred at one of the Copenhagen meetings. Following the usual presentations about health and various approaches to medicine, we duly retired to eat and then to the bar where several colleagues ordered their drinks and smoked cigarettes. For most of the day we had been sitting in a centrally heated room and had taken part in no strenuous activities other than disagreeing with each other in a mild sort of way and occasionally moving our chairs to let others get by. From some perspectives of health care activity, we were behaving quite irresponsibly: smoking, drinking both coffee and alcohol, pursuing sedentary activities and no doubt eating fatty foods. However, those of us partaking in such activities seemed to be paying little attention to 'health' as such and were generally getting on with the day-to-day business of living, part of which was actively pleasurable. As such this is a rejection of an aesthetics of Kantian 'pure' taste and an embracing of a Bourdieuian 'vulgar' taste that returns to the senses. And it is this notion of sensuousness that is at the heart of the original meaning of aesthetic in that it springs from the lower animal passions, a matter of literal taste.

One of the burdens, or joys, of being a conference delegate is that one has to take part in social activities. It so happened that I was invited to the German beer festival in Munich, and not wanting to offend my hosts I duly took part. The festival takes place in a huge park complete with fairground activities that are replete with noise and activity, and charged with the electricity of human beings having fun. Within the festival grounds there are huge barns where people go to be entertained. The group I was with were duly led to such a barn and as the doors opened I was immediately reminded of many of the things my mother had told me not to do as a boy and which seemed enjoyable as a man. From out of the open doors came a billow of smoke, gales of laughter, squalls of music from a German 'oompah' band and the wonderful breezy beery odours of the hall – all the perils of enjoyment captured together in a storm of experience. It will be my own fault if I do not make it to old age. And here lies the crux of the argument – most of the health care debates are moralistic and ignore a profound factor in human existence, repeated from the first example, and that is the simple activity of pleasure.

Another scene occurred in a restaurant. My wife and I had decided to take an early spring walk; the weather was fine and after a gentle stroll we arrived at a hotel in time for lunch, as planned I might add. During the meal, a number of middle-aged women came to sit at the next table. The first topic of conversation was their health and each woman took her turn to talk about current ailments. In doing so she introduced various connected topics such as the state of her family, the well-being of her husband, the relative benefits of being mature, where she had been shopping recently and a general philosophy and outlook on life. While we might as professionals be tempted to look at this as a health care narrative, health being the chosen topic of introduction, we would be missing a valuable point. Health was used as a springboard for a wide-ranging conversation that did not itself remain focused on health. Like the stereotypical greeting 'Hello, how are you?' rarely intends to elicit a conversation about the person's state of health, health as a subject of naturally occurring narratives plays only a minor role. All too often we consider health as if it was the peak of a unified pyramid of rational consonant understandings rather than a topic in a constellation of understandings, some of which may be dissonant. It is knowing the relationships between elements of such a constellation that might help us to understand health as part of daily living, as praxis.

When I was a small boy my grandfather took me to the local park where he sat with his cronies, and I played. To give himself some respite from me, he would suggest that I ran around the bowling green. He would either time me, to see how fast I could run, or he would count how many times I had completed the circuit. This was play and I would imagine myself to be some athletic hero of the day like Chris Brasher or Emil Zatopek. Such play became a sport as I grew up and started cross-country running. In my twenties I played other sports and ran, not only for the simple fun of it, but because I wanted to improve my fitness. Fitness to play sport that is, not as a health activity. In my thirties, I started to study again and as an aid to preparing for my examinations began to run every day after studying. In my forties, my father had his first heart attack and I began running again, not this time for enjoyment, but as a hedge against angina. However, I soon stopped as there was no pleasure in such activity and I was picking up more minor injuries 'jogging' than going for my daily walk. If we take the same activity, in this case running, we can infer differing attributes to it and the benefits that it may have brought for my health. Biddle (1995) refers to this as the 'feel good factor'. Indeed, people had seen my running in my thirties and thought I was doing it for my health. This was quite false. I did it for the sheer pleasure of running like a boy and as a practical activity that would enable me to enjoy playing. Only later did the same activity gain overtones of a health care activity. It is precisely this aspect of understanding such an activity in relationship to a broader field of understandings and activities that is important.

As a final example I would like to refer again to the element of pleasure and how it is ignored in health care thinking. A current debate has been about the implication of cholesterol in coronary heart disease (Evans, Barer and Marmor 1994) where eating a fatty diet is seen to be an unhealthy behaviour. A favourable way of eating has been proposed as the 'Mediterranean diet' that includes less fats, less meat, more fruit and vegetables and carbohydrate – like breads and pastas. Again, in the spirit of academic benevolence, I have eaten in the Mediterranean and holidayed on a Greek island. Apart from the incidence of cigarette smoking that accompanied such meals, there were several cultural factors rarely mentioned in health care directives about diet that might play a significant role. First, the meals were slow affairs often partaken within a large family group that occurred late in the evening. Cultural setting seems to be conveniently forgotten in health care descriptions of diet. Second, the food was enjoyed as an activity amongst a series of activities which might include dancing or going for a stroll outside to take the evening air. Yet the palpable enjoyment of the food as an eating activity and as a social occasion had little to do with the seeming narrow aspect of nutrition. Perhaps the reason for the failing inducements to change dietary habits (Meillier, Lund and Kok 1996; Nguyen, Otis and Potvin 1996) is simply that such inducements demonstrate a poverty of understanding concerning the human activity of eating together as a pleasurable activity and the previously mentioned constellation of activities that make health part of a complex praxis aesthetic. Hamilton *et al.* (1995) refer to vegetarians as eating from a moral menu, and it is this virtuous aspect of acceptable conduct that appears to pervade health care arguments. The dispute of the primacy of reason over sensuousness is not a new argument in European thought and appears also to have ramifications in Chinese political thinking (Gu 1996).

Health as identity

In modern times, health is no longer a state of not being sick. Individuals are choosing to become healthy and, in some cases, declare themselves as pursuing the activity of being well. This change, from attributing the status 'being sick' to engaging in the activity of 'becoming well', is a reflection of a modern trend whereby individuals are taking the definition of themselves into their own hands rather than relying upon an identity being imposed by another. Being recognized as a 'healthy' person is, for some, an important feature of a modern identity. While personal active involvement has always been present in health care maintenance and prevention, in that people have strategies of distress management (Aldridge 1994), a new development appears to be that being a 'healthy', 'creative', 'musical' or 'spiritual' person is considered to be significant in the composition of an individual's 'lifestyle'. Rather than strategies of personal health management in response to sickness, we see an assemblage of activities designed to promote health and prevent sickness. These activities are incorporated under the rubric of 'lifestyle' and sometimes refer to the pursuit of 'emotional well-being' (Furnham 1994). Furthermore, such a lifestyle is intimately bound up with how a person chooses to define him or herself.

Thus I am arguing here that post-modern identities are constructed, and although these identities are bound up with cultural values, they focus primarily on the body. What we need to take heed of as health care professionals is that this 'body work', this embodiment of culture (Kirmayer 1994; Lewis 1995; Starrett 1995; Turner 1995), this corporeality of expression, is a pleasurable activity, often recreational and simply not medical. Bodies are done; they become the material aspect of both the individual and the culture in which he or she is embodied. The presentation of symptoms by a patient, for example, has an articulacy that is based upon the body and its needs. The naming of the entities to which those symptoms refer by the medical practitioner is based upon a different articulacy that is based in language and reason. The somatic has an aesthetic based upon the senses, while diagnosis has an ethic based upon naming (Khushf 1996). For the patient, the process of naming, putting words to a private somatic sensation and communicating that sensation within a context of reason, the medical encounter, changes the experience of that sensation (Cioffi 1996).

The definition of health, who is to define what health is and who is to be involved in healing is not a new activity. Such issues are raised at times of transformation when the old order is being challenged (Aldridge 1991a). In post-modern society, orthodoxies are challenged, and as truth is regarded as relative with few fixed authorities to turn to, identities can be composed from a palette of cultural alternatives.

Health is also appearing in modern society as a commodity. Far from being a simple object, health is concerned with social relationships representing personal worth, market values, existential principles and theological niceties. However, the location of health in modern terms is often within the body (Charmaz 1995; Kelly and Field 1996; Wallulis 1994). People are demanding recognition that they play an active role in their own health care, and that some can act as lay health care practitioners. Indeed, before we ask a doctor or any licensed practitioner, we have been through varying cycles of self-care, asking family and friends or just hoping that the problem will go away. This shift away from authority and orthodoxy towards democratization and choice reflects a change from a belief in the certainties of science and religion to a relativist position where people literally 'make up' their own minds and work on their bodies; that is, we construct our own identities.

As a consequence of challenges to traditional authority, and the collapse of State socialism, here in Europe, there is no longer a possibility for some individuals to relate to a given social order. In the writings of many health care practitioners, particularly in alternative medicine, there are few references to health care as being a social product for the benefit of communities. Instead, rather than a communal argument being voiced, there appears to be an argument for the individual located in an ecological context – the 'green' politic of environmental liberalism. Such a perspective ignores the notion of population and health and the pervading fact that morbidity is correlated with the distribution of wealth (Evans et al. 1994; Vågerö 1994).

Individuals are seeking to treat themselves with a long-term eclectic health strategy that includes a palette of activities with the support of chosen, albeit diverse, informed advisers who can fulfil the role of facilitator. Health care consumers are blurring the role between the traditional health care services delivered at times of crisis, with those of preventive strategies based on consumerism. The idea of community health in these descriptions may be alluded to as an ecological context, but there is little reference to an immediate social or communal context. This is a reflection of the Romantic notion of the individual related directly with the cosmos (Tsouyopoulus 1984).

Medicines as charismatic ideologies

My principal criticism of health care arguments as presented by conventional medicine, and many complementary medical initiatives, is that these approaches are founded upon a charismatic ideology; that is, health is pursued for health's sake. While this may be relevant for religion – life for a divine being's sake – or for art – arts for art's sake – health will be always undermined by the reality of the body. Health, religion and art are presented as metaphysical activities – they are above the physical realm. But, like the body of work in terms of art products, the individual body in terms of physical health is subject to temporality and is not above the substantial plane of existence. Health is temporal and locally corporeal. We may be better advised to defer from the charismatic ideology of 'C' medicines – that is, conventional and complementary – and seek a functional aesthetic relating to the performed body. To be accepted as a performance, a habitus (Bourdieu 1993), there must be an audience and that returns us to a cultural and social field.

While body size and shape are aspects of personal identity, it is how the body is interpreted, the aesthetics of health beliefs, that plays an important role in forming identity. Such beliefs play an active part in how we recognise illness and what therapy form we choose (Aldridge 1992a). Meanings provide a bridge between cultural and physiological phenomena. The diagnosis of a medical complaint is also a statement about personal identity (Stravynski and O'Connor 1995; van der Geest 1994) and the stigma that may be attached to such an identity (Crossley 1995). Symbolic meanings are the loci of power whereby illness is explained and controlled. Such loci are now shifting from the educated health professionals to the increasingly better-educated, and health-conscious, consumers, although that relationship is delicate (Dickinson 1995).

Indeed, in the post-modern era there are ever-increasing producers of symbolic goods as related to health. Various agencies, including consumer groups, now make claims for cultural legitimacy in competition with the orthodoxies of conventional medicine (although it appears sometimes that complementary medical agencies have been incorporated within the body of conventionality). The notions of alternative medicine, consumer groups and self-care groups have struggled to liberate health from the grip of academic control and the monolith of conventional medicine. This has been linked to the development of individual autonomy whereby the health of the individual can be performed as he or she sees fit. Health has the potential of a style and form liberated from a subordination to political and medical interests. To quote Bourdieu:

> ...the mass production of works produced by quasi-industrial methods
> coincided with the extension of the public, resulting from the expansion

of primary education, which turned new classes (including women) into consumers of culture. The development of the system of cultural production is accompanied by a process of differentiation generated by the diversity of the publics at which the different categories of producers aim their products. (1993, p.113)

Definition of health in a cultural context

It is clear that in our modern cultures several belief systems operate in parallel, and can co-exist. Patients have begun to demand that their understandings about health play a role in their care, and practitioners too are seeking complementary understandings. Health itself is a state subject to social and individual definition. What counts as healthy is dependent upon cultural norms. Health and disease are not fixed entities but concepts used to characterize a process of adaptation to meet the changing demands of life and the changing meanings given to living. Negotiating what counts as healthy is a process we are all involved in, as are the forms of treatment, welfare and care which we choose to accept as adequate or satisfactory (Aldridge 1990a, Santiago-Irizarry 1996).

Spickard (1994), in an earlier volume, reminded us that modern people do not merely accept the identities passed down by authorities. Instead, they construct their identities from various sources. Modern identity is eclectic. As in the age of Romanticism, when revolution demanded a new way of being, the primacy of the perceiver is once more being emphasized. Subjectivity becomes paramount, on the one hand reifying the individual, but on the other hand running the risk that the individual will become isolated. Indeed, while post-modernism is perhaps itself characterized by a revolt against authority and tends towards self-referentiality, its very eclecticism leaves the individual valued but exhausted of significance – what Gergen (1991) refers to as 'the saturated self'. This move towards the ability of the individual to control her or himself has led Pinell (1996) to refer to the homo medicus, the sick person who objectivizes her or himself as a medical auxiliary.

Brewster Smith (1994) suggests that the inflated potential for self-hood dislocated from traditional value sources increases the potential for despair, and while individuals may rise to the challenge of pluralism, there are some individuals who will seek to join groups who offer some form of reassurance in a given orthodoxy of beliefs and actions. The danger in modern Europe is that the Romantic notion of individualism becomes perverted into nationalism, and the dislocated individual seeking to construct his or her own identity joins a group intent on the limitation of others' freedom of self-definition whereby he or she can maintain their own security. Consensus is fragile in a context where individual demands are reified.

If the self in modern society is always being constructed to meet the variety of life's contingencies, then we move away from the model of one generation initiating the next generation into the truths of its own beliefs. Instead there is a pool of experts and advisers to whom we can turn when constructing a system of beliefs within a cultural ecology. Ecological, in the sense that those beliefs are connected, and that the consequences of those beliefs, when acted out in the real world, are related one to another. In some modern alternative healing approaches, traditional forms of teaching by initiation and learning by discipline are rejected in favour of an eclecticism that takes techniques and locates them within a culture of meanings improvised according to the situation. This action itself is political. Rejecting given orthodoxies, and demanding freedom to engage in the project of realizing one's 'self', is a 'politics of life-decisions concerning life-styles' (Brewster Smith 1994). A performative and dramatic approach overrides both traditional and deconstructive notions of causality.

Health as functional aesthetic

The notion of lifestyle appears to be important in describing modern approaches to health care use and its delivery. In a Foucauldian sense, the self is not an assemblage of functional components, but a unified style of behaviour (Dreyfus 1987). However, I am challenging such a perspective in this chapter. Rather than there being a human nature, the self-interpreting practice of being human enables us to have varying natures. Our lives have the potential to become a work of art in that our identities are constructed and maintained each day (Aldridge 1989a), thus a performed identity and a functional aesthetic. In this sense the activity of healing is concerned not with restricting us to a one-dimensional sense of being according to an accepted orthodox world view, but the possibility for the interpretation of the self as new, albeit embedded as an identity within a particular culture.

Individuals then seek to make claims about their personal identity to someone else to whom they matter; that is, in interaction. Claiming to be a healthy, fulfilled, empowered, artistic or spiritual person is a way of presenting the self that will elicit a response from others. Schwalbe (1993) interprets this action of deciding which identity to present, and in how we present ourselves, as one of moral agency. In modern descriptions of alternative healing, it is the body that is the stage for the interaction of the self and its interaction with culture.

If the big narratives of modernism are now being replaced by our own personal sets of meaning made locally with those whom we seek to live (Warde 1994), then we need to understand more about the person that sits before us in our consulting room. How that person creates an identity will be indicative of how that person will resolve his or her problems. How that person seeks to be identified will guide his or her health care activities. Some will seek medications, others will imbibe herbal preparations; some will seek to be physically manipulated, others will seek to be psychically manipulated; some will exchange energies both subtle and cosmic, others will search for the laying on of hands in a ritual way, whether it be from a medical doctor or a spiritual healer (both require their own brands of faith); while some will sing to relieve their souls, and others will jog for the heart's content. Each of these, the body-builder and the disciple, the artist and the atheist, the athlete and the allopath, will demand a recognition for whom they are as a person, and for that recognition to be included in treatment decisions. Indeed, the route to treatment will be guided by an itinerary pertinent to personal identity. Health is something that is done, a performed art.

What we singularly fail to see is that our current thinking about health is dominated by a medical thinking that ignores much of the reality of the persons we intend to treat and support. Few people, when they are sick, respond by seeking a health care practitioner (Andersen 1995). Perhaps even fewer consult a health care practitioner about staying healthy. What we appear to do, outside of an academic life thinking about such lofty matters, is eat, drink, amuse ourselves, love our nearest and dearest, walk the dog, chase pieces of leather across field (both dogs and football players), without thinking of medical consequences. Maybe our health care assumptions are so narrow that they have little relevance for others who do not bow down at the altars of epidemiology and empiricism. Many lay appraisals of health care activity seem be based upon holistic considerations that include feelings of mood and vitality (Andersen and Lobel 1995). If changes of mood are ignored, or assessed as potentially pathological by health care practitioners, and the philosophy of vitality is generally regarded as invalid in modern scientific medicine, then we should not wonder that few people come to us for help. If, as in traditional Chinese medicine, for example, health seeking becomes a pleasure, that sequesters 'a body that can not only taste sweetness but be sweet, not only report painful symptoms, but also dwell on and cultivate the quiet comforts of health' (Farquhar 1994, p.493), then maybe we can understand that the seeking of a positive identity in a post-modern world is an activity that can be enjoyed without experts and the grand narratives of science and medicine. We may indeed have to learn to seek out those personal and local truths that our patients themselves are choosing to embody.

It may appear that self and society are being presented as opposing realities. However, in the field of health promotion we know that to choose only one approach would be limited. In this century major changes in health status have occurred as results of improvements in living conditions – clean water, improved sanitation and adequate nutrition. There is also evidence that income plays an important role in maintaining standards of health, that poverty is not only a social burden; for the individual it has consequences for personal health. The field of health influences as they are played out in the community manifest themselves in the bodies of individual persons.

In the last decade of the twentieth century there is a change in relationship between self and society. The individual is becoming disembedded from a traditional commitment to society, a disenchantment with the collective, and a new type of commitment is being seen (Warde 1994). In a liberal ideology, individuals with enough disposable income are becoming personally responsible for their own identity and this is linked to lifestyle as commodity. Individuals are socialized in a post-modern society as consumers with a choice of lifestyles. While on the one hand our autonomy is restricted in the field of employment (if we can find employment), how we choose to define ourselves and with whom we choose to define ourselves is a matter of personal freedom. An anomaly of this situation is that personal perceptions of health, their own well-being and life satisfaction may be at odds with a health professional's assessment of that individual's health status (Albrecht 1994).

The danger of this individual health lifestyle approach, when it assumes that health is the opposing pole of a health–illness construct, is that individuals too can be held as responsible for the causation of their own diseases (Kirkwood and Brown 1995) and lifestyle factors can be seen as the precursors, risk factors, of future illness (Armstrong 1995). Health may then become expressed as a moral debate concerning responsible citizens free from the intervention of doctors. This in turn masks the agenda of restricting access to limited resources. Rather than the sick being labelled as deviant, the sick become labelled as illegitimate users of provision. In England such a situation has occurred whereby advertisements in national newspapers have been taken out on behalf of a medical association requesting patients only to contact their doctor in an emergency.

Promoting and maintaining our health is one such choice in the plethora of consumer activities intimately related to our identity. The body-builder, eating efficiently for the production of a body mass, will consume differently from the computer freak who surfs the Internet and eats fast food for a fast lifestyle. Both these will differ from the jogging yoghurt eater who consumes vegetables to purify his material self, reduce his cholesterol levels and meditates for the salvation of the planet. The young boy who was running for fun in my earlier example, grew up to be the young man running for pleasure, who became the middle-aged man running for his life. While the same activity prevailed through each episode, the needs that were being gratified were different (see also Montelpare and Kanters 1994; Tinsley and Eldredge 1995).

The implication of Bourdieu's work (see Randal Johnson in Bourdieu 1993) is that any analysis that overlooks the social grounds of aesthetic taste tends to establish as universal aesthetic and cultural practices that are in fact products of privilege. So it is of a universal health practice. A pure aesthetic demands keeping necessity at arm's length, and daily life will always subvert such an health aesthetic, thus my call for a functional aesthetic of health understandings based upon the body that legitimates pleasure. Martin (1996, p.53) urges us to an 'understanding of the imagery, language and metaphor operating in our contemporary culture of the body'.

Implications for health promotion

I would like to consider three practical areas of health care that relate to the previous arguments. All are subject to the charismatic ideology that assumes a monolithic perspective on health as applied by experts who know that is often based upon an hidden moral agenda.

The first is concerned with AIDS educational campaigns that are concerned with encouraging safe sex amongst gay men. Such educational material has assumed that there is an homogeneous culture to which gay men belong and that behavioural change will follow as a logical consequence from reasoned exhortation. Gold (1995) argues otherwise. There is not a safe sex culture in existence, and the encouragement to have safe sex has missed out on the reality of hedonism involved in sexual contact. As mentioned previously, health care rationale, for the individual, is not necessarily linked to a carefully planned strategy as health care professionals like to believe. There may be indeed disparities between what people believe and what they do.

For some gay men, the constellation of sexual gratification, recreational pleasure and the maintenance of a particular lifestyle, tied up as it is with a gay identity, does not have health care as a principal strategy for living, even in a climate of AIDS prevention. Human beings live, with optimism and zest, to enjoy life, not necessarily to prevent illness. Any interventions aimed at changing behaviour in gay men to promote a safer sex culture will need to accept that there are groups of men with differing lifestyles and expectations, some of who may not be benign and benevolent towards a wider community.

A second example is in the field of dieting and exercise as they are related to body shape. Females in Western industrialized cultures are expressing not only concern about their bodily shapes but are actively engaged in altering how they appear. The female body is the interface between the woman herself, as a person, and her social identity. Feelings about the self are related to feelings about the body; they are not solely located in the body, but are concerned with how that body appears to others. A vast amount of time and money are spent on consumer activities related to this body image in terms of exercise activities, fashion and diet. Slimness has become popularly associated with elegance, self-control, social attractiveness and youth (Furnham, Titman and Sleeman 1994). Such descriptions are also the motivating factors associated with the sales pitch of many consumer products. While such personal lifestyles of dieting for fitness and the presentation of a powerful potent body may be health enabling, there is also the paradox that it is these very activities that are involved in the generation of eating disorders. Hartley (1996) argues that the advancement of health education encouraging a diet low in fat and cholesterol has a negative effect and may play a role in eating disorders. The aesthetic of near emaciation in conjunction with the modern moral imperative of eating healthily, that is fat-free, may encourage a lifestyle that is life threatening. Health promotion has a social ecology that is all too easily neglected and this neglect of context may be the cause of high relapse rates following health promotion interventions (Stokols, Allen and Bellingham 1996).

The encouragement of the excessive individualism, while promoting autonomy, may be at the expense of her integrity as a whole person. She is connected to a set of cultural values that threaten to destroy her health when disembedded from the relations that may offer a social meaning to her personal identity. This excessive emphasis on the individual body dislocated from the social body is classically reflected in the egoism explanation in Durkheim's explanation of suicide (Warde 1994). Food preparation, the choosing of diet, the presentation of the body and the adornment of the body are never fixed and belong to a complex argument related both to individual identity and to the maintenance of a symbolic capital (Rasmussen 1996).

A third example is concerned with cigarette smoking in the young. While there has been a considerable impact on behalf of educational campaigns to curb adult smoking, those campaigns have failed to make any impact on the prevalence of young smokers (Lynch 1995). Lynch argues that this failure is because educational campaigns singularly fail to understand the reasons why young people smoke. These reasons may not be homogeneous, and certainly will not follow the causal sensible logic of most health care professionals. Image is seen as a powerful factor in influencing smoking behaviour, as is the need to be 'an individual'. Thus campaigns aimed to curb enjoyment, emphasizing a sensible conformity to an artificially constructed target group of adolescent smokers falsely assumed to be homogeneous, will be doomed to failure.

We see that hedonism, the enjoyment of the body, the maintenance of a self-image and pursuing an active, seemingly healthy, lifestyle can be both health promoting but, in some circumstances, deleterious to health. The pursuit of excessive individualism may lead to a disentanglement from social relationships that are vital to bringing some checks and balances to counter extremes of living that may prove to be deleterious. There is no easy reconciliation of this problem.

We must, however, recognize that our health care endeavours must target small groups and individuals. There are no easy global solutions that can be applied from the top down. Struggling to understand the individual and those with whom she is bound is vital. If this is central to the practice of health care in the consulting room, then it can surely be extended to our health care reasoning.

The ramification of all this for health care is that instead of a top-down approach to promoting health care, we must consider targeting interventions aimed at small groups in which individuals are embedded. Even within church groups we know there are small groups of individuals who have differing interpretations and adopt differing lifestyles (Spickard 1994).

We have to understand how people 'do' their lives, not simply what they think and say about their lives. It is in the body that individual identity is expressed, and the body is the interface between the individual and society. It is what people do together that binds them together with the groups with whom they perform their lives. This performance will be bound up with lifestyle, exercise and leisure activities (Johnson, Boyle and Heller 1995; Montelpare and Kanters 1994; Tinsley and Eldredge 1995), home decoration (Madigan and Munro 1996), dieting (Furnham and Boughton 1995; Hamilton *et al.* 1995; Nguyen *et al.* 1996) and dress. In a sense, 'lifestyle' is not something that can be read about in books, it is an activity and also subject to change (Træen 1995). Making sense of the world is an activity achieved through the body. Swimming cannot be learned about by reading about it, or by gathering together a band of expert swimmers together to tell you about their experiences, nor by attending a conference of hydro-physicists. At some time we have to jump into the water and through experience do it. The body grasps what it needs to do. Having a teacher in the water certainly helps. So too with health and a change in 'lifestyle'. If we wish to encourage people to do something differently, we have to understand that it will be intimately connected with their identity as a person and those with whom that identity is validated. Health care professionals are no longer the group with whom our patients wish to identify, and with their rates of suicide, marital disruption and drug abuse, who can blame them. Change is brought about by influencing small groups and understanding their way of being in the world.

One factor that we must take into account is that the serious business of living can also be fun. While we know a lot about health care activities and their impact, we know little about the importance of leisure activities and their ramifications for health. Positive emotions, according to new thinking, influence our health status for the better. Optimism and a sensual pleasure in everyday activities and situations are valuable for promoting personal health, and the absence of symptoms and a sense of enjoyment, coupled with a zest for living, appear to play a significant role in the subjective assessment of health (Montelpare and Kanters 1994; Wenglert and Rosén 1995). Once more, health is an activity that has sensual ramifications that are also concerned with pleasurable activities that are themselves integrated with an overall sense of 'lifestyle' rather than our unilateral exhortations to follow health care prescriptions.

How such optimism and sensual pleasure is passed on to those living in poverty as the urban poor will be the proving ground of the post-modernist argument and its reification of individualism. That the poor may continue to smoke and drink as creature comforts in a harsh world may lend credibility to the argument that sensual pleasures and leisure activities, even when there is no work, are the important arbiters of health care activity as it relates to daily living. The distribution of wealth that has a considerable impact of morbidity is not in the hands of the individual but belongs to a broader political process.

At the beginning of this chapter I used a quote from Pierre Bourdieu that separates the pure aesthetic of a dominant class from that of natural vulgar enjoyment. The same situation occurs in the broader medical discourse, whether it be within the suprematist dogma of orthodox medicine or the moral stricture of complementary medicine, as they have both become established in modern Western health care delivery. There is a pure aesthetic of health related to a dominant moral discourse. What I am arguing for is a vulgar praxis aesthetic that takes health as being done. This reflects both the chthonian mode of knowing (touch and smell) with the Apollonian mode (seeing and being seen) (Bemporad 1996). Rather than separating forms of knowing, perhaps we can turn to a reconciliation that occurs in the practice of everyday life. The body that is done is both seen and smelt in practice. Health care understandings are, then, heterogeneous, combining both sense and reason located in the practice of everyday living. This will have an implication for the methodologies that we use for health care research, as we need to incorporate – literally embody – lay knowledge (Aldridge 1990a, 1992a; Emke 1996; Popay and Williams 1996).

CHAPTER 3

The Clinical Assessment of Acupuncture for Asthma[1]

This chapter is concerned with reviewing the use of acupuncture for the relief of chronic bronchial asthma. The intention is to embark upon a controlled clinical trial of acupuncture therapy in the context of general medical practice. However, a secondary property of this chapter will be a discussion of clinical trial methodology as applied to a complementary therapy.

Acupuncture

Acupuncture is a therapy which has gained some recognition both within the realms of popular practice and, perhaps more importantly, within the realm of medical practice. The practice of acupuncture is a collection of procedures which include the insertion of needles at specific points of the body for both the relief of pain and the treatment of disease, moxibustion and cupping.

Traditional descriptions of acupuncture are concerned with the flow of vital energy, called ch'i, along fixed paths called meridians. These are linked together with each other and the organs of the body. Flow of energy along these paths has a circadian rhythm, so that at times and seasons it may vary. Energy in this context has a bipolar character; it can be positive called 'yang', and negative called 'yin'. The energy within the body, ch'i, reflects both the vitality of the universe and society (Millman 1977).

For a body to be healthy in this system of description then the flow of ch'i in the meridians is normal and balanced. Essentially the process is of maintaining balance, i.e. becoming healthy or losing health. Diagnosis too is seen as a

---

1   This Chapter was written originally in 1985. The references have been superseeded but the methodological argument remains the same.

process and takes into account many factors. It includes a patient history of changes in behaviour, appetite and emotions. The state of the skin, eyes, breath and tongue are noted for colour, consistency and odour. There are special techniques too for the evaluation of the flow of energy in the 12 meridians, electrical measurements of skin resistance, and the palpation of skin and subcutaneous tissue.

Although the mode of action on acupuncture is not known precisely, there are a number of suggestions which propose that the mechanism is linked with the secretion of endorphins. Guillemin, Vargo and Rossier (1977) and Yu and Lee (1976) suggest that acupuncture relieves that part of the broncho-constriction which does not arise from the constriction of smooth muscle as a result of chemical mediators. The effect of acupuncture in asthma is mediated through modification of the reflex component of broncho-constriction. Other writers invoke the proximity of the central nervous system projections of the acupuncture stimulation site and the pain path as the rationale for the selection of treatment loci, humoral-biochemical mechanisms, neuromechanisms, and the bio-electric mechanism. Millman (1977), incidentally, does point out that these descriptions are made by 'scientific apologists'.

It is more likely that acupuncture represents many phenomena and that a primary difficulty, as we shall see later, lies in a treatment modality which is underpinned by an Oriental philosophy being subjected to an explanation by the differing theoretical understanding of modern Western medicine.

Asthma

Asthma is a condition characterized by symptoms which are present over long periods of a patient's life. The number of persons with asthma in the United Kingdom is estimated to be about 2 million. Such a number is too great for the hospital services to provide continuing care. Although the condition is often mild, and readily treated, for those persons with a chronic condition the illness is composed of recurrent crises and debilitation. Gregg (1985) estimates that the incidence of asthma in the population is increasing and in a form which is frequently more severe than in the past. The general practitioner is in a position to identify the incidence of asthma, to be involved in preventive measures and to offer early treatment. Many persons seen in hospital outpatient departments could be as easily managed in the context of the general practitioner clinic (Arnold, Lane and Zapata 1983).

Asthma is often refractory to pharmacotherapy, the side effects of which can be distressing. A low-risk form of treatment such as acupuncture could constitute an advancement in the management of asthma particularly if used in the context of general medical practice that utilizes elements of patient education and a self-care perspective (Dias, Subraniam and Lionel 1982).

Clinical controlled trials of asthma

A literature search was carried out using the Medline database through St Mary's Hospital Medical School library. The criteria for the search were English language papers for the past ten years covering 'asthma therapy' and 'acupuncture'. Eight studies were discovered which used a controlled trial methodology using either a 'placebo' or 'no treatment' control group (Berger and Nolte 1977; Christensen et al. 1984; Dias et al. 1982; Shao and Ding 1985; Takishima et al. 1982; Tashkin et al. 1977, 1985; Yu and Lee 1976).

Although these trials ostensibly used a controlled trial methodology there were many inconsistencies. First, most of the trials had few subjects. The largest trial had 111 subjects but the rest had no more than 25. Second, there was a large disparity in the age ranges. In one trial the ages ranged from 6 to 71 years. Third, the clinical entities were wide ranging.

The predominant conclusion of the controlled trials was that there is only at best a modest improvement in the 'objective' assessment of airway impedance. These objective measures were mainly concerned with expiratory flow rates, airway conductance and thoracic gas volume. A greater perception of symptom relief was made subjectively by the patients using self-report measures and diary techniques. It is this point which will be discussed later in the chapter.

Clinical evaluations

Two trials (Cioppa 1976; Fuller 1974) were essentially evaluations of clinical practice made by clinicians. They covered a range of symptoms associated with asthma and varied their treatment approach according to the presenting symptoms. The number of treatment sessions was not standardized but varied according to the symptoms and symptomatic improvement.

The criteria for improvement were subjective and included the assessments of both practitioner and patient. Cioppa (1976) found that 67 per cent of the patients improved with acupuncture treatment. The conclusions of this research were that acupuncture appears to (a) relieve muscle spasm, (b) be useful in

subacute conditions, (c) be something other than hypnosis, (d) facilitate manipulation, (e) have an immediate effect, (f) give complete remission – not only
palliation – in many cases, (g) give a sense of well-being, (h) be a valuable
adjunct to standard practice. Fuller (1974) also believes that acupuncture is
effective for the treatment of chronic asthma and recommends its use.

The remaining papers were a collection of miscellaneous reports and letters
about the clinical application of acupuncture, the relationship to general
medical practice and as replies to letters (Allen 1983; Bodner, Topilsky and
Greif 1983; Donnelly, Spyykerboer and Thong 1985; Hayhoe 1982; Marcus
1982; Rebuck 1985; Rosenthal, Wang and Norman 1975).

Hossri (1976) describes the use of acupuncture massage in children for the
relief of asthma. This entails a number of techniques using pressure at acupuncture sites, friction and manipulation. Hossri also uses hypnosis in combination
with these techniques. Acupressure, the substitute of digital pressure for
needling at specific sites, has been used in medicine and dentistry both for the
relief of pain and tension (Kurland 1976; Penzer 1985; Weaver 1985).

Discussion

There is a disparity between the claims of acupuncturists as to positive clinical
benefit, and the findings of the clinical trials research which demonstrates little
'objective' change but does emphasize 'subjective' change. Such difficulties
bedevil the assessment of alternative or complementary thera- pies particularly
because there is a confusion between different levels of measurement, i.e.
between that which can be measured in terms of quantity as a gas volume, and
that which cannot be readily subjected to such quantification such as 'feeling
better'.

A more serious critique is that of the controlled trial methodology itself.
The trials in this study failed to provide a sample size with sufficient power to
make any valid conclusions from the statistics (Lewith and Machin 1983). Furthermore the trials really did not investigate 'acupuncture'. The process of
standardizing the treatment approach removed from the practice itself that
which is of the essence of the treatment. By restricting needling sites to specific
loci, limiting the number of treatment sessions and abdicating the use of traditional diagnostic practices, the trials were really reduced to testing the insertion
of needles at particular points. Small wonder then that needling as 'acupuncture' in these trials differed from needling as a 'placebo' or 'sham' acupuncture.
What these trials failed to do was realize that although a methodology can be

applied, if applied without understanding simply as a formula then no significant findings emerge. To do this abdicates both responsibility in science and real discovery. Science is not methodology; methodology serves science.

How can we as scientists say that we have subjected a practice to adequate investigation when we remove from the process that which is essential? When applied rigidly clinical trials remove the interaction bet- ween the subject and the researcher. It is this very interaction which we know is at the very heart of clinical practice, and which cannot be removed no matter how impersonal we may wish to be. The separation of the disease from the person loses those very qualities which we need to understand. Diseases may be treated as aggregates and submitted to statistical analysis but it is individual persons in whom those diseases are located and who confront us in our surgeries.

Another feature of the clinical trial methodology was that asthma was seen as an homogeneous clinical entity. There was no consideration that the symptoms were located within persons who perceived their symptoms differentially, or that asthma in a six-year-old is qualitatively different from that in a 71-year-old.

Asthma appears to be tractable to acupuncture when treated by com- mitted clinicians who use traditional techniques. The clinical trials have not investigated acupuncture as a treatment modality but 'needling techniques'. The challenge for us as clinicians and researchers is to rigorously examine the practical effects of acupuncture treatment but from a perspective which involves the whole person and the totality of the treatment process.

CHAPTER 4

Of Ethics and Education
Strategies for Curriculum Development

There have been continuing demands (WHO 1988) for the renewal of medical education such that the education of medical students will prepare them to met the needs of the communities which they will serve (Prywes 1983). The central emphasis, apart from that of maintaining a standard of knowledge and skills sufficient for licensing medical practitioners, has been on the qualitative aspects of carers.

In any new path that is proposed, it is the philosophical and social questions which gain prominence in the light of ever-increasing technological development. These technological developments bring forth questions concerned with the quality of patients' lives (Tosteson 1990), ethics and morality. The imminent and pressing problems of chronic disease, old age, handicap, abortion, artificial nutrition, withdrawing medical support, organ transplantation, fertility and genetic engineering raise issues relevant for the clinician in everyday practice. Furthermore, the economic costs of medical care underlying the solutions to ethical dilemmas, and the costs of medical testing and intervention, must be included in clinical thinking and thereby included in any new curriculum. In some ways this is uncomfortable knowledge (Stein 1988). The social sciences applied to medicine operate in a charged political arena where information often challenges established clichés and puts in question accepted solutions. Falling fertility in the Western world is occurring at a time when there is increasing longevity. This will shift the fiscal balance necessary for the support of health care, particularly in countries where the 'new consumers' from other lands demand support from a budget to which they have not contributed in the immediate past.

Social considerations in medicine demand a long-term perspective on human relationships requiring knowledge about human nature, family culture, and social welfare. As the 1988 WHO declaration states:

…the aim of medical education is to produce doctors who will promote the health of all people, and that aim is not being realized in many places, despite the enormous progress that has been made during this century in the biomedical sciences. The individual patient should be able to expect a doctor as an attentive listener, a careful observer, a sensitive communicator, and an effective clinician; but it is not enough to treat only some of the sick.

Strong and heady stuff, and for many of us almost impossible to contemplate in its entirety and implement in practice. Such practice requires knowledge from varying disciplines concerning human behaviour. Promoting the health of all people, as recommended, is a social and moral consideration. Attending the individual patient, the central focus of the clinical encounter, is an ethical consideration. While both hang together easily in the above quo- tation, in practice they are not so easily realized.

How can we then contemplate a curriculum for medical education when the breadth of knowledge is so great, and the increasing trend of practitioners is towards specialization? One way would be to educate health professionals to work together such that they can operate as a team to develop and share individual expertise. Some initiatives in medical education have attempted to promote such activity.

For the introduction of any change in a curriculum there are essential conditions for that change. First, it is important that all who are likely to be involved in implementing change are involved in discussions regarding that change. This initiative is essentially a political and relational process. Political, because one party attempts to influence the other by argument. Relational, because the process is dependent upon goodwill and trust between faculty and the students for whom they are responsible. Second, for new methods to be implemented then the teaching staff involved must not be defensive and protective about their own subjects. This second condition requires interdisciplinary and interdepartmental co-operation. The implementation of change is a management task for which few of us are prepared by training.

The strength of this approach is that it mirrors the consultation approach which stresses the activity of the patient. Patients, and sometimes their families, are expected to actively contribute to treatment decisions and identify goals for change. In areas of decision making where ethical considerations play an important role, the negotiation of co-operation within a relationship of trust could be a vital skill for our students to learn. This skill would not entail an encyclopaedic knowledge, but the ability to seek relevant knowledge and apply it in context as the situation demands. Part of this assimilation of knowledge would be social; that is, listening to what others have to say with a different world view.

Sukkar (1986) writes that in order to bring about change in a medical faculty it was important that the teachers were made aware of the educational processes involved and that the teachers had expertise in planning the new educational strategy. To this end members of the teaching staff were asked to participate in a programme of 2–3 day workshops. Junior members of staff were also encouraged if they showed interest in educational activities. Specialized workshops also developed expertise in specific areas of educational activity: curriculum planning, instructional methods, the use of educational technology and other teaching media, and evaluation methods. Small working groups were also set up to implement particular aspects of curriculum development.

This teacher training programme emphasized the role of learners in setting learning objectives. Although integration between departments was encouraged the impact was minimal. The introduction of such change involved three main strategies:

1.   A fellowship strategy which involved and included the teachers.

2.   A political strategy which used power and influence to implement the necessary initial changes.

3.   An academic strategy of considering issues on their intellectual merit and the basis of information rather than the protection of territorial rights.

It is clear from the literature that there are no universal solutions to curriculum change, and each setting must generate its own particular programme, although the process of change with institutions has elements in common. What is evident from the practice of implementing change is that a tutor training programme is mandatory (De Marchais 1990). Tutor skills are paramount in new approaches to medical education. The tutor must stimulate discussion, maintain attention to the problem being discussed and guide the learning of the group, by facilitating group dynamics. This entails the tutor having an overview of the territory of the subject while the students can explore individual features.

What we can learn from this is that although students are in individual control of their own learning, and deciding what they will learn, the faculty determines the methods by which the students will be taught. It is the faculty which remains constant over time and which must maintain the thread of education. The student weaves that thread, according to his or her own particular pattern, into a garment which fits his or her own particular needs.

The central feature of any new approach is that it is based upon set objectives. These objectives are made clear between student and tutor relating to the personal needs of the student and inevitably to the requirements set by the state exam. In the end the faculty is responsible to the community that it will produce doctors of a particular standard fit to serve that community. While the standard itself may be questionable we can accept it as a basic which we can enhance, rather than a ceiling to which we must aspire. This tension will always exist between individual perspectives and state requirements, but it is not necessarily counter-productive reg- arding new teaching approaches (Coles 1987).

Although in recent years a number of medical schools have adopted problem-based learning, so far there is no evidence that problem-based learning is educationally superior to the conventional curriculum. Nor is it inferior, and students appear to like such methods. Output measures are insensitive in detecting the subtle differences that may occur using such methods; although as educators we assume that a problem-based approach may be creating an educational climate which enables students to learn in what seems to be a desirable manner.

Contract learning is also a form of learning by the setting of mutual objectives. The term 'contract' itself is redundant as all learning situations are a contract between student and teacher, or student and faculty. What these methods have in common is that the contract is made explicit, rather than implicit, and given definite boundaries according to the personnel involved.

The assumed benefits of these methods are that learning occurs in a context similar to which the student will practise as a doctor where knowledge is shared and negotiated in a team; that their eventual work as a doctor will be improved because knowledge is understood in clinical and social context; and the conditions are set for lifelong learning (Coles 1990). Students are not only learning how to become doctors, they are also learning how to learn. That further learning, based upon critical thinking, does take place after qualification is open to question. Much practice is based upon eliminating variability and reducing the uncertainty of facts until they fit the familiar view such that a diagnosis can be made. This is the maintenance of medical belief, not the pursuit of scientific argument.

The major implication of this approach is that if we are to implement new methods, and wish to assess the efficacy of those new methods on the standard of medical education, then assessment must occur after graduation when the new doctor is in practice. Apart from this assessment of our teaching methods on the quality of the students we produce, it is clear from the literature that new teaching methods also have a vital component of evaluation during the career of the student at the medical school.

Current thinking in medical education emphasizes the idea that people learn best when they are helped to define their own problems, acknowledge and accept their own strengths and weaknesses, decide on a course of action, and evaluate the course of their decisions. (A situation which also sounds rather like the doctor – patient encounter.) It does not mean using self-administered tests to determine knowledge and skills; what it does mean is helping people to judge their own performance. It is important for students to define their own learning objectives, and the educator's task is to facilitate that learning. While the student identifies what he or she wants, the trainer, or support group, also identifies what the student needs to expand his or her learning objectives. The need of the student is a point which is often missed; it is not only what the student wants (which the student can determine) but what the student also needs (which his or her colleagues, and tutor, must determine).

Any reform of the curriculum will then require a reappraisal of the principles and practices of the evaluation system. The norm-referenced test which is the primary method of evaluation was initially designed to rank students for the purpose of selection. Difficulties arise when it is used, as it currently is, for the assessment of competence. The norm-referenced test 'while it provides information regarding the relative strengths and weaknesses of students in comparison to their peers...does not provide an estimate of the absolute level of performance achieved' (Turnbull 1989, p.145).

As it is the principal responsibility of a medical school to produce competent physicians, and not to rank order them, it is more reasonable to compare student achievement to an external standard of performance or criterion. Criterion-referenced testing is more suitable for the assessment of competence as it best meets the objectives of medical schools by empha- sizing achievement of clearly established external standards and, thereby, ensuring a standard of performance. Evaluation in this sense guides both tutor and learner to the areas which must be developed. These methods are also valuable for those students who may require remedial help, and for encouraging a broad-based platform for student education.

New methods, then, also carry with them a component of assessment. Assessment practices are often the major barrier to developing increasing student responsibility; if students always look to others for judgements of their competence, how can they develop their ability to assess their own learning? Transactions between students and staff are critically affected by the balance of power – where it rests and how it is used determines the quality of learning. Assessment is the clearest example of this power in action. Collaborative forms of assessment are necessary to overcome the problem of authority while still meeting the need for a certificate of intellectual competence. An agreed criterion-referenced test provides the neutral ground for such collaboration. Using peer reference will strengthen internal demands for consistency and respect for individual ways of learning. But the demand of external licensing must be met and faculties cannot shirk the responsibility of meeting that demand and the authority of implementing expected criteria.

It is at this very point where we have the dilemma of the current examination system. If we encourage students to develop their own way of learning, then surely we must encourage them to assess themselves as to their competence. However, as faculty we have responsibility to the wider community in issuing the necessary licences of competence. While the student has the responsibility to learn, we have the responsibility to guide, and ultimately judge. To include the assessment of the student, and his or her peers, is essential in respecting their way of learning and implementing change in the curriculum. As to the criteria necessary for licensing, then it is the faculty of teachers who must conserve and maintain the curriculum such that it is coherent and recognizable to external scrutiny. If both parties are involved in the dialogue of change and conservation, within the context of a respectful and trusting relationship, then we can hope that the dilemma will be resolved satisfactorily.

In the end there is a distinction between the student who is there to learn, and the teacher who is there to guide. If the students knew already they would not be studying. It could well be that in our new methods we are asking the student to be both doctor and educator; this would not be so far from the modern demand made of the medical practitioner, and the old meaning of the word 'doctor'. However, to attain such a social standing requires validation from the community, of which the faculty is representative, that the student when graduated can both teach and heal.

A handicap to the introduction of new teaching methods can be the students themselves. It appears that the pressure of examinations dominate the curriculum no matter how well intentioned the design, or how educationally sensible the underlying philosophy (Carney and Mitchell 1987). This can be overcome, but it is necessary to understand that these new study methods also introduce stress. First there is the stress of having little time for leisure activities. Introducing more areas of study, such as medical ethics, into the curriculum will further compound this problem. Second, any form of assessment, no matter how valuable to the student, is an additional stressor.

Time is an important factor for students. Learning takes time and we must be concerned that students have time to absorb knowledge. Presently there is talk of producing students efficiently, meaning that doctors can be produced in one year less than is currently possible. This is a dangerous trend and totally against the move towards a qualitatively better education. What are we educating our students to become as doctors and carers if we continually stress objectivity, work and production in the shortest time? Furthermore, we are assuming that all students will learn at the same rate. We can promote excellence in all our students, but not all can achieve excellence at the same rate. The way in which we teach is as important as what we teach.

To practise medicine is to solve ethical dilemmas. Medical consultation is a social act where one person intervenes to influence another person utilizing clinical and non-clinical expertise. As Brock (1991, p.45) writes:

> Shared decision-making does not imply a value-neutral role for physicians; it requires of them a more delicate balancing. They must advocate for their patient's health and well being, while also being prepared ultimately to respect patients' self determination, even when they agree with their patients' treatment choices.

Such a statement could be translated substituting tutor for physician and student for patient. Medical or educational interventions are reached by consultations which demand a social understanding lacking in medical education. Learning to make shared decisions based on consultation will be the future of health care delivery. How we implement such an activity, and teach it to our students, is a matter of debate and urgency and runs counter to the modern trend of specialization. Ethics is concerned with the decisions individuals make about their own behaviour. Morality is the set of rules resident in the community which govern individual behaviour. The reconciliation of an individual ethic within the context of a social morality is at the heart of human decision making. Finding solutions to this dilemma is the stuff of education.

CHAPTER 5

Aesthetics and the Individual in the Practice of Medical Research

Art does not reproduce the visible, rather it makes visible. Formerly we used to represent things visible on earth, things we either liked to look at or would have liked to see. Today we reveal that reality that is behind all living things, thus expressing the belief that the visible world is merely an isolated case in relation to the universal, and there are many more latent realities.

Paul Klee, quoted in Grohmann (1987)

There is a demand made of arts therapists by the wider community that they validate their work with clinical studies (Aldridge 1990a, 1990b). This is often countered with the argument that scientific methods are often inappropriate to the study of these forms of creative therapy. A similar cry is also heard in orthodox medicine that the strict methodology of science is often found wanting when applied to the study of human behaviour. This has stimulated calls for innovation in clinical medical research (Hart 1984). A significant factor of that innovation is a growing awareness by the doctor of the patient's social and cultural milieu, and an understanding of health beliefs (Gregg 1985; Underwood, Gray and Winkler 1985; Wilkin 1986). What we may need then in clinical research is to facilitate the emergence of a discipline which seeks to discover what media are available for expressing clinical change. These media may be as much aesthetic as they are scientific, thereby emphasizing the art of healing in parallel with the science of healing (Aldridge 1989c; Gregg 1985; Underwood *et al.* 1985; Wilkin 1986).

Both science and art are activities which attempt to bring certain contents of the world into cognition. The contention of this chapter is that when we study human behaviour, and in particular what it means to be sick, to become well again or to live through the process of dying, then both forms of acquain-

61

tance, artistic and scientific, are necessary for the practice of research in medicine.

In medical research most of the modern initiatives for that research have come from the field of natural science. Such research when applied to the study of human behaviour is partial and neglects the important creative elements in the process, and practice, of healing. This is not to deny the scientific, rather to emphasize the aesthetic such that both may be considered together. Unfortunately the tension of understanding both elements of human understanding results in one or the other being denied. Such is the current situation in modern medicine. However, the continuing problems of chronic illness and human suffering urge us to go beyond our partisan beliefs and look again at *how* we know as well as *what* we know (Aldridge and Pietroni 1987a). This is literally the art of re-search.

The problem facing the clinician is that he or she must often mediate between the personal needs of the patient and the health needs of the community. These needs are informed by differing world views. Similarly there is often a split in medical science between researchers and therapists. One group see themselves as rational and rigorous in their thinking and others as sentimental and biased, which in turn elicits comments about inhuman treatment and reductionist thinking. Neither of these stances is true; each perspective has something to offer. However, the predominating ideas in published medical research are those of natural science as informed by statistical data.

Historical context

The science of statistics developed in eighteenth-century France (Tröhler 1988) as part of the centralized apparatus of the State (Foucault 1989). 'Statistics' as the science of State was the empirical numerical representation of the resources available to the State and formed the components of a new power rationality. Health care became, as it is now, a political objective, as well as a personal objective. Health, from this perspective, is seen as the duty of each member of society and the objective of all. Individual needs are subsumed within the goals of the collective, the private ethic is informed by the public ethic and objective empirical data are the means by which goals are assessed (see Table 5.1). These data are related to the economic regulation of health care delivery (health as commodity), public order (the regulation of deviance), and hygiene (the quality of food, water and the environment).

Table 5.1 Comparative and complementary perspectives on health research

Scientific perspective	Individual perspective
• state regulation of health	• personal regulation of health
• constancy predictability and control: the future is based on past data	• creative irrationality: being and becoming
• technology of the body: observations, examinations and case reports	• techniques of the self: music, art, personal narratives and poetry
• objective statistical reality based on instrumentally monitored data	• subjective and symbolic reality based on the senses and human consciousness
• the health of the body is an imperative of the State	• self maintains its own identity
• scientific	• aesthetic
• time as chronos	• time as kairos

From this viewpoint we have the notion of health care, and knowledge about that health care, which is regulated by the State. The objects of that health care (patients), the practitioners of that health care (therapists) and the providers of that health care (health and State insurance) are informed by the same world view. Such was the strength of modern science, it offered a replicable body of knowledge in the face of the ever-increasing solipsism of metaphysics in the eighteenth century.

From a modern scientific stance the body is to be manipulated as an object of the State to whose ends it serves. Such manipulation is served by the processes of classification and normalization. People are observed, classified and analysed as 'cases' according to their deviance from a given norm. Disease becomes a category like any other rather than the unique experience which it is.

The epistemology of this normative process is that of natural science which emphasizes reason, constancy and predictability. In the face of death and disruption the imperative of health is to maintain continuity and control. It is a philosophical assumption that the positive instance of an hypothesis will give ground for further instances. However, there is no logical necessity which will safeguard our passage from past to future experiences (Ayer 1982).

A critique of scientific methodology

Implicit in many criticisms of art therapy research is the notion that there are 'right' premises for doing science. The implication is that there is a common map of the territory of healing, with particular co-ordinates and given symbols, for finding our way around and that the orthodox map of scientific medicine is the only one. Any different map is seen as deviant, and any challenge to the construction of that map as heretical (Watzlawick 1984).

The implication of such heresy is that those who question the method of mapping human experience, or offer an alternative map, will be excommunicated from the scientific and therapeutic community. Alternative practices are implied to be 'cultish' and at best 'unscientific'. Bateson (1978), however, reminds us that although we think in terms of coconuts or pigs there are no coconuts or pigs in the brain. In clinical research that which we report on is a product of our own perceiving. This is not to put forward a purely nominalist argument (Gillon 1986), which would be to plunge us backwards into the darkness of metaphysical speculation and dogma, rather to emphasize the relativity of perspectives in thinking about healing.

Similarly, when we speak of scientific or experimental validity, that validity has to be conferred by a person or group of persons on the work or actions of another group. This is a 'political' process. With the obsession for 'objective truths' in the scientific community, then other 'truths' are ignored. As therapists we have many ways of knowing: by intuition, through experience and by observation. If we disregard these 'knowings' then we promote the idea that there is an objective definitive external truth which exists as 'tablets of stone' to which only we, the initiated, have access.

Methodological issues

While clinical controlled trial methodology may appear to be scientifically sound, a number of articles have questioned the scientific premises of such methods.

The first of these criticisms is that a random selection of trial subjects cannot be achieved because any group of patients comprises a highly selected non-random group (Burkhardt and Kienle 1980; Editorial 1983). Any results concerning this trial group cannot be generalized to other trial groups. These inductive generalizations, it is argued, are no more respectable than those made from anecdotal experiences.

Second, group generalizations from research findings raise problems for the clinician who is faced with the individual person in his or her consulting room. Individual variations are mocked by the group average (Barlow and Hersen 1984). If a group of 50 patients in a treatment group does statistically better than a control group of 50 patients then such a difference could be due to a small number of patients in the treatment group showing a larger change while the majority of patients show no changes or deteriorate slightly. It is the patients who change significantly which are of interest to us as therapists, and we would want to know the significant factors involved in that change. These factors, however, are lost within the group average.

Third, there are issues of reliability which are linked to the practice of scientific research. The reliability of our knowledge is only as good as the underpinning hypothesis (Dudley 1983). An hypothesis by definition is capable of being disproved. Inevitably the reliability of a trial when extended to a broader population is an act of induction (Burkhardt and Kienle 1983).

Not everything is measurable by numbers

At a fundamental level there is a major fault in much research thinking about human behaviour. This is the confusion of number with quantity. Numbers are the result of counting and can be accurate because there is a discontinuity with one integer and the next. We can count one boy, two boys, three boys and see the difference. When we come to the measurement of quantity then we have greater difficulty in being precise. Quantity is approximate.

It is easier to see three boys than it is to measure exactly three litres of water. This problem has bedevilled clinical measurement. Although methods of measurement are continually being refined, the very process of measuring, when introduced into a clinical trial, influences the trial itself.

The people with whom we work in the therapist–patient relationship are not experimental units. Nor are the measurements made on these people isolated sets of data. While at times it may be necessary to make this split we must be aware that we are making the act of separating data from people.

When we come to measure particular personal variables then we face many complications. Consider a person who sits before a practitioner in a surgery who has been treated unsuccessfully for chronic leukaemia with a bone marrow transplant. The clinical measurements of blood status, weight and temperature are important. However, they belong to a different realm to those of anxiety about the future, the experience of pain, the anticipation of personal and social losses and the existential feeling of abandonment. These defy comparative measurement. Yet, if we are to investigate therapeutic approaches to chronic disease, we need to investigate these subjective and qualitative realms (Clark and Fallowfield 1986; Gold 1986; Spitzer et al. 1981).

In terms of outcomes measurement we face further difficulties. The people we see in our surgeries, or in our clinical trials, do not live in isolation. Life is rather a messy laboratory and continually influences the subjects of our therapeutic and research endeavours. Even more daunting is the fact that subjects influence themselves.

Finally, there is no such thing as a purely 'physical' treatment (Heron 1984). Treatment always occurs in a psychosocial context. Medicine is a social as well as a natural science (Kleinman, 1973; Mechanic 1986). The way people respond in situations is sometimes determined by the way in which they have understood the meaning of that situation (Harré and Secord 1971). By studying the accounts people give of their symptoms in the context of their intimate relationships then we can glean valuable understandings of illness behaviour. The meaning of a headache in the context of a therapist–patient relationship may be a far cry from the meaning of a headache in a husband–wife relationship.

This reflects one of two fundamentally differing approaches to science. One is to develop precise and fixed procedures that yield a stable and definite empirical content. We have this in controlled trial methodology. The other approach to investigation depends upon careful and imaginative life studies which, although lacking some of the precision of technical instruments, have the virtue of continuing a close relationship with the natural social world of people.

Ethical and political issues

The subject matter of our research endeavours, and the way we carry out those endeavours, reflects our views of the society we wish to live in, how we wish to deal with our fellow human beings and how we want to be dealt with by them.

As therapists the concern for the subject prevails over the interests of society at large and scientific medicine as an institution. Individuals are not treated as a means to some collective end in clinical practice, although we may subscribe to a notion of community health. Furthermore, we discover a dilemma for research in that scientific standards of acceptability are juxtaposed with the ordinary therapeutic standards of the therapist. The stan- dards of probability necessary for scientific statistical validity may be more exacting than the standards of probability acceptable to either the patient or the therapist. Such standards can vary according to the context in which they are applied. For the dying person the rigour of the clinical trial and the level of probability in terms of treatment efficacy may be quite different to that of the 'healthy' person, a woman in mid-term or an infant.

A further difficulty of accepting levels of probability is that trials of treatment are often scrutinized or judged by therapists and scientists who have a world view which is different to that of those carrying out the trial. While it is necessary to have questions posed by 'outsiders' it is important that trials of art therapies are assessed by panels which have representatives of these therapeutic directions. By incorporating experts from differing disciplines then it is possible to design procedures whereby any prevailing dogma is not granted a monopoly status as a compulsory 'current status of scientific knowledge' and that minority groups representing other forms of therapeutic practice are not suppressed by the majority vote. This plurality of opinion will enliven research endeavours and offer a broad platform of therapeutic practice (Pietroni and Aldridge 1987).

While trials may be set up to conform to an experimental methodology, those practising within the trial invariably approach their work from a clinical viewpoint. For the subjects of the trial their agenda is likely to be 'clinical' in so far as their expectations are of treatment. Similarly the results of a trial need to be interpreted and applied by therapists. Perhaps what we have failed to ask are the following questions: 'What is the exact nature of therapeutic judgement, what realms of information are used to make that judgement and who is to assess the legitimate outcome of that judgement?'

When controlled trials are carried out in a therapeutic setting then the benefit for the individual is set against the benefit for the group. The Declaration of Helsinki (1975) states:

> In any medical study, every patient – including those of the control group, if any – should be assured of the best proven diagnostic and therapeutic method.

The clinical judgement of the therapist is on the side of the individual patient even if it means the corruption of a research project. When therapists, who are bound by contracts for treatment, take part in clinical trials then the dilemma is revealed. Either they fulfil their individual contract for treatment with the patient, or they abdicate that contract and fulfil their obligations to the research contract which are concerned with group benefit. This raises further the conceptual issues for health care of whether 'health' is an individual or a societal concept. Are we as therapists committed to improving the health of individuals we see, or are we directed to improving the health of the communities we serve?

Meaning and reality

A social science explanation of human behaviour has emphasized that human beings are not solely organisms responding to stimuli from the environment, or simply the sum of their interacting organ systems. The very difficulty of studying such behaviour is that people make sense of what they do, impose different meanings onto reality and alter their behaviour accordingly. When we try to understand social action we have to take into account that there are different available interpretations of that action. Furthermore, these actions take place as processes in natural settings and belong to social contexts. Not all patients have the same means of articulating their problems and concerns as do their therapists.

When a person consults a therapist and presents a problem then that problem can be seen in varying ways according to the perspectives of the patient and the therapist. The presentation of that problem will have occurred after previous discussions with other family members, and previously attempted health care activities (Aldridge 1990a). Similarly the choice of healer and the available treatment is also part of a cultural context which embraces the therapist and the patient (Kleinman and Sung 1979).

Scientific medicine emphasizes one particular way of knowing; this seems to maintain the myth that to know anything we must be scientists. If we consider people who live in vast desert areas, they find their way across those trackless terrains without any understandings of scientific geography. They also know the pattern of the weather without recourse to what we know as the science of meteorology. In a similar way people know about their own bodies and have understandings about their own lives. They may not confer the same meanings as we do, yet it is those meanings and particular beliefs about health to which we might best be guiding our research endeavours. While as therapists we may help to bring about a change in behaviour by technical means, it is the patient themselves who we have to rely upon to describe the meanings and implications of that change. This also leaves out the burgeoning problem for us as scientists in explaining how a change in meaning can bring about a change in behaviour.

The practical difficulty of researching subjective variables is that they are not accessible to quantitative methods, nor are they generalizable; they are indeed subjective. To combat this difficulty and potential disruption of our knowledge we tend to ignore such data and reduce our variables to those which are easily manipulated. To do so reduces the person to simply being a vessel for the containment of a disease. When we include subjective variables such as emotion, we treat them as if they could be weighed (Porter 1986).

When we intervene or treat persons in our research studies then we are engaging in an activity which is not stable. Our intention is to bring about change. This too poses a problem for generalizability beyond that seen in the earlier section. Not only do we have to extrapolate from one group to another, we have to induce meanings from a situation which is in a state of flux.

In natural science studies objectivity is sought by separating the subject from interfering with the experiment. Some authors state that by doing this the person is alienated from the study (Reason and Rowan 1981). Yet we know that the attitudes and belief of the experimenter and the subject are important, and that the experimenter and the subject interact with each other. When we study health then we have to take into account biological, psychological and social factors (Engel 1977; Schwab and Schwab 1978). They are not independent factors but interact with each other. It is we as researchers who separate the world into categories, yet social life occurs in natural settings quite different from the artificial ones created for research.

Single-case designs

There are ways of researching the person scientifically in the form of single-case studies, where the possibilities for blind intervention and randomization are retained (Aldridge 1988a). In this practice the patient is their own statistic. These single-case approaches may be a useful middle ground from which art therapists can begin their research endeavours as therapists researching their everyday practice (Aldridge 1990c). These forms of clinical study can collect multivariate data over time. They therefore lend themselves to the study of regulatory processes within the individual, where any deviance is from the norm of the person themselves. The person becomes their own statistic – they are not compared with the group.

Art and science

Research from this standpoint is not science in that has no generalizable reference. The importance of such work is in its particular subjective and unconventional reference. While the aesthetic may appear to occupy a pole opposite to the scientific, we may propose that both poles are necessary to express the life of human beings.

Both art and science bring an appreciation of form and the expression of meaning. Maps, traces and graphs are articulate forms of an inner reality. So are the objects of art. They exist as articulate forms; they have an internal structure which is given to perception. However, while the graph is a regularized form whereby the individual, as content, is charted upon given axes, the object of art is both the expression and the axes of that expression, i.e. form and content.

In expressive art sensory qualities are liberated from their usual meaning. While science requires the graph for regularity, art requires that forms are given a new embodiment; they can be set free to be recognized. In this way qualitative form can be set free and made wholly apparent, in direct contrast to the questionnaire method where inner subjective realities are submitted to an external objective form. This is not to deny the use of the questionnaire, rather to emphasize the possibility of considering expressive forms when we wish to discover the quality of life. Sensual qualities then become of vital import to the whole, not to be rated on a scale, but intrinsic to the total gestalt.

In this way of researching we are concerned with showing rather than saying. For example, there are important factors in heart disease related to the Type A behaviour which can be discovered by interview. However, the picture of the individual gained from such interviews is rather negative (Aldridge 1990c) and may be an artefact of the assessment method. A more neutral stance may be to allow subjects to improvise music.

Expression

The artistic symbol negotiates insight not reference. It expresses the feelings from whom it stems and is a total analogue of human life. The symbol and that which is symbolized have some common logical form, i.e. they are isomorphic. Science, in contrast, negotiates reference not insight. That which is within the individual is placed within a context.

Music and art are concerned, not with the stimulation of feeling, but the expression of feeling. It may be more accurate to say here that feelings are not necessarily 'emotional states', more an expression of what the person knows as inner life, which may exceed the boundaries of conventional categorization. By encouraging non-verbal forms of expression we can learn and utter ideas about human sensibility. A reliance on verbal methods alone assumes that we can know and speak about all that we are. A reliance on machine expressions of our inner realities assumes that all that we are is measurable and material.

The art form presents the whole intelligible form as an intuitive recognition of inner knowledge projected as outer form: subjective is made objective but in the terms of the subject. In artistic expression we have the possibility of making perceptible an inner experience.

Conclusion

A time has come when we can judge our research on whether it makes a powerful and important contribution to the cumulative evidence (Pringle 1984) on a particular issue rather than whether or not it formally proves a point. This recognition of subjective data is occurring at a time when an emphasis is being placed on the 'whole' patient rather than fragmenting the person into organ systems (Pietroni 1984).

Balint showed us that is not solely scientific skills which help us to fully understand the patient. It is possible to have a descriptive science of human behaviour which can be based upon the aesthetic. In this way we can ask of our research that it expresses what it is to be human, what it is to be well and what it is to fall sick.

As modern living provokes ever-more anxiety then the present search for scientific solutions based upon predictability, and the attempted control of nature by technology, continues. This retreat from the anxiety of dying and its emphasis on the material prevents us from understanding the true process of living. How can we then offer hope and comfort to the sick and the dying (Aldridge 1987a,b,c,d)?

A phenomenological perspective on research concerns itself with the person as they are 'coming into being' rather than the verification of hypotheses which are predicated on observations of the past. To say that the future will be as the past was is a cultural artefact of our dominant scientific epistemology. From such a deterministic view of the past how can we account for change and all that is new?

The mistake made by empiricists is to introduce sense data as objects, whereas it is a pre-objective realm we have to explore in ourselves if we are to understand our experience and that of others. Consciousness becomes not a matter of 'I think that', but a matter of 'I can'. This is the important element of intentionality which cannot be measured but can be heard, seen and demonstrated.

The politics of medicine, and the technology of modern medicine which serves it, places the existence of the individual in question. Personal means of health are concerned with a subjective reality which is symbolic. As human beings we are capable of self-regulation, and the foundations of this regulation are not confined to objective criteria. In many cases we are mysterious to ourselves. We have properties which are concerned with a created knowledge.

As therapists and researchers, then, how are we to face the problem of how to constitute an ethics of existence not solely founded on a scientific knowledge of the self which is comparative to group norms, but one in which the principal act is creative? Our task is to ask of ourselves, and then of our patients, 'How can we create ourselves as a work of art?' (Rabinow 1986).

The implications of this thinking for research practice is that we can encourage people to develop an articulacy of self based on their own expressive realizations. These may be expressed in the form of music, or pictures or stories. We can encourage people to document their journeys through life not as the accumulation of material quantities of flesh and blood but in sounds, words and pictures. The documentary of a life's journey through a chronic illness may be realized in a series of case notes. However, it can also be possible to document that journey as a series of photographs which are far more eloquent for the travellers. The preservation of the values of humanity within our culture are as much in the hands of the clinician/researcher as artist as they are in the clinician/researcher as scientist.

Human behaviour cannot be studied from one point of view only. Within the total repertoire of psychological medicine it is necessary to have different approaches to understanding the world: the scientific and the aesthetic. This position, of multiple understandings, offers an acceptance of orthodox clinical trials together with a promotion of new understandings (Touw-Otten and Spreeuwenberg 1985). By doing so differing studies inform each other.

It is vital that we pursue academic rigour in our experimentation – but not by burying our heads in the sand. Rigour without imagination leads to stagnation just as imagination alone leads to anarchy. Modern clinical research can combine the two. A combination of rigour and imagination is necessary to meet the challenges of health care. Our intellectual endeavours should be astute enough to see that science can accommodate multiple viewpoints (Freeling 1985; Howie 1984; Rose 1984) and search for a reconciliation of difference within the framework of the scientific, which is Truth, and the aesthetic, which is Beauty.

CHAPTER 6

Clinical Research, the Individual Patient, and the Limits of Randomized Controlled Trials

A combination of rigour and imagination is necessary to meet the challenges of health care. Within the total repertoire of medicine, it is necessary to have different approaches to understanding the world. This pluralist position offers an acceptance of orthodox clinical trials together with a promotion of new understandings and methods. In this way, differing studies inform each other. It is not a retreat to old methods, but the development of what is new, including new ideas in statistics. Our intellectual endeavours should be astute enough to see that science can accommodate multiple viewpoints and thereby develop a wide range of therapeutic possibilities.

A discussion on the possible detrimental use of randomization in studies of psychosocial interventions for cancer (Le Shan 1991) has highlighted the recurring controversy of methods appropriate for medical research with human subjects. The contention of this chapter is that while the large scale, randomized, controlled clinical trial (Phase III) is clearly of importance in medical research, it has limitations and is only one of the possible methods available for researching the health of human beings.

Critics have argued that the strict methodology of natural science is often found wanting when applied to the study of human behaviour (Aldridge and Pietroni 1987a,b; Burkhardt and Kienle 1980, 1983), and stimulating calls for innovation in clinical medical research (Aldridge 1991a; Cvitkovic 1992; Freireich 1981, 1990). A significant factor in this perspective is a growing awareness by doctors of the importance of a patient's social and cultural milieu, and a recognition that the health beliefs and personal understandings of a patient should be incorporated in treatment. What we need in clinical research are methods that identify clinical changes as they occur in the individual rather than methods that reflect a group average. How clinical change occurs, and is recognized, will depend upon not only the view of the researcher and clinician, but also the beliefs and understandings of the patient and his or her family (Aldridge 1990a).

The difference between clinical research and clinical validity

There is often a split in medical science between researchers and clinicians. Researchers see themselves as rational and rigorous in their thinking, and tend to see clinicians as sentimental and biased, which in turn elicits comments from clinicians about inhuman treatment and reductionist thinking. We are faced with the problem of how to promote in clinical practice research that has scientific validity in terms of rigour and, at the same time, a clinical validity for the patient and clinician.

The randomized trial is theoretically relevant for the clinical researcher, but too often it randomizes away what is specifically relevant for the clinician and patient. A comparative trial of two chemotherapy regimes assumes that the treatment and control groups contain evenly balanced populations. What is sought from such a trial is evidence that one regime works significantly better than another when comparing group averages. Yet, as clinicians, we want to know which method works best for the individual patient. Our interest lies not in the group average, but with the patients who do well with a particular treatment and those who do not respond so well.

Furthermore, randomizing patients with specific prognostic factors obscures different therapeutic effects. Rather than searching for a non- specific chemotherapy treatment of a particular cancer, we may be better advised to seek out those factors that allow us to deliver a specific treatment for particular individuals with a particular cancer.

This is not to argue against randomization in general but to note that we have randomized the patient rather than the treatment. As Weinstein (1974) says:

> ...randomization tends to obscure, rather than illuminate, interactive effects between treatments and personal characteristics. Thus if Treatment A is best for one type of patient and Treatment B is best for another type, a randomized study would only be able to indicate which treatment performs best overall. If we wanted to discover the effect on subgroups, one would have to separate out the variable anyway. (p.1280).

Today, molecular biologists identify specific cytogenetic targets for cancer therapy, and oncopharmacologists develop site-deliverable cytotoxic drugs (Gutierrez, Lemoine and Sikora 1992). In cancer studies, the continuing random assignment of patients to treatments groups misses two vital points: first, that the non-specific chemotherapy of specific cancers lacks both scientific rigour and clinical validity; and, second, that human metabolisms, while sharing common characteristics, may also have idiosyncratic responses to challenges.

The limits of 'objective' contemporary scientific medicine

As discussed in the previous chapter, modern science implies that there is a common map of the territory of healing, with particular co-ordinates and given symbols for finding our way around, and that the map of scientific medicine is *the* map. We need to recognize that scientific medicine emphasizes only one particular way of knowing. Although this approach maintains that to know anything we must be scientists, many examples show this to be a myth. People who live in vast desert areas find their way across those trackless terrains without any understanding of scientific geography. They also know the pattern of the weather without recourse to what we know as the science of meteorology. In a similar way, people know about their own bodies and have understandings about their own lives without the benefit of anatomy or psychology. They may not confer the same meanings on their experiences of health and illness as we researchers do, yet we might most wisely be guiding our research towards an understanding of personal and idiosyncratic beliefs.

When we speak of scientific or experimental validity, we speak of a validity one group of people confers on the work or actions of another group. This is a 'political' process. With the obsession for 'objective truth' in the scientific community, other 'truths' are ignored. As clinicians we have many ways of knowing: by intuition, through experience, and by observation. If we disregard these ways of 'knowing' then we promote the idea that there is an objective–definitive–external truth that exists as written in stone and only we, the initiated, have access to it.

The people with whom clinicians work in the therapeutic relationship are not experimental units. Nor are the measurements made on these people 'independent' of the person. While at times it may be necessary to treat the data this way, we must be aware that we are doing this – otherwise, when we come to measure particular personal variables, we are likely to face many complications.

Consider a person who has been treated unsuccessfully for chronic leukaemia with a bone marrow transplant. The clinical measurements of blood status, weight and temperature are important. However, they belong to a different realm of understanding than do issues of anxiety about the future, the experience of pain, the anticipation of personal and social losses and the existential feeling of abandonment. These defy quantitative measurement. Yet if we are to investigate therapeutic approaches to chronic disease, we need to investigate these subjective and qualitative realms. While we may be able to make little change in blood status, we can take heed of emotional status and propose initiatives for treatment. The goal of therapy is not always to cure; it can also be to comfort and relieve. The virtually exclusive involvement of today's physician with the biologic dimension of disease has resulted in a blindness to the need to understand suffering in the patient (Cassell 1991).

In terms of outcome measurements, we face further difficulties. The people we see in our clinics do not live in isolation, apart from the world of meaning. The way people respond in situations is sometimes determined by the way in which they have understood the meaning of that situation. The meaning of hair loss, weight loss, loss of potency, loss of libido, impending death and the nature of suffering will be differently perceived in differing cultures. To this balding middle-aged researcher, hair loss is a daily occurrence. To my Greek neighbour it would be a source of constant distress. When we deliver a powerful therapeutic agent, then, we are not treating a 'free-standing' clinical entity but intervening in an ecology of responses and beliefs which are somatic, psychological and social. Indeed, as others have noted as well, the whole notion of 'placebo' presumes that belief can exert an influence on the body.

In a similar way, what Western medicine understands as surgery, intubation and medication, others may perceive as mutilation, invasion and poisoning. Cultural differences regarding the integrity of the body will influence ethical issues such as abortion and body transplants. In a given culture, treatment initiatives may be standardized in terms of the sub-culture of the administrating researchers, but the perceptions of the subjects of the research and their families can differ variously. Actually, we know from studies of treatment options in breast cancer that the beliefs of physicians vary, and these beliefs influence the information the physicians give to their patients (Ganz 1992).

Challenges to the orthodoxy of controlled clinical trials

The controlled clinical trial is regarded as the basis of modern medical practice, but this belief is largely based upon mythology. Many practices of modern medicine have been introduced without the benefit of controlled trials, and treatments are often introduced because doctors believe they are of value – chemoprophylaxis for infective endocarditis (*The Lancet* 1992b) is an example, as is the type of bypass called 'warm heart surgery' (*The Lancet* 1992c) – or because professional groups and opinion leaders decide they are of value (Nattinger *et al.* 1992). Again, this is not to argue against controlled studies overall, but rather to show that the practice of medicine is not exclusively a scientific enterprise based upon systematic research.

Randomized controlled trials are sometimes inappropriate to detect small changes in outcome, or to discover what is useful for the clinician. In a prospective observational study of the prophylactic administration of antibiotics in surgery (Classen *et al.* 1992), the authors remind us that 'randomized clinical trials do not provide data on the way in which clinicians use interventions in clinical practice' (p.285). The Classen *et al.* study points out that the appropriate administration of antibiotics would have prevented wound infection in a number of cases, as could be noted by observation. Observational studies allow the clinician to assess what kind of care brings what kind of results. The point here is that the appropriate research method is the matter to be determined, and that one should not blindly adopt randomized controlled studies simply to perform the liturgy of conventional research.

In regard to the use of antibiotics, we should note also the problem of emerging resistance to such drugs (O'Brien 1992). Resistance to any drug occurs after a time, as we are seeing with anti-bacterial agents on a community scale and cytotoxic agents on an individual scale. That such resistance is a product of misapplication both in terms of specificity and dosage should alert us to our scientific myopia, the poor link between medicine as it is practised and the ignorance of research results in the literature, and our singular failure to understand the ecology of pharmaceutical activity whether on a world scale or an individual basis.

Vitamin supplements have a particularly interesting history in illuminating the value of observational studies, the dogged insistence of some scientists on controlled trials and the challenge of clinicians to research orthodoxy. In 1980, Smithells and colleagues suggested that vitamin supplements could possibly be used in the prevention of neural tube defects (Smithells *et al.* 1980). There then followed a vigorous debate in the medical press about the necessity for clinical controlled studies. However, as the vitamin supplements seemed harmless, both clinicians and mothers of future children boycotted controlled studies. Mothers were not willing to accept a placebo control, and the ethics of withholding vitamin supplements were seen as dubious. An observational study comparing incidence of neural tube defects before and after the supplements could have provided a satisfactory solution. A recent world congress of scientists and health officials have now recommended the elimination of Vitamin A deficiency throughout the world to promote child health and decrease morbidity and mortality, although 'the precise mechanisms by which Vitamin A exerts its impact on mortality are not yet known' (Sommer 1992, p.864).

While controlled trials do have their use, they are not necessarily the ultimate stage in medical knowledge. On the basis of controlled clinical trials, bronchodilators are extensively prescribed for asthmatic children with an episode of wheezing. Yet the prescription of such bronchodilators seems to be involved with the worldwide increase in asthma prevalence – the 'cure' has become a cause (Crane et al. 1992). Observational studies which sought to understand the appropriate clinical application of such bronchodilators, careful research into child and family ideas of when to use a bronchodilator, and long-term studies of asthma episodes including self-management techniques may have generated substantial clinical data.

'Informed consent'

Randomized trials also present a problem for the patient. We label this problem 'informed consent', but in many instances such consent cannot truly be informed.

Paradoxically clinical practice requires no informed consent, while inclusion in a controlled study does. Yet sometimes the data to inform such consent are limited, and often the data cannot be understood by the patient. Patients cannot be easily informed when, as is often the case, they lack the intellectual background and cultural perspectives of clinical researchers.

If we consider ductal carcinoma in situ (Joslin 1992) – that is, cancerous cells that lack the behavioural characteristics of cancer – as an example, most of the evidence about the clinical significance of the lesion comes from uncontrolled studies done before mammographic screening was widespread. Thus, the patient is asked to make a decision on a treatment about which the doctor can give little objective advice; the advice available is dependent on the doctor's beliefs and prejudices, and the patient may have a limited ability to assess it.

Thornton (1992) presents a patient's view of being asked to take part in a randomized trial of breast cancer treatments. She was given a diagnosis of which she had never previously heard, a leaflet offering four different treatment options, and two weeks in which to seek further information and come to a decision. She reasonably asks 'what is informed consent?' (p.44). With radiotherapy, which was involved in two of the possible treatment options, appearing to offer no improvement in survival, and carrying the possibility of serious after-effects and a possible reduction of quality of life, she was being offered alternatives that to her were unacceptable.

A trial by its very nature is an investigation of the unknown, and the clinician is asked to advise the patient to choose uncertainty at a time of maximum anxiety. Informed consent about inclusion in a clinical trial would best be served by intensive counselling at the time of diagnosis, followed by the clear presentation of treatment alternatives (Warren 1992). Yet we need to remember that the priorities of patients are often different from those of their medical informants. The mental state of a patient after a diagnosis is rather different from that of the doctor, and the implications of the diagnosis for the patient and the patient's family are likely to influence how the patient reacts.

One way in which a clinician can help a patient in arriving at informed consent is by interpreting research findings published in the professional medical press. However, for the clinician in daily practice, it is questionable whether such evidence can be assessed and understood without spending a large amount of time reading.

An analysis of the systemic treatment of early breast cancer (Group 1992) has highlighted the clinician's problems of understanding the relevant research. First, it is difficult for the clinician to interpret the findings of large group studies: (a) there is a tendency for clinicians to draw conclusions based on indirect comparisons (for example, ovarian ablation vs. polychemotherapy) (Bonadonna and Valaguassa 1992), and (b) substantial efficacy can be masked in the research when results are pooled. Second, although differing therapies have different consequences for life quality, this issue is rarely addressed. For example, although the benefits of hormonal and cytotoxic adjuvant therapy appear to improve with time (Editorial 1992), other considerations might be equally important on long-term follow-up: ovarian ablation shows an advantage of the same order as that achieved by chemotherapy (Powles and Smith 1992), cytostatic treatment leads to a certain rate of secondary leukaemia

(Reizenstein 1992), and chemotherapy has a devastating effect on female sexual response (Kaplan 1992). Low toxicity, as one patient remarks (Thornton 1992), depends upon your point of view and whether you are giving the treatment or receiving it.

Or, again, while some authors urge the use of alternative endocrine therapies, noting that they do not compromise the cardiovascular system, the bones (Love *et al.* 1992) and the psychosexual function of women (Fitzgerald, Eelstein and Mansel 1992), other authors warn about the side-effects of such therapies: 'hot flushes' (Rostom and Gershuny 1992), cessation of menstruation in 50 per cent of premenopausal women, and alterations of the singing voice (Goodare 1992).

The question we may then ask is, 'How can we offer informed consent when being informed is a major problem?' Even when there may be particularly successful interventions, such as in the case of Hodgkin's disease, for which there is a 75 per cent cure rate (Urba and Longo 1992), it is possible that in some patients the therapy will cause a second cancer. The longer chemotherapy is given, the higher the risk of leukaemia. Furthermore, in the case of small cell lung cancer, it is clear that the curative effect is weak, and the haematological effects of chemotherapy are worrying; further survival time has not been increased in the last decade (Carney 1992; Hansen 1992).

All this raises doubt about the indiscriminate use of randomized controlled trials. Eventually we must bring into this debate treatment strategies that enhance life quality, studies that offer specifically targeted therapeutic agents, clinical research that is flexible, and a recognition that the individual response to chemotherapy is an important factor.

Advantages and limitations of single-case designs

As mentioned briefly in the last chapter, single-case designs (Barlow and Hersen 1984; Guyatt *et al.* 1986; Louis *et al.* 1984) are one way of meeting both patient needs and the standards of scientific rigour. Such designs appear to satisfy clinicians who see their patients as individuals rather than statistics (Watts 1992), patients who prefer to be treated as individuals (Goodare 1992), and researchers who would recommend life quality as an important variable.

In a single-case design the patient is his or her own control. Single-case approaches may be a useful middle ground from which clinicians can begin to research their everyday practice. These forms of clinical study can collect multivariate data over time and they therefore lend themselves to the study of regulatory processes within an individual, in whom deviance is departure from a personal norm (Aldridge 1991b).

Such designs do not have a uniform approach. There are differing levels of formality and experimentation. A common feature of the designs is that they stay close to the practice of the clinician, minimizing the dilemma of clinical priorities or research priorities. In some cases patient and clinician are the researchers. An important feature of single-case trials is the identification of a specific evaluative index (or a battery of tests), challenging the clinician to link clinical changes to the treatment.

Guyatt (Guyatt *et al.* 1986) describes the single-case trial using oral theophylline and a placebo for the treatment of uncontrolled asthma in a 65-year-old man. Specific targets were self-rated by the patient at the end of each ten-day treatment period: laboured breathing on bending, hurrying, and climbing stairs; the patient's perceived need for albuterol during the day; and the extent to which breathlessness disturbed the patient's sleep. When the code was broken and the placebo periods appeared to be superior, the medication was discontinued and a further randomized single-case trial of ipratropium and a placebo began. This time the active treatment was superior to the placebo. Thus doctor and patient, through controlled observation, found a suitable treatment regime. We can say that the treatment was randomized within the patient rather than randomizing the patient to treatment.

I am not suggesting here that such a single-case trial would be appropriate for all diseases – advanced breast cancer, for example, when there would likely not be enough time to move from one therapy to another. As with all clinical research, it is important to find the appropriate method according to a number of various factors: the treatment being used, the attitude of the patient being treated, and the nature, and stage, of the disease being treated.

Single-case study designs are an attempt to formalize clinical stories. These designs take as their basis the clinical process of diagnosis, treatment, monitoring and evaluation. It is possible to vary systematically the management of the patient's illness during a series of treatment periods using randomization of treatment periods and blind assessment where appropriate. Effective treatments are linked with specific patient characteristics which are immediately relevant to the clinician and the patient. Any decisions about the design of the trial and the choice of outcome measures can be made with the patient (and the patient's family if need be). The primary focus of the research is upon the treatment benefit for the individual, whereas conventional studies are more concerned with changes in groups of patients.

A weakness of single-case designs is that they make it difficult to argue for the general validity of a treatment. To overcome this problem, groups of co-operating practitioners could collect single-case data according to a common format and then analyze the data as a group (although the problem of pooled data remains). If a case study is to be part of a systematic research approach, the measure of course will need to be replicable. Similarly, if the research is intended to speak to other practitioners, it is important to develop a measure that they too can validate.

Where the patient and clinician cannot be blind to the treatment intervention, an outside assessor can be blind to the treatment period. Such an external assessor can also act as a monitor of the trial and can halt the trial if this is in the best interests of the patient.

Statistical analysis can be used to identify subtle changes occurring in the data that are not immediately apparent, or when many variables from an individual need to be correlated with each other. A time series analysis – which traces change over time – can provide important information, sometimes clinically relevant information. The time series analysis of data has proved to be relevant clinically. For example, a time series analysis of serum cretonne levels in renal transplant patients is sensitive enough to detect rejection of the transplant before this is observed by experienced clinicians (Gordon 1986). Time series analysis can also be sensitive to the circadian rhythms of physiological processes and can influence the administration of drug regimens.

In all, the advantages of single-case research designs are their flexibility of approach, the opportunity they provide to include differing levels of rigour, and the possibility of incorporating ethical considerations pertinent to the individual case. Such designs are appropriate for clinicians who wish to introduce research into their own practice, particularly in developing hypotheses to be tested by other methods of clinical validation. Furthermore, with the development of statistical methods suitable for monitoring subjective, rhythmic or episodic data – methods that are not dependent upon the collection of equally spaced recording and that not only can detect change but also can discriminate between changes – clinicians and researchers have an opportunity to validate their clinical findings with a standard approach.

What we must keep in mind is that the pattern of reactivity in an individual is like a weather pattern: it constantly changes, never arriving at a steady state. A time series analysis of outcome changes is pertinent to the individual in that the changes are always compared to their own physiology (Aldridge 1991c). The person acts as his or her own norm. Furthermore, as in the previously mentioned study of transplant rejection (Gordon 1986), physiological changes relevant to clinical change can sometimes occur in the normal range of reactivity. When this happens it is possible to act before a crisis occurs.

If the clinician needs to relate data from single-case studies to other forms of research, then it is possible to develop a prognosis from the baseline data and clinical history and then examine it in the light of group statistics – for example, survival data based on cancer site and staging. By using an outside assessor, the prognosis can be made blind to the patient and practitioner.

To facilitate further studies, it is imperative that we develop two things:

1. A central research agency for the consultation, co-ordination and analysis of single-case designs, with connections between different countries (such an agency would co-ordinate research initiatives in smaller institutions, give advice and support on research methods, and help with the analysis of data).

2. Methods of data acquisition, statistical analysis, and data presentation suitable for clinicians to use in their daily practice (for example, the time series analysis of multivariate data).

Conclusion

It is vital that we pursue academic rigour in our research. But we must not bury our heads in the sand of dogma. Rigour without imagination leads to stagnation, just as imagination alone leads to anarchy. Modern clinical research can combine the two. A combination of rigour and imagination is necessary to meet the challenges of health care. Within the total repertoire of medicine, it is necessary to have different approaches to understanding the world. This pluralist position offers an acceptance of orthodox clinical trials together with a promotion of new understandings and methods. In this way, differing studies inform each other. This is not a retreat to old methods, but the development of a new approach, including new ideas in statistics. Our intellectual endeavours should be astute enough to see that science can accommodate multiple viewpoints and thereby develop a wide range of therapeutic possibilities.

CHAPTER 7

A Community Approach
to Cancer in Families

This chapter focuses on the management of terminal illness in the context of the family. Several important issues are raised. The first is a consideration of who is a family member. The second is the consideration of critical junctures in the process of dying. And the third is a discussion of the way in which community professionals can co-ordinate their practice.

A feature of working with the terminally ill is that there are various individual and relational problems which have to be resolved and accommodated. The family has to adapt to the process of losing a loved one, and then life continuing without that person. The overriding emphasis in this chapter is on assisting families to use their own resources to accommodate change. However, they are helped in this by a network of community support and professional expertise.

This approach attempts to integrate the physical, psychological, spiritual and social dimensions of a person's life. The concept of whole person medicine is a part of general medical practice already, but the community approach offers beyond that, first, a way of working with people to encourage their own innate healing properties and, second, the involvement of those persons with whom they live in the management of the process of dying. The focus of the work is on the quality of life for the patients and their family. Patients are regarded as active partners in health care rather than passive recipients of that care. However, this raises difficulties for assessing outcomes. Qualities of lives are difficult to compare.

In the management of terminal illness using this approach there is a particular emphasis on understanding family change. The specific activities offered are: family counselling, meditation and visualization, formal and informal hypnosis for the management of pain, prayer and the administration of the sacraments in the home. All families are offered these activities at varying times, but they are not all taken up. For example, some families who are not Christians will not want to celebrate the Eucharist, yet some will want to be introduced to prayer. The choice resides with the patient and the family.

In the course of working with the patient and the family the principal practitioners involved are the family doctor, the parish priest, the specialist hospital consultants and, in the case of leukaemia, the specialist nursing sister. Apart from these persons there are lay parishioners who offer a range of necessary support activities which include home visiting, child minding, shopping, transport and friendship.

The function of the author in this work has been to co-ordinate the family work and the endeavours of the lay helpers with that of the practitioners. This informal role could be carried out by any of the practitioners involved. The emphasis is upon mutuality and co-operative endeavour to meet the needs of the patient. The medical practice is complemented by counselling and community support. To do this does not mean endless group meetings but requires one person to be able to communicate with all involved persons and facilitate their co-operation.

First contact

The first contact, after referral, is at the patient's home or in the hospital. At this first meeting the foundations of the future contacts are established. Any interventions are made from a basis of shared information with both partners and are under the influence of the patient and his or her spouse. The reason for this is that in families where terminal illness is present, they express a loss of control over the therapeutic endeavour, and the process of dying itself also comes to be seen as beyond their control. When we talk with them about potentials and therapeutic possibilities then the process of therapeutic intervention, the management of information and social support is brought into the realm of their influence. In this way responsibilities are shared and the process of change becomes a co-operative endeavour. In this sense, practitioners who are involved act as guides and facilitators.

Both partners are seen together and are told what can be offered in terms of social support, complementary interventions for pain management and initiatives for family counselling. At this time they are asked which medical practitioners are involved and if they can be contacted to discuss co-operation. The family are usually expected to initiate this meeting with the general practitioner, or with the hospital consultant. Most of the following interventions take place in the home of the patient. This process of finding out who does what and why is itself important and helps the patient to clarify how decisions are made, and where further information can be gathered from which to make those decisions.

Once practitioners are contacted and their permission gained to work with the family then those practitioners are contacted by the author to discuss what is to happen next. In the cases of hospital treatment, access to specialist consultation by the author is informal and often occurs during routine visits with the patient for treatment; for example, when platelets are replaced.

For the general practitioner either consent is given because the family doctor knows the author already or the general practitioner comes out to see how the author practises. This is a reflection of the genuine desire of some practitioners to learn about 'complementary' practice.

Who is family?

The family are asked who 'in the family' would help in time of need and in terms of general support. The concept of 'family' varies from family to family. Some people have an 'instrumental' concept of family. These family members are those who could be called upon for quite specific activities; that is, distant relatives who would be seen as 'close' may be appropriate for telephone conversations to talk over difficulties. At the same time there are geographically close relatives who can be used for transport but who are not seen as 'close family'.

Other families are far more 'sentimental' in their construing of 'family'. In this way anyone who is involved with these families on a regular basis, who visits regularly and who listens to problems, is 'family'. The author is adopted into such networks on the grounds of regular listening. Any such person becomes temporarily 'one of the family'.

A third group of families are 'restricted'. They are tightly knit with a small membership. Their boundaries are drawn around the marital pair and the children (regardless of age or geographical distance). Their perspective is to 'get by without too much outside help'. Any help is inevitably outside. These families are predominantly professional and express great store on being autonomous. Friends, however, are seen as separate from the family.

Family membership appears to be a function of 'instrumentality'; that is, those who can carry out particular supporting functions. This instrumentality is modified by 'sentimentality'; that is, by a willingness to make a benevolent and fraternal contact with the family. Close friends can attain the status of family membership by fulfilling particular functions. For the 'restricted' families most of their needs are met by their self-sufficiency.

These distinctions are important in helping such families. By discovering the style of families it is possible to offer help which can be accepted. For example, with 'instrumental' families it is possible to define the help offered in terms of specific functions such as counselling, pain relief and childminding. For 'sentimental' families the initial approach is made and delivered in terms of social contact, of attending large family meetings and using the resources of family structure to provide emotional support and practical help.

In 'restricted' families it is important to tread carefully and avoid overtones of welfare. These families in some ways are handicapped by their self-sufficiency in that their contacts for support are few. However, they do understand professional roles and respond to such an approach. The skill then lies in promoting permeability of the family boundary whereby social support can be accepted without the family perceiving themselves as becoming 'dependent'.

Family change

The sources of distress in the families of patients who are dying are located in the interaction of the physical, psychological, social and spiritual changes (Table 7.1). In working with the patient in the context of the family it is possible to meet the needs not only of the person who is dying but also of the survivors. In some ways the process of handling death is a preparation for handling life for those who remain.

Whether the course of dying is seen as a lingering death and tragic loss, or an opportunity to resolve existential issues and prepare for a future, depends very much upon the family's construing of death and the input of external support.

There are 'critical junctures' during this process where it is possible to meet the needs of the family. Some practitioners see the main approach of working with families where there is cancer as being one of crisis management. If critical junctures are appreciated then there is less need of 'crisis' work.

An important critical juncture for many patients and their families is the hospital interview, particularly when a diagnosis is offered, or the results of tests are presented. One way of supporting the family is to go through their last hospital interview, discover what they understand, and then discuss the questions that understanding raises. These questions can then be written down

Table 7.1 Changes in personal and family coping	
Coping with physical changes	• Anticipation of pain • Management of pain • Change in physical appearance • Management of the physical sequelae of treatment
Coping with personal changes	• Loss of hope, fitness, identity • Anxiety and depression about the future • Loss of role in the family and in employment • Frustration and helplessness
Coping with family and marital changes	• Resolution of conflict • Change in parental roles • Anxiety about future welfare (financial and emotional) • Anticipated hospital contacts and treatment • Anticipated loss of family member • Handling hospital contacts and treatment • Planning the future • Social isolation • Loss of sexual activity • Negotiation of dependence/independence • Negotiation of marital and family distance • Saying 'goodbye' and talking about dying • Planning the funeral
Coping with spiritual changes	• Feelings of loss, alienation and abandonment • Understanding suffering • Accepting dependency • Handling anger and frustration • Forgiving others • Discovering peace • Discussing death • Grieving

and asked at the next consultation or used as a focus for discussion and counselling.

Some families want to read about their problem and it is useful to have a library of resource material to meet such needs.

Hospital appointments can be times of difficulty. Throughout an illness these important junctures deliver information about the efficacy of treatment and always include decisions about what to do next. As the illness progresses there is a lack of certainty when attempts at treatment fail. Not only is there a sense of diminishing control but also the realization and anticipation of physical deterioration and death. This is often exacerbated by the debilitating effects of the treatment itself.

At these times it is important to meet with families after appointments and discuss issues of the awareness of death, disintegration and loss of self; the anticipation of pain and the implications for pain management; the physical sequelae of both treatment and the disease process, and their management (nausea, incontinence, change in physical appearance); the expressions of frustration, helplessness, anxiety and depression; the change in family roles and structure during the process of dying and after death; the future welfare of the family after death (financial and social); and the spiritual and existential questions raised at this time about the nature of suffering and feelings of abandonment, guilt or punishment.

All of these issues have ramifications for the rest of the family. Feelings of hopelessness are not necessarily limited to the patient. The management of pain and the basic nursing of the patient are often managed at home by a spouse. Pain is not only an internal response to tissue damage; it is an experience which exists within an emotional and relational context.

Nursing and the physical support of the patient can mean a change in relationships within the family. A former breadwinner has to become dependent and this can challenge both the personal identity of the patient and that of other family members. This causes particular difficulty when medication is used for pain relief, or the patient becomes so debilitated that the process of decision making changes.

For example, in one family the author saw, the husband decided that to gain his wife's attention he would ring a bell by his bedside. His wife was then expected to attend to him. When she did not, he became distressed. His distress was not only related to his lack of ability to cope with his increasing physical problems but also with the understanding that his wife was taking over more and more activities and making more and more decisions within the home. This was not an attempt to wrest power from her husband but a reflection of the burgeoning demands upon her time. Time to sit and debate over decisions was seen as a luxury and a painful reflection of his loss of abilities. This loss was painful for both partners and signified a change in the relationship. Their plans for a long and fruitful life together had become truncated. The immediate future appeared to be filled with difficulty and distress.

The expression of dissatisfaction was also used as an opportunity to discuss the loss of physical potency. Although this discussion took place with both partners together it stemmed from separate interviews with each partner. When sexual activity becomes painful or impossible it is possible to encourage partners to lie together and hold each other. The maintenance and encouragement of intimacy is important at a time of impending isolation and loneliness.

Relief and comfort

Other than the negotiation of family changes, the principal area of work with the terminally ill is that of bringing comfort and relief. For example, the author was asked to see a woman who had a continuing pain in the right side of her body. This woman was taught a number of relaxation techniques, introduced to meditation and encouraged to use self-hypnosis. Each of these sessions was recorded on audiotape for the person to use at any time for the relief of pain, and for gathering strength to face the day. However, various family members would attend these sessions. The reason they gave for this was that they gained their own comfort and relief from using the techniques, and from knowing that the patient was gaining relief too.

The main reasons for using such methods for pain relief are to avoid the confusion and drowsiness and other side-effects of some medication; to avoid the memory of pain by using amnesia; to limit the anxiety of a future threatening event; and to bring sleep or rest.

These techniques are not used as replacements for medication but as complementary approaches. With medication there is always a trade-off between pain relief and consciousness. By using both together it is possible to keep patients alert and responsive while removing the experience of pain. The effect upon the family is that they no longer see a loved one suffering and, perhaps as importantly, that loved one is not as irritable when rested and pain free.

In the author's practice meditation, prayer, visualization, hypnosis and relaxation are all used for strengthening the patient's resolve, bringing hope, relieving boredom and rehearsing difficult future events. This is done in the context of the family. Family members are encouraged to be present. At each session each person present is asked what needs to be focused on during that session. By using an audiotape and encouraging self-reliance the therapeutic contact is minimized and the patient given some control over his or her problems. Such techniques allow the patient and the family to have a choice of alternatives.

Some of these concepts, like 'hope', may seem rather vague. However, it is these issues which are raised by families. As general practitioners we must be responsive to such issues. It is important that we do not dodge these existential issues either out of ignorance or a desire for simplicity of practice which is concerned solely with symptomatic relief. It is the tackling of some of these issues which brings relief.

For example, a woman was in the late stages of cancer. Her general practitioner had terminated her hospital treatment because the treatment was hastening her death faster than the course of the disease. The woman and her husband were both worn out by the management of her pain and the constant round of hospital visits. The main problem presented by this family was that the woman, when she woke up each day, could not face the day itself after a sleepless night. She had lost the will to live. By using meditation and visualization techniques this woman discovered a resource within herself which gave some comfort. As a secondary problem her husband, the general practitioner and the parish priest were concerned that she was not talking about dying. They would talk to her about many things in her daily life but then go outside the house to discuss her slow decline and whether or not to tell her that she was dying. By talking to the general practitioner, the husband, the priest and the patient together, the issue of dying was addressed. The woman was simply told of the concern of the men in her life that she was dying and not being given the opportunity to talk about it. Her reply was that she knew that she was dying but was more concerned with 'living' to the full the days she had remaining with her family and children.

With all the interventions this woman participated in, from the learning of visualization techniques and prayer, to family counselling, various family members would make themselves present. Other family members were allowed to join in. After the first session to teach her a relaxation technique to promote rest, both her husband and her mother asked to sit in on the sessions, not to scrutinize the author, but for the benefit they gained for themselves. The result was a creative use by these family members of the technique. Her mother used it to gain rest while sitting with her daughter at night. Her husband used it for calming himself down before hospital visits with the consultant oncologist, and after his wife's death when he thought he could not cope with the children.

The main emphasis in this approach is on developing a family culture where needs can be expressed and where the family can learn to formulate their own solutions to problems.

Social activity and support

By using a community network, the family can be supported without the intrusion of too many professionals. A common feature seems to be that on the diagnosis of a life-threatening illness, or the development of worsening and publicly evident symptoms, the family reduce their social contacts. Sometimes friends simply stop visiting.

In the author's practice the family are encouraged to join home groups within a Church community. These groups are held regularly in a parishioner's home and are not set up specifically for the support of the patient but are for the encouragement of nurturing relationships within the community. Each group is different. Some groups have a set format and discuss issues. Other groups are social. The patients and their families are encouraged to make friends or develop old acquaintances.

A man, who became a close friend of the author, said that the knowledge that he could make a friendship, although he was in the process of dying, helped him to make sense of dying. From these contacts friendships grow and the family are open to being visited at home. All of this is under the control of the patient and the family. No person is coerced to join a group.

Another way that families are supported, and which uses this home group contact, is the celebration of the sacrament of the Eucharist in the family home. The parish priest attends to the spiritual needs of the patient and family, prays with them regularly and guides them in their reading if requested. Once a month friends and family, according to the wishes of the patient and their family, gather together in the patient's home to celebrate the sacrament of the Eucharist together. This is one more tie into a network of support. It is an activity which allows people to share their common faith but also to express their common concerns.

The friendships forged during these activities are helpful in the short-term support of the patient and the family, but are significantly important in the long-term support of the survivors.

Bereavement

When death occurs much of the therapeutic support ends. However, the ties and links of friendship are appropriate at the time of the funeral and in support-ing the family in their grief. These links of friendship endure. In the author's practice the continuing support of the survivors is managed not therapeutically but informally by the naturalistic means of friendship in a context of community.

Community support in this form is based on the idea of mutuality. No person is referred to a group for support as such but invited to join a group for their own benefit and the support of others. These groups are not run by profes-sionals, although occasionally someone may be invited to address a group or share a cup of coffee. As these groups continue over the years there are inevita-bly widows and widowers who can support and understand new members whose spouses are dying. In this way expertise is not resident in one person but becomes a communal attribute.

Co-ordination of support

For a practitioner working in this way it is important to consider the needs of the person as a whole, and the needs of those with whom that person lives.

In the author's practice most of the preliminary work and a large part of the continuing work is in co-ordinating other professionals and community initia-tives. The most important understanding we can have here is that of boundary. Professionals often have clearly defined tasks and are happy to work with others who have complementary roles with clearly defined tasks. This defini-tion is not always apparent with lay helpers, and as co-ordinator it is important to negotiate a clarity of understanding about what helpers can do.

Of course, it is inappropriate to define friendship. It is appropriate to suggest that too many 'counsellors' with differing aims can make things worse, or at least introduce confusion at a time of uncertainty. To counter this the author has concentrated on identifying tasks with professionals and then meeting with families and friends to determine who is doing what. A by-product of this is that one person sees where activities are being duplicated.

Following on from this there are times when it is appropriate to restrict access to the family. Sometimes the needs of nursing have to take precedence and it is the presence of a person with a long-term and comprehensive picture of what is happening who can make such a decision.

For example, a friend was dying and his physical needs were becoming more and more demanding. Both his wife and the nursing sister from the hospital were attending him through the night. On hearing of his imminent death many people wished to see him and say goodbye. Each person was concerned to minister to him in his time of need. However, being visited is a very taxing business, particularly if you are meeting the needs of others too. It was necessary for the nurse to ask some people not to visit as the patient was becoming weaker and weaker. Similarly, it was important to emphasize the need for the family to spend time together and for the professionals to withdraw.

In contacting other professionals it is important to be clear about what we say we can do and make sure that we say it in terms that they understand. Medical practitioners understand the need for counselling. There is some hesitancy on their part about the use of hypnosis and visualization techniques. This hesitancy disappears if we take time to either demonstrate or discuss exactly what we do. All these activities are part of building a system for further interventions with other families.

The initial months of the author's practice were spent with practitioners as much as with families. Once practitioners understood what the author was doing, and the author understood them, then working together became easier.

Summary

The characteristics of this community service to the terminally ill are:

1. An 'holistic' perspective which is concerned with developing comprehensive programmes to meet the physical, psychological and spiritual needs of those who come for help.

2. Programmes which are responsive to family style and promote family coping mechanisms and strengths. Self-care and education are emphasized before treatment and dependence.

3. A way of working which emphasizes practitioner co-operation and utilizes lay networks.

4. Pharmacological and surgical remedies are talked about with the family.

5. An active partnership is encouraged between caregivers and consumers.

6.   Change as a process is accepted and understood as having ramifications for many family members. Crises are anticipated at critical junctures in the process of dying.

7.   Continuity of care is seen as extending beyond death and within the realm of informal community support.

8.   Communication with other professionals and community groups is seen as important in fostering the development of such a service.

This response is less concerned with family pathology, and more with promoting family strengths. We must face the challenge of working with other practitioners of differing theoretical persuasions. To do so will mean that we can fully meet the needs of those whom we serve.

CHAPTER 8

Music Therapy References Relating to Cancer and Palliative Care

Hospitals and clinics worldwide have incorporated music therapy when working with cancer patients and in palliative care (Aldridge 1995, 1999, 2000a; Amies 1979; Bellamy and Willard 1993; Bonny and Pahnke 1972; Cai *et al.* 2001; Gallagher and Steele 2001; Hoffmann 1998; Magill 2001; Mramor 2001; Munro 1984; Munro and Mount 1978; Porchet-Munro 1988, 1993; Rykov and Salmon 1998, 2001; Xie *et al.* 2001), particularly as part of multidisciplinary teams (Mandel 1993). As the music therapy profession has developed internationally, so has its role in palliative care (O'Kelly 2002). Music is a highly versatile and dynamic medium lending itself to a variety of music therapy techniques used to benefit both those living with life-threatening illnesses and their family members and caregivers. Indeed, music has been a palliative modality used over the centuries to comfort the dying. 'Infirmary music' was an intimate expression of French monastic medicine in 11th-century Cluny and anticipated the current hospice and palliative medical movements (Schroeder-Sheker 1994).

Standley's (1995; Weber 1999) review of the literature relating to music therapy makes a meta-analysis from 55 studies utilizing 129 dependent variables, and concludes (p.4) that the average therapeutic effect of music in medical treatment is almost one standard deviation greater than without music (0.88). Music therapy appears to have an indication for the management of pain and, as we will see further, for the relief of suffering.

The nursing profession has seen the value of music therapy (Cook 1986; Coyle 1987; de Vries 2001; Foxglove 1999; Harcourt 1988; Richardson 1992; Shatin 1980; Sheldon 1998), particularly in Canada and the United States, and championed its use as an important nursing intervention even when music therapists are not available. A clinical nurse specialist (Bechler-Karsch

1993) made an overview of 14 articles on audioanalgesia, concluding that music has no adverse effects on ill patients when used as an adjunctive non-invasive therapy. Music can touch patients deeply and transform their anxiety and stress into relaxation and healing. Patients with cancer who undergo surgical procedures are highly stressed; in such a situation music therapy helps (Cunningham, Monson and Bookbinder 1997; Sander Wint *et al.* 2002), as it does in the intensive care unit (Johnston and Rohaly-Davis 1996). The anxiolytic effect of music has experimental support, albeit using a healthy student population (Knight and Rickard 2001).

Music therapy has found an acceptance in the field of palliative care and the hospice movement (Aldridge 1996, 1999, 2000b, 2000c). This acceptance has been partly related to the developments within health care delivery that utilize family medicine (Aldridge 1987b, 1988b, 1990a), complementary approaches (Arai *et al.* 1999; Bunt, Burns and Turton 2000; Hirsch and Meckes 2000; Nakagami 1997; Nicholson 2001; Petterson 2001; Vickers and Cassileth 2001; Watt and Verma 1998) and the arts therapies (Bailey 1997; Brandenburg 1988; Deeken 1995; Griessmeier 1990; Heyde and von Langsdorff 1983; Jochims 1981; Karambadzakis and Muthesius 1997; Mango 1992; Olofsson 1995; Steidle-Röder 1993). Furthermore, the arts and creative arts therapies are being seen as a form of spiritual care in health care settings, particularly where individuals are confronting life-threatening illnesses. By offering opportunities to engage in the arts and creative expression, persons with cancer can be enabled to mourn, grieve, celebrate life, be empowered to endure their situation, and find healing and meaning (Bailey 1997; Magill 2002; Marr 1999). When people suffer, they are in danger of losing their dignity, which makes the relief of pain and suffering a matter of aesthetics (Aldridge 1991a; Pullman 2002), hence the importance of arts therapies.

Cancer therapy, pain management and hospice care

The goal of palliative care is to achieve the best quality of life for patients and their families (WHO 1990). From a holistic perspective, palliative care 'affirms life and regards dying as a normal process; neither hastens nor postpones death; provides relief from pain and distressing symptoms; integrates the psychological and spiritual aspects of patient care; offers a support system to help patients as actively as possible until death; offers a support system to help the family cope during the illness and in their own bereavement' (p.11).

From what we see above, cancer and chronic pain relief require complex, co-ordinated resources that are medical, psychological, spiritual and communal. Hospice care in the United States and England has attempted to meet this need for palliative and supportive services that provide physical, psychological and spiritual care for dying persons and their families. Such a service is based upon an interdisciplinary team of health care professionals and volunteers, which often involves outpatient and inpatient care. While palliative care has pioneered improvements in pain management, having confirmed unnecessary suffering among cancer patients, because of the inadequate use of analgesic medication and other effective interventions, effective non-pharmacological strategies like music therapy are an important part of treatment plans for the relief of cancer pain (MacLean 1993; Zaza *et al.* 1999). O'Callaghan cautions us that music used inappropriately can also aggravate pain (O'Callaghan 1996b).

In the Supportive Care Program of the Pain Service to the Neurology Department of Sloan Kettering Cancer Center, New York, a music therapist is part of that supportive team along with a psychiatrist, nurse-clinician, neuro-oncologist, chaplain and social worker. Music therapy is used to promote relaxation, to reduce anxiety, to supplement other pain control methods and to enhance communication between patient and family (Bailey 1983, 1984; Magill Levreault 1993). As depression is a common feature of the patients dealt within this programme, then music therapy is hypothetically an influence on this parameter and in enhancing quality of life. In advanced stages of cancer, music therapy is used in pain management as an important intervention for relieving suffering (Ferrell, Rhiner and Rivera 1993; Foley 1986; Kerkvliet 1990; Magill 2001; Magill, Chung and Kennedy 2000). Some studies have attempted to demonstrate that music therapy brings about a change in mood (Walden 2001) and for improving mood and quality of life (Burns 2001) in adult oncology patients with modest results.

Bailey (1983) discovered a significant improvement in mood for the better when playing live music to cancer patients as opposed to playing taped music, which she attributes to the human element being involved. Gudrun Aldridge (1996), in a single-case study, also emphasizes the benefits of expression facilitated by playing music for the post-operative care of a woman after mastectomy, and Deborah Salmon has emphasized the relationship between music and the emotions (Salmon 1993, 2001). Given the increasing research into the treatment of breast cancer and gynaecological cancer, then music therapy is also responding with studies that complement medical initiatives and address the emotional needs of women (Jackson 1996; Jacobsen 1993; Tobia, *et al.* 1999).

A better researched phenomenon is the use of music in the control of chronic cancer pain, although such studies abdicate the human element of live performance in favour of tape-recorded interventions (Zimmerman *et al.* 1989).

In addition to reducing pain, particularly in pain clinics, music as relaxation and distraction has been tried during chemotherapy to bring overall relief, and to reduce nausea and vomiting. Using taped music and guided imagery in com-bination with pharmacological antiemetics, Frank (1985) found that state anxiety was significantly reduced resulting in a perceived degree of reduced vomiting, although the nausea remained the same. As this study was not con-trolled the reduced anxiety may have been a result of the natural fall in anxiety levels when chemotherapy treatment ended. However, the study consisted of patients who had previously experienced chemotherapy and were conditioned to experience nausea or vomiting in conjunction with it. That the subjects of the study felt relief was seen as an encouraging sign in the use of music therapy as a treatment modality.

In a crossover study to evaluate to what extent the therapeutic use of music would decrease pain in patients with cancer who were receiving scheduled analgesics (Beck 1991), subjects were assigned randomly to listen to their pref-erence of seven types of relaxing music or a control (a 60-cycle hum) twice daily for three days. There was an inconsistent relation between pain and mood and there was a significant decrease in pain from using either the music or sound, but there was no effect on mood. Although the mean percentage of change in pain for music was twice that for sound, the results did not differ sta-tistically.

Trygve Aasgaard, a Norwegian music therapist, has focused on songs, song writing and singing in paediatric cancer care (Aasgaard 1994, 1999, 2001; Abrams 2001). He emphasizes that children are more than their disease by offering children the chance to be creative – then they become something other than patients. They become expressive beings. We hear this same theme of creativity re-occurring throughout the world of music therapy in cancer care. One of the attractive features of music therapy when it is practised in hospital settings is that it draws in other members of the family, nurses and clinicians, who are encouraged to take part.

Song writing is a favoured method for helping patients to express them-selves in palliative care (O'Callaghan 1996a, 2001; Weber 1999). Australian music therapists have taken this song production further both in end-of-life settings (Hogan 1999) and when working with children in hospital (Dun 1999). At the same time, Barbara Griessmeier was pioneering music therapy for children suffering with cancer in Germany (Griessmeier 1995, 2001; Griessmeier and Bossinger 1994) and Trygve Aasgaard was also producing similar work in Norway (Aasgaard 1999). Music therapy has also found an important role as a complementary therapy in the treatment of bone marrow transplantation in children (Pfaff, Smith and Gowan 1989) and in hospitalized haematology patients (Barrera, Rykov and Doyle 2002; Lane 1994; Robb 2000).

Throughout the ages, songs have been an important vehicle for the expression of the deepest human feelings. While the use of sacred songs has reflected the spiritual dimension, it is popular songs that reflect the everyday sentiments of ever-lasting love, missing a partner, cherishing a friend and gratitude for all that has happened. Music therapists sing such songs at the bedside or compile tapes of selected songs for family and friends.

In a study at the Bristol Cancer Help Centre, United Kingdom, music therapy increased well-being and relaxation and lessened tension during the listening experience, and there were increased levels of salivary immunoglobulin A and decreased levels of cortisol in listening experiences and improvisation. The authors suggest that maybe the benefit of improved mood is also beneficial for the immune system (Bunt, Burns and Turton 2000; Burns *et al.* 2000, 2001), an impression that other researchers are also investigating (Bartlett, Kaufman and Smeltekop 1993; Duocastella 1999). Such studies are an extension of findings earlier in this chapter that music therapy is an effective anxiolytic and reduces stress (Hanser 1985).

Memories of past events can be elicited through song (Weber 1999) and music therapy is particularly indicated in the management of emotional trauma (Weber, Nuessler and Wilmanns 1997). Experiences of past events are often linked to particular songs that were being played at the time. Through playing such songs, lives can be reviewed and people can be encouraged to say what is important. From this basis, patients are encouraged to talk about what happened to dreams and plans that they once had. In the various song repertoires there are as probably as many songs about regret as there are about promise. Somehow using the words of others is a way to make a statement about personal feelings. For those patients that are inarticulate in the face of strong emotions, then pre-composed songs are a vehicle for expression and reminiscence. For others, struggling to find what they want to say, with their own voice, then composing songs, or melodies even, is another important musical activity leading to self-expression. Having the skills to use both composed and improvised material is vital to the ability of a music therapist.

In many studies we find that music therapy is used with family and care-givers (Aldridge 2000c; Gallagher *et al.* 1998, 2001; Magill 2001; Murrant *et al.* 2000; Porchet-Munro 1993). In addition, music therapists also emphasize the importance of music for their own healing in meeting personal needs when working with the dying (Hartley 2001; Rykov 2001; Salmon 2001), and for working in a broader hospital milieu of colleagues and friends (Aasgaard 1999, 2001).

There is a rapidly developing literature related to working with children with cancer (Brodsky 1989; Camprubi Duocastella 1999; Daveson and Kennelly 2000; Fagen 1982; Froehlich 1984, 1996; Marley 1984; Slivka and Magill 1986, 1993; Standley and Hanser 1995) that also focuses on specific issues like the management of paediatric pain (Loewy 1997; Stevens *et al.* 1994), hospitalization (Froehlich 1996), terminal care in children (Frager 1997), and special needs groups like paediatric HIV patients (McCauley 1996). The World Health Organization emphasizes that parents will need strength to support their children, and that both children and parents may need help to find peace (WHO 1998).

Some music therapists work in situations with adult patients, or clients, who are living with the challenge of the Human Immune-deficiency Virus. Both Nigel Hartley (1999) and Lutz Neugebauer (1999) present work in such situations. There is a pioneering literature in this field of work initiated by Colin Lee (1995) and Ken Bruscia (1991, 1995), who use music creatively in therapy to address the problems of both living with HIV/AIDS and coping with dying. Indeed, there is a growing use of varying creative arts therapy approaches in both this field (Frego 1995) and cancer care in general (Heyde and von Langsdorff 1983; Higginson *et al.* 2000).

Hope, meaning and a sense of purpose

Stimulating the awareness of living, in the face of dying, is a feature of the hospice movement, where being becomes more important than having. The opportunity, offered by music therapy, for the patient to be remade anew in the moment, to assert an identity that is aesthetic, in the context of another person, separate yet not abandoned, is an activity invested with that vital quality of hope. Hope, when submitted to the scrutiny of the psychologist and not con-forming to an established reality, can easily be interpreted as denial. For the therapist, hope is a replacement for therapeutic nihilism enabling us to offer constructive effort and sound expectations. Sometimes hope is not for a prolonged life but for a peaceful death reconciled with self and family (Aldridge 2000c).

One of the problems facing a patient with the diagnosis of cancer is the seemingly hopelessness of the future. Expectations of health and longevity are challenged. Maintaining or promoting hope is an important contribution to health care, both for motivation to engage in treatment and for general well-being. Music therapy, with its emphases on personal contact and the value of the patient as a creative, productive human being, has a significant role to play in the fostering of hope and a sense of purpose in the individual (Aldridge 1995). Hope involves feelings, thoughts and requires action; that is, like music it is dynamic and susceptible to human influence. Hope changes too; patients knowing that the hope of a long life has gone can, however, hope that they will be reconciled to their families or hope that they can tell their feelings to their friends. Discerning these subtle dimensions of hope and offering the means for their expression is a central part of palliative care.

Any therapeutic tasks must concentrate on the restoration of hope, accommodating feelings of loss, isolation and abandonment, understanding suffering, forgiving others, accepting dependency while remaining independent and making sense of dying. Music therapy can be a powerful tool in this process of change by offering means for the expression of loss and negative emotions but also for the expression of positive emotions. Change can be accommodated within the overall rubric 'quality of life'. While the elusive life qualities inherent in creative activities, joy, release, satisfaction and simply being are not readily susceptible to rating scales, we can hear them when they are played and feel them when they are expressed. Music therapy assists palliative care patients and families cope with grief and loss, pain and anxiety, disorientation and dementia, lack of meaning, and hopelessness (Hilliard 2001). Not only does music therapy allow for expression that brings relief, it also brings emotions into a form that can be discussed. There is also enough evidence that music therapy is a powerful anxiolytic and is an important agent in the management of chronic pain. Furthermore, we can also use songs that express existential doubts about what alternative meanings there may be for living; this was the traditional role of psalms and sacred music. By expressing difficult emotions and finding a way of resolving those emotions through music then we can propose that music therapy is a way of coping.

Music therapy appears to open up a unique possibility to take an initiative in coping with disease, or to find a level to cope with near death. It is this opening up of the possibilities which is at the core of other existential therapies. Rather than the patient living in the realm of pathology alone, they are encouraged to find the realm of their own creative being, and that is in the music. In Lucanne Magill's four themes in music therapy, we see the power of music to build relationship, enhance remembrance, be a voice to prayer and instil peace (Magill 2002). Experiencing the spirit of being human, and transcending the vagaries of a failing body or a fearing mind in a fragile world, is an activity that music making, like prayer and meditation, encourages (Aldridge 1987a; Magill 2001; Salmon 2001).

The World Health Organization (WHO 1990) makes a list of recommendations that we should consider in cancer relief and palliative care; as we see from the previously cited material, music therapy has the potential to meet all of those recommendations (see Table 8.1).

Coda: Case vignette

Lois was admitted with an advanced stage of cancer. She had recently suffered the loss of her eldest son. Her professional life had been very active and remained so until her hospital admission. Although Lois had become fractious and uncooperative with the treatment team, they asked for music therapy. Her physician felt that some of her needs were being unmet and her expressions of dissatisfaction were a symptom of unmet need rather than Lois being a 'difficult patient'.

We first visited Lois in her hospital room where she was surrounded by very lively friends, all of whom were more than willing to act as advocates of her well-being. Her friends were being confronted with Lois's physical deterioration and suffering and this complicated the situation further. As often occurs, we have to deal not only with the needs of the patients but also those of the family and friends. People seldom suffer alone, they suffer with others. On asking what music both she and they liked they said, 'Anything, from flamenco to Broadway musicals.' So we played a selection of songs. This focused an already lively gathering of disparate voices into some sort of coherent atmosphere where people were listening rather than speaking.

Between songs, she began to tell us a little about her life and what she needed. This changed the nature of the session to a meditative theme where we improvised a meditative chant about peace and waiting.

Table 8.1 World Health Organization (1990, p.11) recommendations and music therapy responses from the literature

WHO recommendations	Music therapy responses
Affirm life and regard dying as a normal process	Life is performed until we die
Provides relief from pain and distressing symptoms	Music therapy is recognized as an anxiolytic and as a medium for pain relief
Integrate the psychological and spiritual aspects of patient care	The spiritual needs of patients are reconciled with their psychological needs
Offer a support system to help patients as actively as possible until death	Patients and their families are actively supported to cope during the illness
Offer a support system to help the family cope during the illness and in their own bereavement	Many music therapists offer aftercare for bereavement, sing at the funeral or make tape recordings of the favourite music suggested by the person who has died

At our next session, which both physician and patient requested, the focus was on this meditative music. Only her closest friend was present. While talking with Lois, we heard several themes that were important for her. These themes included a relief from pain, a need for peace, concern for her family and her anxiety about the near future – particularly concerning the process of dying and reconciliation with her loved ones.

Her physician too had concerns that maybe her resistance to treatment was bound together with unspoken existential needs. Her physical condition was indeed deteriorating – she was receiving intravenous medication for the relief of pain that she controlled by a hand-held device. Yet the relief of pain is not the same as the relief of suffering. While the patient was receiving strong medication for her pain, the treatment team also recognized that she was also suffering. In the cancer centre where this took place, such an integrated approach to music therapy and medicine is standard procedure in the pain and palliative care team.

We then repeated a 16 minute sung meditation accompanied by guitars on themes raised from the conversation that we had previously had. These themes were transposed into imaginative situations between her and her family members. As she had asked for reconciliation, we used the words 'Reaching out to you' and 'I will take you in my arms'.

During the improvisation her son entered the room, spoke with Lois's friend and then too sat down to listen to what we were singing. Her physician also came to listen to what we were doing.

After the song, her physician asked her where she was, as she had clearly relaxed and the expression on her face suggested that she had changed her state of consciousness. She said, 'I am in Beauty, I am in Peace.' This proved to be a turning point in her therapy as expressed by the palliative care team. Lois's son and close friend also said that was an important intervention for them too.

In this short vignette, we see several aspects of the WHO recommendations taking place (see Table 8.1): the relief of pain and suffering, affirming the process of dying as normal and integrating psychological and spiritual needs while being aware of the needs of friends and family (see also Aldridge 1987a, 1987b, 1988b).

But there was also another function taking place. The palliative care team asked us to present this material at their grand rounds meeting as they too wanted to hear about the treatment strategy from a different perspective. Music therapy is also an aesthetic form of therapy and within a treatment team it is important to bring other aspects of knowledge complementary to the scientific.

In the cancer centre itself, doctors and nursing staff ask music therapists to sing for patients. Family members and the administrative staff also ask the music therapists to sing. Boundaries of music as therapy have traditionally been broken in this setting but are also just as easily maintained when necessary. Music is seen, or rather heard, as a medium appropriate to the healing culture of the cancer centre. The boundaries that it is given sometimes as 'music therapy' is necessary as a focus for the treatment activity. When staff, however, ask that the door be left open so that they can hear what is being sung, or sing along while entering the room – sometimes staying awhile – to perform a check on medication, or ask that the therapist drop by because they need a song for themselves at the end of a long day, then the boundaries are being extended and moved. Making music is extended into a broader ecology of healing that encompasses patients, family, friends and carers. While we may concentrate on music therapy as an anxiolytic and as pain relief, we may be in danger of forgetting that there are subtle and existential aspects of music therapy that are as important. While not being immediately accessible for measurement they are discernible and are accepted by other clinicians as valid. This has been so practised in the cancer centre for the last 25 years.

CHAPTER 9

Music Therapy and Spirituality
A Transcendental Understanding of Suffering

In the field of music therapy, particularly for those working in the ecology of palliative care, there has indeed been an emerging interest in spirituality (Aldridge 1995, 2000b; Bailey 1997; Lowis and Hughes 1997; Magill 2002; Marr 1999; West 1994). In *Music Therapy in Palliative Care: New Voices* (Aldridge 1999), several authors reflect the need for spiritual considerations when working with the dying (Hartley 1999; Hogan 1999). Nigel Hartley has developed this work particularly in hospice settings (Hartley 2001) and with Gary Ansdell ensured that the theme was prominent at the last Music Therapy World Congress in Oxford. In the world of music therapy, the importance of spiritual considerations is evident in the early work of Helen Bonny as a central plank of her approach (Bonny and Pahnke 1972) and Susan Munro's pioneering work in palliative care (Munro and Mount 1978).

Lucanne Magill responded to Michael Mayne at the last World Congress in Oxford (Magill 2002). She reflects on what she believes is really the heart of what we do – music therapy in spirituality – when she says, 'So much of what we do is beyond words and it is really because of this transcendental nature of music that important healing in music therapy can and does occur.' In her four themes in music therapy, she proposes that music builds relationship, enhances remembrance, gives a voice to prayer and instils peace. She concludes: 'In the presence of music, when transformations begin to occur and healing begins, that it is in the lived moments of music therapy that the essence of our work – music therapy, spirituality and healing – is experienced and known.'

Her response is made from a long career of experiences with cancer sufferers and their families (Bailey 1983, 1984; Magill Levreault 1993, Magill 2001; Magill, Chung and Kennedy 2000). Both of us emphasize the importance of the immediate family and the people working in the hospital ward. We refer to this as the 'ecology of singing in an hospital setting' as this fits into both our career experiences in clinical practice and community work (Aldridge

1986). This ecology will also include the palliative care culture, as a broader team and the ethos of the centre as a whole. Anyone working with Lucanne will have seen that there are possibilities to make music from the head physician to members of the ancillary staff. Music making is not solely for the patients in this setting – healing lies in the whole culture (culture here also includes praxis).

These considerations of spirituality are not unique to music therapy; there is, and has been, over the last decade, an increasing vigorous debate over the need for spiritual considerations in health care delivery (Aldridge 1987a, 1987c, 1988b, 1996; Bailey 1997). There is an overlap between music therapy and several other integrative medicine approaches, particularly in the use of breath and how this is applied in altering consciousness (Aldridge 2002). Based on this published work, Nigel Hartley asked me to speak at a series of symposia held at the hospice where he works in Oxford, and we have presented together at various venues. Our intention has been to sponsor the discussion of spirituality as a legitimate topic in music therapy, just as I have tried to do in the field of medicine (Aldridge 1987c, 1991b, 1991c). In clinical practice, I am pursuing this work further with Lucanne Magill at Memorial Sloan-Kettering Cancer Center.

The ecology of dying

As a former community worker, promoting the arts with different people and their communities, music therapy was no strange practice to me when I first came across it in 1985. From my work with the dying in the community, and people who were suicidal, I understood that we must implement an ecological approach to understanding these phenomena (Aldridge 1987a, 1987c, 1991b, 1991c). Indeed, the reason why modern medicine is failing to meet the needs of people is because it lacks such a perspective. Taking a spiritual perspective did not remove from this ecological approach but added another dimension to that ecology of ideas. I had also been advocating the importance of the aesthetic in research at this time (Aldridge 1991a).

For those of us involved in the family therapy movement, core texts had been the books of Gregory Bateson (Bateson 1973, 1979). Everything became process, system and ecology with the intention of stamping out nouns. We see this perspective in Christopher Small's book *Musicking* (Small 1998), where he also references the same discourse as I have done in my earlier work. Indeed, I use culture as an ecological activity in a systemic perspective binding the meanings of individuals in relationships together – what Gregory Bateson refers to as an 'ecology of mind' (Bateson 1972). What we do as individuals is understood in the setting of our social activities and those settings are informed by the individuals that comprise them. Here, too, the body, and the presentation of symptoms, is seen as an important non-verbal communication that has meaning within specific personal relationships that are located themselves within a social context. Symptoms are interpreted within relationships. The process of healing facilitated through music therapy must also be located in such an ecology.

In practice, when Lucanne Magill sings with her patients she also sings with the family members that are present. Ward staff that are present will also join in. Nurses will request their favourite songs and doctors will ask her, or her colleagues, to sing for them too. Music is seen as a natural activity located within an ecology of healing (Aldridge and Magill 2002). Trygve Aasgaard refers to this as milieu (Aasgaard 1999).

Health as performed: A praxis aesthetic in an immanent context

My thesis is that health, like music (Aldridge 2002), is performed. Indeed, the process of 'healthing' can be understood as a dynamic improvised process like that of Small's 'musicking' (Small 1998). How health is performed depends upon a variety of negotiated meanings, and how those meanings themselves are transcended. These meanings are concerned with body, mind and spirit. My intention is to set about the task of reviving a set of meanings given to the understanding of human behaviour that is termed 'spiritual'. It is legitimate to talk about spirituality in a culture of health care delivery. Human beings perform their lives together in meaningful contexts of significant others that are nested within broader social contexts. The different contexts of performance are related to an ecological understanding of what it is to be a human being amongst other human beings and is an argument for a return to a sacred understanding of human beings and nature. In these instances, 'God', 'the divine', 'the cosmos' or 'nature' may be the name given to a meaningful immanent context in which life is performed.

Spiritual meanings are linked to actions, and those actions have consequences that are performed as prayer, meditation, worship, healing and, in our approaches, music healing. What patients think about the causes of their illnesses influences what they do in terms of health care treatment and to whom they turn for the resolution of distress. For some people, rather than consider illness alone, they relate their personal identities to being healthy, one factor of which is spirituality. The maintenance and promotion of health, or becoming healthy, is an activity. As such it will be expressed bodily – what I refer to as a *praxis aesthetic*. Thus we would expect to see people not only having sets of beliefs about health but also actions related to those beliefs. Some of these may be dietary, some involve exercise and some prayer or meditation. Some will be musical.

Religion and spirituality

There is a link between religion and spirituality, that I argue extensively in my book *Spirituality, Healing and Medicine* (Aldridge 2000d), although the two definitions are often confused. The same difficulty has prevailed in the medical and nursing literature where spirituality and religion are confounded.

All major religions recognize a spiritual dimension, and that is the relationship between the human being and the divine. We see this reflected in the yin and yang symbol of traditional Chinese medicine that emphasizes the vertical relationship between the human and the divine, each in their manifestation containing a seed of the other and uniting together to form a whole. Similarly, the Christian cross reflects both the realms of horizontal earthly existence and vertical divine relationship. The difficulty lies in the explanations that are used for understanding when either a sacred ecology or the divine relationship is used; one is assumed to supersede the other according to the interpreter of events. Both are partial. Indeed, what many spiritual authors seek is to take us beyond the dualisms of material and spiritual, beyond body and mind, to realize that in understanding the relations between the two then we leap to another realm of knowledge. Indeed, the Buddhist concept of the 'middle way' is not to find some mid-point between the two but to transcend the two ideas, unifying them in a balanced understanding. This leap that goes beyond dualism is the process of transcendence. In its simplest form, there is a change of consciousness to another level of knowledge; in short, the purpose of spirituality is achieved.

Spirituality in a late modern sense is used consistently throughout the literature related to medical practice as an ineffable dimension that is separate from religion itself. A person may regard herself as having a spiritual dimension but this may not be explored in any religious practice. Central to these arguments is the concept that spirituality lends a unity and purpose to life (see Table 9.1).

Table 9.1 Definitions of spirituality from journal articles

'Spirituality is defined in terms of personal views and behaviors that express a sense of relatedness to a transcendent dimension or to something greater than the self... Spirituality is a broader concept than religion or religiosity... Indicators of spirituality include prayer, sense of meaning in life, reading and contemplation, sense of closeness to a higher being, interactions with others and other experiences which reflect spiritual interaction or awareness. Spirituality may vary according to developmental level and life events.'	(Reed 1987, p.336)
'Spiritual elements are those capacities that enable a human being to rise above or transcend any experience at hand. They are characterized by the capacity to seek meaning and purpose, to have faith, to love, to forgive, to pray, to meditate, to worship, and to seek beyond present circumstances.'	(Kuhn 1988, p.91)
'The spiritual dimension of persons can be uniquely be defined as the human capacity to transcend self, which is phenomenologically reflected in three basic spiritual needs: (a) the need for self-acceptance, a trusting relationship with self based on a sense of meaning and purpose in life; (b) the need for relationship with others and/or a supreme other (e.g., God) characterized by nonconditional love, trust, and forgiveness; and (c) the need for hope, which is the need to imagine and participate in the enhancement of a positive future. All persons experience these spiritual needs, whether or not they are part of a formal religious organization.'	(Highfield 1992, p.3)
'Spiritual: pertaining to the innate capacity to, and tendency to seek to, transcend one's current locus of centricity, which transcendence involves increased love and knowledge.'	(Chandler, Holden and Kolander 1992, p.169)
'Six clear factors...appear to be fundamental aspects of spirituality...those of the journey, transcendence, community, religion, "the mystery of creation", and transformation.'	(Lapierre 1994, p.154)
'Spirituality...pertains to one's relationship with others, with oneself and with one's higher power, which is defined by the individual and need not be associated with a formal religion.'	(Borman and Dixon 1998, p.287)
'...spirituality refers to the degree of involvement or state of awareness or devotion to a higher being or life philosophy. Not always related to conventional beliefs.'	(Lukoff et al. 1999, p.65)
'Spirituality is rooted in an awareness which is part of the biological make-up of the human species. Spirituality is present in all individuals and it may manifest as inner peace and strength derived from perceived relationship with a transcendent God or an ultimate reality or whatever an individual values as supreme.'	(Narayanasay 1999, p.124)

My position is that if spirituality is about the individual, ineffable and implicit, then religion is about the social, spoken and explicit. Definitions are an attempt to explicate the practices whereby spirituality is achieved, although the source may be ineffable. Spirituality lends meaning and purpose to our lives; these purposes help us transcend what we are. We are processes of individual development in relational contexts, that are embedded within a cultural matrix. We are also developing understandings of truth; indeed, each one of us is an aspect of truth. These understandings are predicated on changes in consciousness achieved through transcending one state of consciousness to another. This dynamic process of transcendence is animated by forces or subtle energies, and music is a primary example, in some contexts, of such subtlety.

To remain authentic to both traditional sacred texts and to the earlier part of this commentary, I would suggest the use of 'truthing' rather than truth, in the way that I use 'healthing' rather than health. Truth(ing) is a cosmic activity related to the breathing out and breathing in of the creator, and thus my previous remarks about life being analogous to music, 'living as jazz', where we are constantly being performed as living beings (Aldridge 1989b, 2000b). Thus, truth is an activity; truthing is constantly being performed, and we are its living explicated examples. It is as if each one of us is a song continually being sung. This leads some to ask who the singer is.

'Religion' is used as an operationalization, or outward manifestation, of 'spirituality' (see Table 9.2). There are spiritual practices that people engage in; these often take place in groups and are guided by culture. As a cultural system, religion is a meaning-seeking activity that offers the individual and others both purpose and an ability to perceive meaning. We have not only a set of offered meanings but also the resources and practices by which meanings can be realized. However, as Idries Shah reminds us, we must be wary of confusing 'spirituality' with what is manifested outwardly: 'The poetry and the teaching to which you have referred is an outward manifestation. You feed on outward manifestation. Do not, please, give that the name of spirituality' (Shah 1969, p.115).

The social is what is common to all religions; it offers forms for experiencing nature and the divine, and for transforming the self that is the goal of human development. Consciousness, achieving truth, is a social activity dependent upon its embodiment in individuals. Culture is the specific manifestation of such social forms in symbols, language and ritual, localized for temporal and geographical contexts – thus specific cults and cultures. In globalization, we have the dissemination of culture but without social forms related to

Table 9.2 Definitions of religion from journal articles

'The term religiousness has been used in operationalizing spirituality.'	(Reed 1987, p.336)
'By religious we mean practices carried out by those who profess a faith.'	(Doyle 1992, p.303)
'...the term religious will be used to denote the part of the process when spiritual impulses are formally organized into a social/political structure designed to facilitate and interpret the spiritual search.'	(Decker 1993, p.34)
'Religion has a beneficial effect on human social life and individual well-being because it regulates behavior and integrates individuals in caring social circles.'.	(Idler 1995, p.684)
'Religion is considered by some to be of divine origin with a set of revealed truths and a form of worship.'	(Long 1997, p.500)
'Religion will not be defined in strict terms, but will be used to denote experiences, cognitions and actions seen (by the individual or the community) as significant in relation to the sacred.'	(Ganzevoort 1998, p.260)
'Religiosity is associated with religious organizations and religious personnel.' 'Religion involves subscribing to a set of beliefs or doctrines that are institutionalized.' 'People...can be religious without being spiritual by perfunctorily performing the necessary rituals. However, in many cases, spiritual experiences do accompany religious practices.'	(Lukoff et al. 1999, p.65)
'Religion is the outward practice of a spiritual system of beliefs, values, codes of conduct and rituals.'	(King and Dein 1998, p.1259)
'Religion encompasses that which is designated by the social group as nonroutine and uncontrollable and that which inspires fear, awe, and reverence, that is, the sacred. Through ritual, one gains carefully prescribed access to the sacred, which is carefully protected from the mundane, routine, instrumentally oriented beliefs and actions of the profane realm. Because sacredness is socially confirmed, stemming from the attitude of believers...political ideologies, value systems and even leisure activities such as sports and art [are viewed] as sacred activities.'	(Park 1998, p.407)
'...religious life is an expressive, world-building activity through which we get ourselves together and find a kind of posthumous, or retrospective, happiness.'	(Cupitt 1997, p.xiv)
'Religion is a comprehensive picturing and ordering of human existence in nature and the cosmos.'	(Joseph 1998, p.220)

human contact. Therefore we may spread the idea of spirituality but offer no forms for the achievement of spiritual understandings, which is the traditional role of religious forms in everyday life. The same goes for the idea of music therapy; the idea of musicking as a performative praxis is useless unless we find cultural forms (as in perFORMance) such that healthing may be realized and recognized.

The process of truthing behind the spirit of music therapy will be expressed socially in its practice forms and the names that they are given. These forms will be inevitably corrupted, like religious forms, as they appear at specific times and in specific places for particular peoples (even though the time may be centuries, the places inter-continental and the peoples varied). Only spirit remains. We have the same situation about the naming of music therapy currently and inevitably where forms have to be recognized (literally *re-cognized*) (Aldridge 2000a). Forms have to come into being; the process of forming is at the heart of perFORMance. This process, calling a religion by a name, and its associated divinity, is a political activity. So too is the naming of the performance of therapy.

Beyond meaning: Transcendence and suffering

'Medicine', from the Latin root *medicus,* is the measure of illness and injury, and shares the Latin *metiri*, 'to measure'. Yet this measurement was based on natural cycles and measures. 'To attend medically', Latin *mederi,* also supports the Latin word *meditari,* from which we have the modern *meditation,* which is the measuring of an idea in thought. The task of the healer in this sense is to direct the attention of the patient through the value of suffering to a solution which is beyond the problem itself. In this sense, the healer encourages a change in the sign of the patient's suffering from negative to positive. We are encouraged to see the benefit of suffering in bringing us beyond our present understandings, which is also an understanding of the transcendental. This is what happens in music therapy, particularly in the context of palliative care.

Transcendence is a 'going beyond' a current awareness to another level of understanding. This does not necessarily imply a conventional set of beliefs; it is based upon an innate capacity that we have as human beings to rise above the situation.

The process of spiritual development can be seen as a 'quest' or a journey. In medieval times, the quest for the Holy Grail was not for a material chalice but symbolized the search for knowledge as a vessel in which the divine may be contained. However, what confounds this issue today is that we equate questioning as an activity rather like the chatter of infants. Many spiritual traditions emphasize the importance of silence and non-activity where the appropriate question may be framed and, as importantly, the answer may be heard. Meditation, prayer and music have all been used to fulfil these functions. Silence is the core of music and was the reason that I gave my first music therapy book the subtitle *From out of the silence* (Aldridge 1996).

Religious practice

While the spiritual dimension may be separate from the religious, religious practices are said to provide a bridge to the spiritual, thus assuming that the spiritual is a realm beyond the religious (Lukoff *et al.* 1999). This spiritual dimension is seen as a relationship with a higher power, experienced as internal and intensely personal, that need not be associated with the formal external aspects of religion; the transcending sense of phenomena, rationality and feelings lead to a heightened state of consciousness or awareness. The danger is that what may be seen as 'spiritual illuminations' in the raw condition of altered states of consciousness are imagined to be spiritual experiences. These can become addictive (Shah 1983, 1990), preventing any developmental change – thus the need for a spiritual guide, emphasized in the great traditions, and reflected too in secular psychotherapy as a wise counsellor, to prevent the interpretation of emotions as spirituality. The same confounding of emotion and spirituality may also occur in the use of music, hence the prohibition of musical experiences in some religions and at some stages of spiritual teaching.

The ability to rise above suffering, to go beyond the present situation to a realm where life takes on another, perhaps deeper, significance, is an important factor in palliative care. In the treatment of alcoholism, it is the recognition of personal suffering and the need to transcend the limitations of the self, to understand that we are 'Not-God' (Kurtz 1979), as a process of spiritual awakening that brings about one of the vital steps in recovery. Deborah Salmon (2001) refers to music therapy as a containing or sacred space that facilitates the process of connecting to that which is psychologically and spiritually significant for the patient, thereby transforming experiences of suffering into those of meaning.

Transcending the current situation

From the literature it is possible to piece together a process of spiritual change that emphasizes the need to transcend the current situation. To achieve this there has to be a change both in thought and feeling, accompanied by appropriate actions. This is expressed as a process of questioning, as a search for meaning. Such meanings take the searcher beyond what she is to a higher consciousness, or state of awareness, that is connected to the truth, which people refer to with varying names like 'god', 'the divine', 'the supreme power', or simply 'that'. This is a spiralling process of development based on revealed personal understandings achieved through transcendence, which leads to other understandings. Idries Shah refers to this process as a removal of veils to the truth (Shah 1978). These veils that obscure the truth are formed either through indoctrination, that blinds us, or through the base aspirations of our subjective selves preventing subtle perceptions and higher visions. Religion itself may be a veil that hides the truth, although it claims to offer a public perspective into the truth. The task we face is how to make those veils transparent, or remove them.

Suffering and the loss of a coherent self

We suffer when we fail to make sense of our experience. One of the difficulties faced by people in the advanced stages of cancer, or the neurodegenerative disease, is that they lose their sense of dignity. Pullman argues that this is an aesthetic perspective on suffering (Pullman 2002) and proposes that maintaining a meaningful life is an aesthetic project. This ties in with my perspective of a performed life and why music therapy is so important – we are returned to an aesthetic of living.

The spiritual elements of experience help us to rise above the matters at hand such that in the face of suffering we can find purpose, meaning and hope. It is in the understanding of suffering, the universality of suffering and the need for deliverance from it that varying traditions of music therapy and religion meet. Suffering is embodied as pain. While we may temporarily relieve pain with analgesics, our task is also to understand, and thereby relieve, suffering. Music therapy has the potential to relieve suffering and to achieve the aesthetic. Referring to Lucanne Magill's Oxford presentation, her patient replied, when asked where she was after we had sung with her, 'I am in Beauty, I am in Peace' (Magill 2002).

While we may strive for the eradication of major diseases, the presence of suffering will be a part of the human narrative. So too, then, the relief of that suffering. How that relief is achieved is not dependent solely upon a medical narrative but, as the major religions have offered throughout the ages, also upon spiritual understanding. Through music, in the setting of music therapy, we can encourage such understanding. While the management of pain is often a scientific and technical task, the relief of suffering is an existential task. It can also be a musical task. In the major spiritual traditions suffering has always had the potential to transform the individual. As Tournier (1981) reminds us, it is love that has the power to change the sign of suffering from negative to positive. To that end, music has also been a traditional medium of transformation for the relief of suffering.

Music therapy facilitates the process of connecting to that which is spiritually significant for the patient, thereby transforming experiences of suffering into those of meaning. This has been traditionally termed 'transcendence' – to rise above the immediate situation – and is the basis of hope (Aldridge 1995, 2000b).

Coda: Therapist heal thyself

There are different methods to approach truth. If we accept that in a modern, vibrant culture there is a pluralism of truth claims, then a major task will be for us to reconcile what may appear to be disparate ideas. The argument here is not for some kind of homogeneity of thought but for an acceptance of the tension between ideas as a creative arena that pushes us beyond what we know. Thomas Merton (1996) writes in his journal for 28 April 1957:

> If I can unite in myself, in my own spiritual life, the thought of the East and West of the Greek and Latin fathers, I will create in myself a reunion of the divided Church and from that unity in myself can come the exterior and visible unity of the Church. For if we want to bring together East and West we cannot do it by imposing one upon the other. We must contain both within ourselves and transcend both. (p.87)

The whole concept of pluralism, often invoked for justifying differing positions within the world of music therapy, is itself a term borrowed from theology. The basis of the understanding is that not one of us as human beings can begin to claim a full understanding of the divine (or whatever you may choose to call him or her); thus we have to recognize that we have only parts of the picture. Surely the same goes for music therapy; no one group can claim hegemony nor absolute understanding of the truth of what music therapy is. A challenge is for us all to come together and merge those various understandings. This is recognized in the Christian perspective of 'Though we are many, we are one body' (Aldridge 1987b). The difficulty lies in the fact that although we may all be moved by that same spirit of music therapy, in its localized practices, we begin to operate as religions. Religions are only temporal manifestations and become corrupted – they are eventually replaced by new forms. Surely this is the strength that is music therapy, the ability to adapt to new situations without becoming fixed. While our schools of thought may be necessary religions for the propagation of temporary dogmas, for initiating disciples and accomplishing, we are urged not to lose the spirit through political strife.

My hope is that we can go some way to uniting the 'East' and 'West' of thinking in music therapy such that there is a reunion of thought about healing and the possibility of transcendence. This perhaps is the basis of healing and the core of hope. As Merton suggests, one cannot be imposed upon the other; it is the containment within ourselves that brings the change. This is simply an argument for diversity in the culture of music therapy that includes the many facets of its performance.

This following story illustrates the unity of knowledge and how illusive it is to the ordinary intellect. It is taken from a story told by Rumi, a 13th-century mystic from Afghanistan. I use the symbol of the elephant in my projects as a reminder of the partiality of our knowledge, and the importance of including the knowledge of others when attempting to understand the elephant of therapy.

The Blind Ones and the Matter of the Elephant

In World Tales, Idries Shah recounts the story of the blind ones and the elephant (pp.133–135).

There was a city where everyone was blind. A king, with a mighty elephant, camped nearby.

The people of the city were anxious to experience the elephant and some from among this blind community ran like fools to find it.

Of course they did not even know the form or shape of the elephant, so they groped around touching different parts of it.

Each person who touched a part thought he knew what an elephant was.

When they returned to the city, groups of people gathered around, each anxious to learn the experiences of those who had touched the elephant.

They asked about its shape and were told by the man whose hand had reached an ear that an elephant is a large, rough thing, wide and broad, like a rug.

The man who had felt the trunk said that an elephant is like a straight and hollow pipe, awful and destructive. Another, having touched its feet and legs, said that it is mighty and firm, like a pillar.

Each had a partial experience and based their description of the whole on the partial. All imagined something about the whole by surmising from an experience with the part. No mind knew all and thus knowledge is not the companion of the blind.

If each one of us is a living performed truth in itself, then other truths are made possible through relationship as encounter. Through this encounter with a living universe, we expand into an ecology of knowledge. Through music we have the possibility of performing this encounter; we literally bring truth into a temporal, albeit ephemeral, form. This is the unity of consciousness, becoming whole, and the basis of the healing endeavour. As each person progresses, wholeness is achieved at a different level of understanding. These understandings may be horizontal in a natural ecology, vertical in a divine ecology, or both. Spirituality enables the transcendence from one level to the next, incorporating new perspectives and reconciling contradictions. Thus we become whole as a person: realizing that our relationships have to be healed, we become reconciled as a community; realizing that there is strife and discord, we search for political accord; realizing that there is imbalance and a lack of harmony, we search for a reconciliation with nature; and realizing that we are alone we reach out to the cosmos.

CHAPTER 10

Prayer and Spiritual Healing in Medical Settings

If you can't handle your feelings, how can you avoid harming your spirit? If you can't control your emotions, but nevertheless try to stop yourself following them, you will harm yourself twice over. Those who do this double injury to themselves are not counted amongst those with long life.

Chang Tzu, Quoted in Palmer (1996, p.256)

Thus far you have harmonized with your body, having the usual nine apertures, and you have not been struck midway through life with blindness or deafness, lameness nor any deformity, so in comparison to many you are fortunate. So why do you wander around grumbling about Heaven? Be gone, Sir!

Chang Tzu, Quoted in Palmer (1996, p.164)

Prayer in medicine

Prayer is becoming increasingly used in approaches to healing. The use of prayer is related to specific health outcomes (Duckro and Magaletta 1994; McCullough 1995) and is acceptable within medical practice (Magaletta and Duckro 1996). VandeCreek, Rogers and Lester (1999) found that there was an interest in, and a practice of, prayer as a complementary therapy for breast cancer outpatients.

Although initial clinical research into the benefits of prayer was inconclusive (Collipp 1969; Joyce and Welldon 1965; Rosner 1975), more recent studies, from a broader medical perspective and with larger study populations, have shown that intercessory prayer is beneficial. Several authors argue that religious variables are relevant, even if not beneficial, and that physicians should choose to attend to them (Dossey 1993; King 1997; King and Dein 1998; King, Speck and Thomas 1999; Magaletta and Duckro 1996).

Saudia *et al.* (1991) investigated the helpfulness of prayer as a directaction coping mechanism in patients before having cardiac surgery was examined. Ninety-six subjects indicated that prayer was used as a coping mechanism in dealing with the stress of cardiac surgery, and 70 of these subjects gave it the highest possible rating on the Helpfulness of Prayer Scale. Prayer was perceived as a helpful, direct-action coping mechanism and was independent of whether individuals believed that their lives were controlled by themselves or a powerful other. The importance of this study is that it emphasizes prayer as direct action that the individual uses as a coping strategy.

In a coronary care unit the prayer group had an overall better outcome requiring less antibiotics, diuretics and intubation/ventilation than control (Byrd 1988). For renal patients, prayer and looking at the problem objectively were used most in coping with stress (Sutton and Murphy 1989). It is interesting to see that at the pragmatic level of the patient, prayer and looking at the problem objectively are not exclusive but complementary activities in a system of beliefs. This is stress relief using prayer as a coping strategy.

In the treatment of alcoholism there has been an historical influence of spiritual considerations being included in treatment plans (Bergmark 1998; Carroll 1993; Eisenbach-Stagl 1998; McCarthy 1984) apart from the temperance movement. Such treatments for alcohol abuse were often composite packages using physical methods of relaxation, psychological methods of suggestion and auto-suggestion, social methods of group support and service to the community, and spiritual techniques of prayer. These procedures are still in use today and have been extended into the realm of chemical dependency and substance abuse (Buxton, Smith and Seymour 1987; Green, Fullilove and Fullilove 1998; Mathew *et al.* 1996; Miller 1998; Navarro *et al.* 1997; Peteet 1993). Individuals suffering from substance problems are found to have a low level of religious involvement, and spiritual engagement appears to be correlated with recovery (Miller 1998) while religiosity may be an advantageous coping factor (Kendler, Gardner and Prescott 1997).

Prayer is described by several authors as valuable in terms of care for the elderly across several cultures (Chatters and Taylor 1989; Foley, Wagner and Waskel 1998; Garrett 1991; Gorham 1989; Koenig, Bearon, and Dayringer 1989; Koenig *et al.* 1997; Markides 1983; Reed 1987; Taylor and Chatters 1991).

Medical help seeking and prayer are not mutually exclusive (Bearon and Koenig 1990), as prayer is considered to be an active coping response in the face of stressful medical problems. A study of 160 physicians found that physicians believe that religion has a positive effect on physical health, that religious issues should be addressed and that the older patient may ask the physician to pray with them (Koenig *et al.* 1989). An influential factor in this questioning is the belief system of the practitioner, which may influence in turn the willingness of the patient to talk about such matters.

Byrd's study

Randolph Byrd's (1988) study at the San Francisco General Hospital has achieved landmark status in the topography of healing research. He asked whether intercessory prayer to a Judaeo-Christian God has an effect on the patient's recovery and medical condition while in hospital, and if there is an effect, what are its characteristics. The hypothesis is that intercessory prayer mediates the process of healing.

Intercessory prayer was taken as the treatment method for the 192 randomly allocated patients; another 201 patients formed a control group. All 393 patients had standard medical care as expected. The intercessors were 'born-again' Christians with an active Christian life of daily devotional prayer who partook of fellowship in their local churches. Each patient was randomized to between three to seven intercessors, who were given the patient's first name, diagnosis and general condition. The prayer was done from outside the hospital – prayer at a distance. Each intercessor was asked to pray daily for a rapid recovery and for the prevention of complications and death. Physicians were informed of the trial but did not know to which group the patients belonged.

Standard medical treatment was given throughout to all patients. Thus prayer was an adjunct to standard medical care, not an alternative.

At first glance the statistical results of Byrd's study are impressive, with an overall improvement being attributed to prayer. It does indeed show a touching faith on the behalf of medical scientists in statistical results, partly because the results make medical sense. There is less congestive heart failure, cardio-pulmonary arrest and pneumonia, fewer antibiotics are needed, less diuretic medication and less ventilator support.

My concern with these studies is that while they do demonstrate causally the effect of prayer, they miss an important aspect of prayer which is not instrumental, and is spiritual. While this spiritual change becomes explicit, the time frame for that explication may not conform to the time scale of the trial itself. Indeed, many of the changes that can be related to change may be at first hidden.

Spiritual healing research in medical settings

Prayer is only one form of healing that is regarded as spiritual. There are a variety of other forms of spiritual healing and these are comprehensively described by Dossey (1993), Benor (1990, 1991, 1992), Solfin (1984) and Wirth (1995; Wirth and Cram 1997; Wirth, Richardson and Eidelman 1996; Wirth et al. 1996). The National Federation of Spiritual Healers in England (NFSH 1999) define spiritual healing as restoring the balance of body, mind and spirit in the recipient 'with the intention of promoting self-healing, and to bring a sense of well-being and peace to the recipient' (p.2). A further description concerns itself with finding an inner peaceful core, connecting with a universal source of peace and love that is channelled for the benefit of another. This connection with a universal force is also at the centre of 'therapeutic touch' and belies its connections with ancient systems of healing (Fischer and Johnson 1999).

While the state of mind necessary for healing has been elusive to research there has been quite extensive research into the physical sequelae of spiritual healing phenomena, which has included investigations using controlled trials (Benor 1990). Enzymes and body chemicals *in vitro* have been studied, as have the effects of healing on cells and lower organisms (including bacteria, fungus and yeasts), on human tissue cells *in vitro*, on the motility of simple organisms and plants, on animals and on human problems. While spiritual healing is often dismissed as purely a placebo response, the evidence from studies of lower organisms and cells would indicate that there is direct influence. Even if we introduce the idea of expectancy effects as an influence on experimental data we are still left with a body of knowledge which begs understanding (Solfin 1984; Wirth 1995).

General practice

At the level of daily practice some general practitioners have been willing to entertain the idea of spiritual healing and incorporate it into their practice, to use spiritual explanations for some of their patient contact, or as part of their referral network (Aldridge 2000a; Brown 1995; Brown and Sheldon 1989; Cohen 1989; Dossey 1993; Pietroni 1986). Cohen (1989) emphasizes the value of touch, time and compassion which the healer can offer, and the benefits of referral. Such practice points out the value of working together as a referral network of practitioners.

King *et al.* (1992) focused on patients who use faith healers and physicians to care for their medical problems to learn about how often physicians see patients who are involved in faith healing, and to learn more about physicians' attitudes about, and experiences with, faith healing. Approximately one half (52%) of the 594 participating physicians were aware of at least one patient in their practice who had had a faith-healing experience. Most physicians came in contact with such patients no more frequently than once a year. Fifty-five per cent agreed and 20 per cent disagreed that reliance on faith healers often leads to serious medical problems. However, 44 per cent thought that physicians and faith healers can work together to cure some patients, and 23 per cent believed that faith healers divinely heal some people whom physicians cannot help. Family physicians were divided in their views about faith healing, with a majority expressing scepticism about faith healing and a sizeable minority favourable toward it.

Chronic complaints and recalcitrance

In Brown's (1995) study of chronic problems in an English general practice of six doctors, adult patients with chronic complaints were referred by their general practitioner to a healing clinic. In choosing the patients, the general practitioner included those who had had a problem of six months' duration and had not responded well to usual interventions, other secondary referrals or counselling. Treatment sessions lasted 20 minutes once a week for an eight-week period. The spiritual healing used a 'laying on of hands approach' to 'channel healing energies' and was assessed using a validated quality of life questionnaire that has established population norms for comparison (SF-36). There were significant changes after eight weeks in what was a group of patients with poor health status in role limitations, social function, pain, general health and vitality. These improvements were not extended to an assessment after 26 weeks from the beginning of the study. As the author says, we cannot make any specific conclusions regarding the healing approach as there were no treatment controls. However, for a group of chronic patients, recalcitrant to previous intervention, there was improvement.

Chronic symptoms in general practice are also the focus of Dixon's (1998) study. Like the above study with several general practitioners working together, patients with a condition that had lasted for six months, which was unresponsive to treatment, were referred to a healer. The patients were told that they were going to see a healer, rather than a faith or spiritual healer, who would pass her hands close to the patient visualizing the passage of light through the patient accompanied by relaxing music. We are not told of the control condition, and the use of relaxing music confounds the treatment, given that the use of music as music therapy is a known anxiolytic (Aldridge 1996). However, compared to the control scores, there was an improvement in anxiety and depression scores after three months that was maintained at six months for the treatment group. Functional improvements on the Nottingham Health Profile at three months were not maintained at a significant level after six months. These patients were previously unresponsive to treatment and the improvement in general mood state scores indicates a general setting for recovery that is of worth for clinical practice.

A broader ecology of care

The demand for whole person treatment has been strenuously adopted by some nursing groups, who remind us that in caring for the patient there is a need to include spiritual needs and to allow the expression of those needs (Boutell and Bozett 1990; Burkhardt 1989; Clark and Dawson 1996; Dossey 1999; Ferrell *et al.* 1998; Grasser and Craft 1984; Harrington, Lackey and Gates 1996; Labun 1988; Magaletta and Duckro 1996; Potts 1996; Rukholm *et al.* 1991; Rustoen and Hanestad 1998; Soeken and Carson 1987). Within these approaches there is a core of opinion which accepts that suffering and pain are part of a larger life experience, and that they can have meaning for the patient, and for the caregivers (Aldridge 2000a,c; Nagai Jacobson and Burkhardt 1989). The emphasis is placed upon the person's concept of God, sources of strength and hope, the significance of religious practices and rituals for the patient and their belief system (Soeken and Carson 1987).

When the goal of treatment is palliative, in terminally ill cancer patients with a prognosis of six months or less, the most important outcome is improving patient quality of life (Greisinger *et al.* 1997). Interviews with 120 terminally ill cancer patients show that their most important concerns encompass existential, spiritual, familial, physical and emotional issues, and that throughout their illness these concerns were rarely a focus of their care. What is of further concern is that doctors underestimate symptom severity 15 per cent of the time (Stephens *et al.* 1997), and this has important implications for palliative interventions and the way in which patient understandings are taken seriously.

Doctors, nurses and clergy have worked together to care for the dying (Conrad 1985; Greisinger *et al.* 1997; McMillan and Weitzner 1998; Reed 1987; Roche 1989), and a community team approach which includes the family of the patient and his or her friends appears to be beneficial (Aldridge 1987a, 1987b, 1987c, 1987d). These principal benefits are concerned with a lessening of state-trait anxiety, general feelings of well-being and an increasing spiritual awareness for the dying person regardless of gender, marital status, age or diagnosis (Kaczorowski 1989). This does not imply that each practitioner has to address all of these components, rather that those involved identify that which is necessary for the patient and can call upon the appropriate resources. The nurse specializing in pain management works with the priest understanding suffering and together with the patient that is in pain. But the patient plays an active contributory role. Technical support is vital but optimal care involves emotional support, and these may include techniques of relaxation, visualization and meditation (Peteet *et al.* 1992).

Caregivers need care

Increasing numbers of patients with cancer are being cared for by home caregivers (Hileman, Lackey and Hassanein 1992). The primary purpose of Hileman *et al.*'s study was to identify, categorize and assess the importance of needs expressed by 492 home caregivers and to determine how well these needs were satisfied. Caregivers, unpaid people who helped with physical care or coping with the disease process, were selected from the records of two non-profit community cancer agencies and two hospital outpatient oncology clinics. Six need categories were identified: psychological, informational, patient care, personal, spiritual, and household. Those needs changed over time and required frequent reassessment, but it was the caregivers as well as the patients who were seen as in need. If we continually refine our outcome measures to assess the individual patient then we are committing a big mistake by ignoring his or her ecological milieu.

In a three-month study of the perceived needs and anxiety levels of 166 adult family members of intensive care unit (ICU) patients (Rukholm *et al.* 1991), family needs and situational anxiety were significantly related. Worries, trait anxiety, age and family needs explained 38 per cent of the variation of situational anxiety. In addition, spiritual needs and situational anxiety explained 33 per cent of the variation of family needs. In threatening situations families need strategies to cope. As Zigmond (1987) writes: 'On our own, or in our most intimate groups, we devise more personal and idiosyncratic beliefs, rituals and protocols to ward off the potential storms or deserts of uncertainty' (p.69). The spiritual dimension, while perhaps not warding off uncertainty, offers a satisfactory strategy by which uncertainty may be understood and coped with.

Spiritual factors are also important for the caregivers. Chang, Noonan and Tennstedt's (1998) study examines how religious/spiritual coping is related to specific conditions of caregiving and psychological distress among informal caregivers to community-residing disabled elders. Spiritual coping strategies influence caregiver distress indirectly through the quality of the relationship between caregiver and care recipient. Caregivers who used religious or spiritual beliefs to cope with caregiving had a better relationship with those who were being cared for, which is associated with lower levels of depression and an increased dedication to the role of caring.

Spirituality in the treatment of persons living with AIDS

Comprehensive treatment programmes for people living with AIDS recommend that the spiritual welfare of the patient, and its influence on their well-being, is included (Belcher, Dettmore and Holzemer 1989; Flaskerud and Rush 1989; Gutterman 1990; Hall 1998; Holt, Houg and Romano 1999; Kaplan, Marks and Mertens 1997; Ribble 1989; Sowell and Misener 1997; Warner-Robbins and Christiana 1989). Individuals who were spiritually well and able to find meaning and purpose in their lives were also found to be hardier (Carson and Green 1992). Cooke (1992) reminds us that the care of HIV-infected patients is demanding, and the emotional consequences of caring for HIV-infected people, as it effects the givers of that care, should be directly addressed. Other authors, while supporting an emphasis on the spiritual, also direct our attention to the confounding problem of religions that condemn various aspects of sexuality and the ramifications this has for the person living with HIV or AIDS (Jenkins 1995).

While the term 'spiritual healing' is used here within the context of orthodox medical practices as a complementary or adjuvant approach, the term 'spirit' has other applications. In the absence of a medical cure for AIDS, HIV-infected individuals may seek alternative treatments in folk healing practices. In inner-city New Jersey, HIV-infected Hispanics receiving care at an HIV/AIDS clinic believed in good and evil spirits, and that such spirits had a causal role in their infection, either alone or in conjunction with the AIDS virus (Suarez, Raffaelli and OLeary 1996). They sought spiritual folk healing for physical relief, spiritual relief, and protection from evil. A minority hoped for cure. We must be aware of the prevalence of folk beliefs and alternative healing practices and cannot assume that when we talk of spiritual healing that it will fit into the conventional views of Western approaches.

Ambiguity in outcomes

Richards and Folkman (1997) found spiritual phenomena were spontaneously reported in interviews of 68 of 125 recently bereaved HIV-positive and HIV-negative partners of men who died from AIDS. Spiritual understandings helped assimilate the deaths and were seen as sources of solace. Those reporting spiritual phenomena also showed higher levels of depression and anxiety and lower levels of positive states of mind, used more adaptive coping strategies, and reported more physical health symptoms than those who did not report spiritual phenomena. While these findings are with partners of patients, it reflects the work of King *et al.* (1999), who found that stronger spiritual belief is an independent predictor of poor outcome at nine months for patients admitted to the acute services of a London hospital. Chronic pain patients who endorse a greater use of prayer to cope with their pain also reported a greater degree of disability (Ashby and Lenhart 1994).

A distinct danger of promoting understandings, and calling them spiritual, is that they may deflect from pragmatic understandings that are necessary for daily life. An essential element of spiritual understanding is discernment of reasonable and proper applicability, not the repetition of ritual exercises and wishful thinking. The guiding impulse behind the development of modern analgesics may be as divine as the exercise of meditative techniques. Knowing when and how to use them is the important factor (Aldridge 2000a).

Discernment

There are other dangers in spiritual healing. Some patients are promised fantastic healings by spiritual healers. Others are told that they are not recovering either because they do not want to, or that they do not love others enough, or that they are secretly resisting the healer. Some healers have been known to advise patients to refrain from conventional medical treatments. Such approaches are simply wrong. Discernment is the key. For those seeking miracles or some sort of magical intervention through healing powers, this cautious, reasoned approach may be disappointing. Discernment involves no dressing up in special clothes, nor any fancy hand-passes or magical incantations. Dressing up in clothes inappropriate to the period or the local culture is a warning of spiritual bankruptcy, not enhanced powers (Marsham 1990), as is the use of languages strange to the culture. For those seeking the subtle and the hidden, this approach remains less dramatic but no less effective. The attitude of enhancing discernment is one that can be adapted for all healing modalities, including conventional medicine. Discernment can return the spiritual to the subtle level at which it exists. For spirit to be manifested in material effects requires the discernment of practitioners and of those whom they serve.

An integrative perspective

If we are to submit prayer to a test, then we should at least be certain that the observations we will make will incorporate the relevant criteria for assessing recovery. Prayer not only brings relief but the expectation of a new understanding – literally a change in consciousness.

We saw earlier that spirituality is the search for the divine and the achievement of unity. Prayer is the vehicle for this achievement. You can still pray with a broken leg. You cannot run with a broken leg. Knowing the difference between the two seems to be an elementary knowledge. The intention of prayer is to be with the divine; all other cares will fall away. For the sick, illness takes on a different meaning. It too may disappear. To look for a direct cause and effect with prayer is defying the spiritual teachings throughout the centuries, as it fails to see the purposes of both sickness and prayer itself.

That the mind influences healing is becoming apparent. This is a knowledge of the world concerned with laws of cause and effect called science. There is also a knowledge that some call spirituality. Both are important. Neither are to be neglected. Learning the relationship between both forms of knowledge *heals*. In both perspectives of knowledge, science and spirituality, attainment is achieved through teaching and guidance. If the world is given to us by the divine in all its myriad of richness, then surely the blessings of medical knowledge, and the dedication of varying practitioners, are provided by the same source.

CHAPTER 11

A Qualitative Research
Perspective on Healing

Once, when travelling on a ship, a young Italian came to me and said, 'I only believe in eternal matter.' I said, 'Your belief is not very different from my belief.' He was very surprised to hear a priest (he thought I was a priest) saying such a thing. He asked, 'What is your belief?' I said, 'What you call eternal matter, I call eternal spirit. You call matter what I call spirit. What does it signify? It is only a difference in words. It is one Eternal.'

Inayat Khan (1974, p.32-33)

Within recent years there have been a series of studies about the meaning of spirituality in health care delivery and intentional healing. In support of the demand to include spiritual concerns within integrated medical practices there has been a corresponding need to include research that will underpin such a demand. One of the ways in which we can begin to understand intentional healing approaches, and the concept of spiritual healing, is through the broad spectrum of research approaches called *qualitative research*.

Health care is invariably defined in positivist terms as an object, phenomenon or a delivery system. Knowledge gained through scientific and experimental research is objective, quantifiable, stable and measurable (at best measurable by instrumentation, reducing human error). In qualitative approaches, however, we have a shift in paradigm. Knowledge about health is considered to be a process, a lived experience, interpretative, changing and subjective (at best gleaned through human interaction as personal relationship). Indeed, from this qualitative perspective, we may be encouraged to think of the gerund form of the word 'health' as 'healthing'. In the same way, we can also consider what we do as professionals, and what our patients are involved in continually, as the relationship of healing.

While being human is to err, the collection of data through human interaction is not in itself an error. Qualitative research is not a testing mode of enquiry but a discerning form of enquiry requiring the collaborative involvement of those participating in that healing relationship. This emphasis on the verb 'healing' rather than on the noun 'health' goes some way to explain why qualitative approaches have found such resonance in nursing research, with its emphasis on nursing and caring as relational activities, rather than health care research, which is by definition nominal and objective.

If healing is a relationship, then we have to ask ourselves how we evaluate relationships. Would we take friendship, for example, and rate it on a one-to-five Likert scale or would we value our friendships for their various qualities? It is possible to meaningfully explain to another person what the value of a relationship is without quantifying it if we wish to demonstrate the nature of that friendship. So too for the relationship that is healing.

As the reader will have noticed, there is a major opposition between scientific paradigms, and the first question often asked of qualitative research in medicine is: 'Is it scientific?' The short reply to this is: 'Yes, it is social science.' Medicine, being a social activity, is susceptible to being understood by a social science paradigm as much as it is by a natural science paradigm (Kleinman 1973; Mechanic 1968). To fulfil the functions of health caring adequately, we need both quantitative and qualitative approaches.

Social psychology, ethnography and medical anthropology are acceptable scientific approaches for studying human behaviour, and qualitative research takes much of its methods from those fields. Indeed, suffering, distress, pain and death are experiences relevant to understanding health care but elusive to measurement. Similarly, well-being, hope, faith, living a full life and satisfaction are experiences central to health care but not immediately amenable to quantification. But they can be apprehended by understanding (Lewinsohn 1998), and these understandings are gleaned in relationship, the central activities of which are listening and telling stories. As stories are central to the therapeutic relationship, and a vital part of qualitative research, I shall develop in some length within this chapter the concept of narrative (Aldridge 2000a).

Health care narratives: Context and meaning

In modern scientific terms, physicists, in their pursuit of understanding the nature of physical reality, have reached a stage where they have lost the concept of solid matter; they can't come up with the real identity of matter.

So they are beginning to see things in more holistic terms, in terms of interrelationships rather than discreet, independent, concrete objects.

Dalai Lama (1999, p.351)

Our lives are dynamic and performed in defining contexts that lend them meaning. The context of life in the cell will be the organ, the context for the organ will be the body, that of the body will be the 'environment'. This environment may indeed be the physical environment, but it will also be a social environment, a broader ecological environment of nature and also an environment of ideas. Thus meaning is central to understanding health care behaviour.

Our lives gain their meaning in interaction and the interpretation of events. In this sense, identity is performed in various social arenas with a variety of purposive actors that lend meaning to what is performed. Culture is an ecological activity binding the meanings of individuals in relationships together, what Gregory Bateson refers to as an 'ecology of mind' (Bateson 1973). What we do as individuals is understood in the setting of our social activities, and those settings are informed by the individuals that comprise them (Browner 1998; Hsu 2000; Voss *et al.* 1999). Here, too, the body, and the presentation of symptoms, is seen as an important non-verbal communication that has meaning within specific personal relationships that are located themselves within a social context. Symptoms are interpreted within relationships.

Spiritual meanings are linked to actions, and those actions have consequences that are performed as prayer, meditation, worship and healing. What patients think about the causes of their illnesses influences what they do in terms of health care treatment and to whom they turn for the resolution of distress. For some people, rather than consider illness alone, they relate their personal identities to being healthy, one factor of which is spirituality. The maintenance and promotion of health, or becoming healthy, is an activity. As such it will be expressed bodily, a praxis aesthetic. Thus we would expect to see people not only having sets of beliefs about health but also actions related to those beliefs. Some of these may be dietary, some involve exercise and some prayer or meditation. In more formal terms they may wish to engage in spiritual healing and contact a spiritual healer amongst the health care practitioners that they consult. Indeed, some medical practitioners refer patients to spiritual healers.

What we have to ask, as health care practitioners, is, does the inclusion of spirituality bring advantages to understanding the people who come to us in distress? As soon as we talk about life being something which we can cherish and preserve, that compassion for others plays an important role in the way in which we choose to live with each other, that service to our communities is a vital activity for maintaining well-being, that hope is an important factor in recovery, then we have the basis for an argument that is spiritual as well as scientific. Essentially I am arguing for a plurality of research understanding in healing. How do we make meaningful connections that form the narratives we make as patients and practitioners, and how do those narratives inform each other?

Anecdotes: The applied language of healing

Complementary medical approaches are often dismissed as relying upon anecdotal material, as if stories are unreliable. My argument is that stories are reliable and rich in information. While we as medical scientists may try and dismiss the anecdote, we rely upon it when we wish to explain particular cases to our colleagues away from the conference podium (Aldridge 1991a, 1991b). Even in scientific medicine, it has been the single-case report that has been necessary to alert practitioners to the negative sideeffects of current treatment.

While anecdotes may be considered as bad science, they are the everyday stuff of clinical practice. People tell us their stories and expect to be heard. Stories have a structure and are told in a style that informs us too. It is not solely the content of a story, it is how it is told that convinces us of its validity. While questionnaires gather information about populations, and view the world from the perspective of the researcher, it is the interview that provides the condition for the patient to generate his or her meaningful story. The relationship is the context for the story and patients' stories may change according to the conditions in which they are related. This raises significant validity problems for questionnaire research. Anecdotes are the very stuff of social life and the fabric of communication in the healing encounter. As Miller writes: '...every time the experimental psychologist writes a research report in which anecdotal evidence has been assiduously avoided, the experimental scientist is generating anecdotal evidence for the consumption of his/her colleagues' (1998, p.244). The research report itself is an anecdotal report.

Stories play an important role in the healing process, and testimony is an important consideration. Indeed, we have to trust each other in what we say. This is the basis of human communication in the human endeavour of understanding; it is the central plank of qualitative research. When it comes to questions of validity, then we have the concepts of trustworthiness in qualitative research. Testimonies are heard within groups that challenge veracity.

Multiple perspectives

What I shall be arguing for here is a multiple perspective for understanding health care delivery that is not solely based upon a positivist approach but also upon an interpretative approach. To take such a position is political in that it challenges the major paradigm of scientific research in medicine, a paradigm that is often transparent to those involved. Quite rightly, the qualitative paradigm is also seen as being critical; it challenges both the power and privilege of a dominant scientific ideology (Aldridge 1991a,d, 1993c; Trethewey 1997).

An advantage of qualitative research is that it allows us to see how particular practices are being used. We can discover the meanings attached to activities as they are embedded in day-to-day living. The terms 'healing', 'spirituality', 'intentional' and 'energy' are subject to dictionary definition but also defined by their practice. Qualitative research helps us to understand how such terms are understood in practice; this is a political activity, as the feminist movement has reminded us. We have the right to call our experiences by what terms we wish without a dominant group telling us how that term 'should' be used. While many of us may question the use of the term 'energy' in healing, the word is used by both patients and healers alike, and we might be better directed to discovering its use in practice if we wish to understand it better. When we come to discuss the meaning of healing itself – what role spirituality has in health care, the nature of intentionality – then we are discussing the role of meaning in people's lives. One way to discover those meanings is to ask the participants. The rigour of the asking and the way those meanings are interpreted is the scientific method – methodology – of qualitative research.

To understand the health implications of prayer, for example, we can discern the effect of prayer by experiment. However, I shall argue later in this chapter that the impact of prayer from a spiritual perspective is better understood in its subjective interpretation as a qualitative study. Both complement each other. If we successfully argue for a complementary medicine, that is increasingly being called an integrative medicine, then surely we can have a congruent paradigm for health care research that is complementary and integrative.

A way of seeing how these differing perspectives can be applied to a common problem would be to study those patients who fail to complete a course of treatment – what is sometimes referred to as non-compliance. A positivist paradigm may hypothesize that compliance with the prescribed treatment regime is a matter of patient education. By designing a patient education programme to raise an understanding of the treatment then compliance would be improved according to specific criteria for evaluation. We could design an experiment that would randomize identified non-complying patients to a taught education programme, a leaflet education programme and to no education. Their compliance with medication could then be measured by an assessor blind to the education programme itself.

A qualitative approach would not initially set up an experiment, nor would it try to measure anything. In this instance we would be interested in the experience of patients consulting practitioners, listening to what the practitioners say, prescribe and advise, and then ask whether patients have complied with that advice. We would be asking where, when, with whom and on what grounds is the decision made not to comply with medical advice. In this case it is the perspective of the non-complier that is as important as the practitioner. Similarly, we may ask patients who also complete a course of treatment and compare them with those who fail to complete. This includes interviews, observations in various settings such as the consulting room and the home, and maybe written material such as diaries. Once we knew the circumstances of non-complying, then we could design what initiatives to investigate experimentally. Non-compliance may be located in the patient, it may be located in the practitioner, or it may be an artefact of their relationship. Unless we discern with whom and when, then our experimental work will be inevitably limited.

From a critical research perspective, we would be interested in how a clinic is so organized that some groups fail to have their treatment needs met and where some patterns of treatment response are endemic. This may mean a collaborative enquiry with a self-help patient group and entail some form of advocacy between the clinic and the group (Aldridge 1987d; Reason and Rowan 1981). This latter approach reflects the strong participatory action component of early social science research.

Qualitative research is an umbrella term. Some of these lean towards an emphasis on analysing texts and interviews (like content analysis and discourse analysis), while others rely upon descriptions of interaction, that may use a variety of media, and are based upon ethnography, ethnomethodology, symbolic interactionism and phenomenology. Other methods set out to build theories. Other approaches may set out to discover a particular historical background and locate this within an ideological or political perspective – the assimilation of acupuncture within modern Western medicine, for example, and contrasting its acceptance in various European states.

Qualitative research as constructed meanings in context

Qualitative research covers a variety of approaches. What characterizes these approaches is an emphasis on understanding the meaning of social activities as they occur in their natural contexts. These are interchangeably called field studies, ethnographies, naturalistic inquiries and case studies. A central plank of these approaches is that we can discern the meaning of social behaviour like healing and prayer from the experiences that people have in particular contexts, and that these meanings themselves are constructed. Constructed, in the sense that people make sense of what they do. The difficulty these approaches face, from a perspective of positivist science, is that because sense is continually being made, and this sense may vary from context to context, there are no universally applicable laws of human behaviour but a series of locally constructed meanings in specific contexts where cultures of healing exist.

Participant observation

Participant observation is a generic term for a qualitative approach where the researcher observes what is happening from an insider position. Rather than administering a set of pre-formed interviews, the participant observer works alongside the staff and patients, asking what is going on and listening to what is spontaneously said. Julia Lawton (1998) worked directly alongside patients, their families and staff in a hospice to see what was happening. She observed 280 different patients in an intensive study of the dying patient and the dying process, in an attempt to answer why some patients are admitted to hospital and others are not. She found that patients are admitted to a hospice when bodies begin to disintegrate such that contemporary concepts of the hygienic, sanitized, bounded body become challenged. This builds on the original works of Glaser and Strauss, who studied the process of dying, that gave rise to qualitative research as grounded theory (Glaser and Strauss 1967). What Lawton does is to challenge the homogeneous concept of the hospice as a place for the dying patient and the dying process. She see the hospice as a place where marginalized cancer patients are referred when they experience difficult symptoms and their bodies deteriorate beyond a socially acceptable boundary.

This reflects the challenging nature of qualitative research, its location in practice and personal experience.

Narrative analysis

Researchers from a wide variety of disciplines have found narratives to be useful in explaining cross-level psychological phenomena (Mankowski and Rappaport 2000). Narratives with different sources and functions occur at the group level and as individual levels of analysis. Research on narratives is particularly useful for understanding the relationship between social process and individual experience, especially in spiritually based communities (Aldridge 1986, 1987a, 1987b, 1987d). Narratives in spiritual settings appear to serve a variety of functions in community life. They define community and facilitate personal change (Aldridge 1987c). As such, local community narratives are vital psychological resources, particularly where dominant cultural narratives fail to adequately represent the lived experience of individuals.

In a family-based treatment approach for suicidal behaviour (Aldridge 1998), what the patient tells as a story, and the narratives of those involved with the patient, generate important bases for treatment initiatives, as well as providing an important source or research material. When analysing family narratives of illness, it was possible to identify specific family features that led to suicidal behaviour; a situation where a family was about to change (by someone leaving or joining), where the identified patient could only do wrong (even when they tried to put things right), and where that person has always been the 'sickly' member of the family. Personal narratives, while being individual, are also located within family narratives, which themselves are located within social contexts. However, these narratives are not accessible to a questionnaire approach – people have to tell them to a listener.

As we have seen earlier, the understanding of patients' stories is vital. Stories, in the hospice, offer the context for elucidating hidden meanings. Little *et al.* (1998) investigated the illness narratives of patients who had undergone a colectomy for colorectal cancer. They asked patients to tell the story of their illness from its first intimations, in their own words with minimal prompting. These interviews were then transcribed, and analysed using a grounded theory approach. From this observational material emerged two phases of subjective experience: an initial phase of disorientation and a sense of loss of control, followed by an enduring adaptive phase where the patient constructs and reconstructs his experience through narrative. This last phase they call liminality – a dynamic process of adapting to the experience of being ill as expressed in a narrative account of a body that must accommodate the disease and the self.

Potts (1996) examined the role of spirituality in the cancer experiences of 16 African-Americans living in the southern United States. Without any investigator-initiated mention of spirituality, participants referred to many categories of spiritual beliefs and practices that were relevant in their experiences with cancer. When spirituality was specifically explored, there was an even greater elaboration on the initial categories. Key findings included a belief in God as the source of healing, the value of prayer as an instrumental practice, a strategy termed 'turning it over to the Lord', and locating the cancer experience within the context of a greater life narrative. The willingness of care providers to address spiritual and cultural dimensions of cancer enhances therapeutic relationships and the efficacy of psychosocial interventions.

Such narratives are not only important for understanding the process of a disease, but they can also make an important contribution to understanding what helps in the process of recovery (Aldridge 1998; Garrett 1997; Spencer, Davidson and White 1997). People of faith find meaning in their struggle. Black's (1999) study of the spiritual narratives of 50 elderly African-American women found that those women 'believed their hardship had meaning, because they interpreted it as a measure of their strength, imbued it with divine purpose, and foresaw a just end' (p.372). If we are engaged in countering hopelessness as a precursor to failing health, then surely the narratives of these women, and the understandings that we can glean from them, are important factors for consideration in health care research?

Ethnographic studies

Qualitative researchers are often engaged in field work. They have to physically visit the people in the clinic, their homes, the hospital ward, the street or the village. The forms of documentation necessary for these studies too will vary. Anthropologists have pioneered these methods in learning about other cultures and we too are being challenged to learn about other cultures of healing. At the heart of these approaches is an emphasis on the researcher being a primary instrument in the research process for the collection of data and for analysing that data. The researcher is involved in the context in which he or she works; there is an expectation that he or she is sensitive to non-verbal communication and that he or she will be interpreting what he or she experiences. These will be referred to here as ethnographic studies.

For example, in a study of mental disorder in Zimbabwe (Patel *et al.* 1995), 110 subjects were selected by general nurses in three clinics and by four traditional healers from their current clients. The subjects were interviewed using an interview schedule. Mental disorder most commonly presented with somatic symptoms, few patients denied that their mind or soul was the source of illness and spiritual factors were frequently cited as causes of mental illness. Subjects who were selected by a traditional healer reported a greater duration of illness and were more likely to provide a spiritual explanation for their illness. Most patients, however, showed a mixture of psychiatric symptoms that did not fall clearly into a single diagnostic group, and patients with a spiritual model of illness were less likely to conform to criteria of 'caseness' and represented a unique category of psychological distress in Zimbabwe.

The significance of healing rituals is important for understanding how health care may best be implemented. An ethnographic study of a churchbased healing clinic in Jamaica (Griffith 1983) shows how mixing spiritual, psychological and conventional medical needs, with their heterodox beliefs and values, creates tension. While a new ritual format needed to be introduced, it is difficult to transform traditional formats of healing. Such an ethnographic qualitative perspective could be used to discern how complementary medicine approaches are used within modern healing cultures within health care clinics.

Ethnographic approaches have investigated interdisciplinary work (Sands 1990), experience of the intensive care unit from a patient's perspective (Rier 2000), the traditional health beliefs and practices of black women (Flaskerud and Rush 1989), the experience of caring for elderly parents in the home (Lewis, Curtis and Lundy 1995), pregnant adolescents' responses to the preparation for motherhood class curriculum (Lesser, Anderson and Koniak-Griffin 1998), and adapting to chronic diseases like asthma (MacDonald 1996) and AIDS (Kotarba and Hurt 1995).

Phenomenology

While experience and interpretation are at the heart of all qualitative methods, there are also particular phenomenological approaches that look to the essence of a structure or an experience. The assumption that an essence to an experience exists is similar to the assumption by an ethnographer that culture exists. Prior beliefs are first identified and then temporarily set aside so that the phenomenon being studied may be seen in a new light. In a study of the phenomena of prayer we would want to know what constitutes the consciousness of praying, what the sensory experiences of prayer are, what our thoughts are and what emotions are involved. Setting and context would also be central to this phenomenological understanding. In this way, we see that the lives of the mystics would provide documentary evidence of a phenomenological approach to understanding prayer and meditation.

DoRozario (1997) used a hermeneutic and phenomenological perspective to understand how individuals with disability and chronic illness survive and cope successfully with their lives in spite of overwhelming odds. The lived experience of 35 informants and 14 autobiographers, who represented a wide range of people with disability and chronic illness, was used as the basis for understanding the phenomenological world of chronic conditions. Five factors that facilitated coping and adaptation were identified. The combined elements of spiritual transformation, hope, personal control, positive social supports and meaningful engagement in life enabled individuals to come to terms with their respective conditions. The research identified processes by which people reconcile their outer forms of disability, decay or suffering and discover an embodiment of their own inner resources and strengths.

Phenomenological studies are well suited to understanding the world of the sufferer. An interpretive phenomenological study, which began as a study of the meaning of being restrained, offers a glimpse into mental illness (Johnson 1998). Ten psychiatric patients were interviewed and the audiotaped interviews transcribed. The resulting texts were analysed using a process methodology developed from Heideggerian hermeneutical phenomenology. Two major themes emerged – 'struggling' and 'why me?' – revealing what it was like for the participants to live with a serious mental illness. As part of their struggling, patients asked the existential question 'Why me?' – a question that was repeatedly heard when working with the dying. This study underscored how important it is for the nurse caring for a psychiatric patient to enter into, and try to understand, the world of patients with mental illnesses, emphasizing the practical application of research for practice. Similarly, Savage and Canody (1999) found that for patients with a life-sustaining device, then spirituality, humour and strong family relationships were essential to a positive outlook.

Grounded theory
The strategy of research is inductive where theories are gleaned from experience. This is not theory testing but theory generation, where either existing theories are lacking or fail to explain the phenomenon satisfactorily. Given that a placebo, for example, is a concept in common use by practitioners, qualitative research would ask, and observe, those practitioners when they believed a

placebo to be occurring and what they understood a placebo practice to be. Similarly, they would ask patients about their understandings of what is happening. This breaks the cycle of abstract definitions being brokered amongst scientists and locates explanations in everyday practices. In this way theories are generated that match the data gathered from experience and has led to the approach known as 'grounded theory' (Strauss and Corbin 1990). Grounded theory elucidates substantive theories applicable to understanding localized practices that have a high internal and content validity, rather than grand theories of medicine.

In Camp's (1996) study of coronary artery bypass grafting spiritual issues are extremely important. The operation is perceived by the patient as a life-threatening event and the study aimed to discover the spiritual needs of patients undergoing surgery and how these needs are met during hospitalization. Postoperative data were collected through interviews with 17 adults, aged 34 to 83 years. What emerged was that spiritual needs centred around having faith in their own decision making, in the hospital staff (especially the nurses) and overwhelmingly in God during a time of great stress, alongside feelings of being 'pulled apart' and fragmented. Consequently, patients needed to recover a sense of wholeness, that included physical, psychological and spiritual aspects of their experience.

Research in healing

Medical professionals are becoming aware that there are aspects of health that do not fall within their range of knowledge. For those elements to be incorporated into practice, a realm of quantitative clinical evidence is being demanded that is quite inappropriate. I am not saying that spirituality and its influence on health care practices should be accepted simply because it is a good idea, rather that the means of gathering and displaying evidence is discussed, particularly when we know that existential matters are important for human well-being. We do not need to validate such a position from scientific studies – we have some residual knowledge within our cultures of healing that we need not abdicate. Scientific medicine is but one pillar of the culture of healing; the aesthetic and the spiritual are two others.

Critics have found the strict methodology of natural science is often found wanting when applied to the study of human health care behaviour (Aldridge and Pietroni 1987a,b; Burkhardt and Kienle 1980, 1983), and this critique has stimulated calls for innovation in clinical medical research and therapy

(Aldridge 1993c, 1996; Reason and Rowan 1981). A significant factor in the desire for innovation is a growing awareness by doctors of the importance of a patient's social and cultural milieu, and a recognition that the health beliefs of a patient, and understandings of personal meanings, should be incorporated in treatment. What we need in clinical research is a discipline that seeks to discover methods that express clinical changes as they occur in the individual rather then methods which reflect a group average. How clinical change occurs, and is recognized, will depend upon not only the view of the researcher and clinician, but also upon the beliefs and understandings of the patient and their family (Aldridge 1998).

There is often a split in medical science between researchers and clinicians. Researchers see themselves as rational and rigorous in their thinking, and tend to see clinicians as sentimental and biased, which in turn elicits comments from clinicians about inhuman treatment and reductionist thinking. We are faced with the problem of how to promote in clinical practice research that has scientific validity in terms of rigour and, at the same time, a clinical validity for the patient and clinician.

The randomized trial appears to be theoretically relevant for the clinical researcher, but has all too often randomized away what should be specifically relevant for the clinician and patient. A comparative trial of two chemotherapy regimes assumes that the treatment or control groups to which patients are randomly assigned contain evenly balanced populations. What is sought from such a trial is that one method works significantly better than another comparing group averages. Yet, as clinicians, we want to know what method works best for the individual patient. Our interest lies not in the group average, but with those patients who do well with such treatment, and those who do not respond so well. Furthermore, it is randomizing of patients with specific prognostic factors which obscures therapeutic effect. Rather than searching for a non-specific chemotherapy treatment of a particular cancer, we may be better advised to seek out those factors which allow us to deliver a specific treatment for recognized individuals with a particular cancer. This is not to argue against randomization exclusively, rather that we have randomized the patient rather than the treatment. As Weinstein says:

> ...randomisation tends to obscure, rather than illuminate, interactive effects between treatments and personal characteristics. Thus if Treatment A is best for one type of patient and Treatment B is best for another type, a randomised study would only be able to indicate which treatment

performs best overall. If we wanted to discover the effect on subgroups, one would have to separate out the variable anyway. (Weinstein 1974, p.1280)

We may well say the same of the non-specific use of prayer; we do not know the use of prayer already by the patient in a group, nor those praying for her. Nor do we know what stage that person is in in terms of suffering such that prayer will bring not only relief but a new understanding. Prayer is not like a medication; as yet no dose-response formula has been discovered.

Science and medicine: What science does not know

Modern science implies that there is a common map of the territory of healing, with particular co-ordinates and given symbols for finding our way around, and that the map of scientific medicine is that map. We need to recognize that scientific medicine emphasizes one particular way of knowing amongst others. Scientific thinking maintains the myth that to know anything we must be scientists; however, people who live in vast desert areas find their way across those trackless terrain without any understandings of scientific geography. They also know the pattern of the weather without recourse to what we know as the science of meteorology.

In a similar way, people know about their own bodies and have understandings about their own lives without the benefit of anatomy or psychology. Furthermore, people know of their own god or connection to a higher power without the benefits of an elaborated theology, as we saw in Chapter 5. They may not confer the same meanings on their experiences of health and illness as we researchers do, yet it is towards an understanding of personal and idiosyncratic beliefs to which we might most wisely be guiding our research endeavours. By understanding the stories people tell us of their healing and the insights this brings, then we may begin to truly understand the efficacy of prayer. That health and the divine are brought together in such spiritualities is a challenge for renewal of our understanding in health care, not a ground for dismissal as invalid.

When we speak of scientific or experimental validity, we speak of a validity that has to be conferred by a person or group of persons on the work or actions of another group. This is a 'political' process. With the obsession for 'objective truths' in the scientific community then other 'truths' are ignored. As clinicians we have many ways of knowing: by intuition, through experience, and by observation. If we disregard these 'knowings' then we promote the idea that there is an objective – definitive – external truth that exists as 'tablets of stone' and that only we, the initiated, have access to it. This criticism applies also to the dogma of religion that refuses to consider what other evidence the world provides. Simply saying that the world is evil will not resolve the need for the necessary dialogue for transcending seemingly opposing views.

The people with whom clinicians work in the therapist – patient relationship are not experimental units. Nor are the measurements made on these people separate and independent sets of data. While at times it may be necessary to treat the data as independent of the person, we must be aware that we are doing this, otherwise when we come to measure particular personal variables, we face many complications. The clinical measurements of blood status, weight and temperature are important. However, they belong to a different realm of understanding than do issues of anxiety about the future, the experience of pain, the anticipation of personal and social losses and the existential feeling of abandonment. These defy comparative measurement. Yet if we are to investigate therapeutic approaches to chronic disease, we need to investigate these subjective and qualitative realms. While we may be able to make little change in blood status, we can take heed of emotional status and propose initiatives for treatment. The goal of therapy is not always to cure, it can also be to comfort and relieve. The involvement of the physician with the biologic dimension of disease has resulted in an amnesia for the necessary understanding of suffering in the patient (Cassell 1991).

In the same way, we can achieve changes in existential states through prayer and meditation, the evidence for which can only be metaphorically expressed and humanly witnessed. Are we to impoverish our culture by denying that this happens and discounting what people tell us? What, then, are we to trust in our lives, the dialogue with our friends or the displays of our machines? This is not an argument against technology. It is an argument for narrative and relationship in understanding what it is to be human; that is, the basis for qualitative research.

In terms of outcomes measurement, we face further difficulties. The people we see in our clinics do not live in isolation. Life is rather a messy laboratory and continually influences the subjects of our therapeutic and research endeavours. The way people respond in situations is sometimes determined by the way in which they have understood the meaning of that situation. The meaning of hair loss, weight loss, loss of potency, loss of libido, impending death and the nature of suffering will be differently perceived in varying cultures. To this balding, ageing researcher, hair loss is a fact of life. My Greek neighbour says that if it happens to him it will be a disaster. When we deliver a powerful therapeutic agent then we are not treating an isolated example of a clinical entity, but intervening in an ecology of responses and beliefs which are somatic, psychological, social and spiritual.

In a similar way, what Western medicine understands as surgery, intubation and medication others may perceive as mutilation, invasion and poisoning. Cultural differences regarding the integrity of the body will influence ethical issues such as abortion and body transplants. Treatment initiatives may be standardized in terms of the culture of the administrating researchers, but the perceptions of the subjects of the research, and their families, may be incongruous and various. Actually, we know from studies of treatment options in breast cancer that physician beliefs also vary, and these beliefs influence the information the physicians give to their patients (Ganz 1992). If we return to the concepts of placebo and non-compliance, then it is surely a qualitative research paradigm that will encourage a practical understanding of the patient – practitioner relationship.

Difficulties in researching prayer and spiritual healing

We know that there are major difficulties with intentional healing research.

First, achieving transcendence, an understanding of purpose and meaning as a performed identity, is an activity. It occurs in a relationship and that is informed by culture. Research initiatives that concentrate on the healer fail to understand the activity of the patient, lose sight of the relationship and ignore the cultural factors involved. I am using culture here to refer to the system of symbolic meanings that are available, not demographic data. Losing this nesting of contexts fragments the healing endeavour, emphasizing a passive patient that receives healing rather than an active patient participating in a common enterprise. A qualitative approach would emphasize the involvement of the patient and that healing is a relational activity.

Second, much research is carried out using a conventional medical science paradigm, but the intention of that research is not always made clear. If the intention is to demonstrate the efficacy of spiritual healing approaches and prayer, then the methodology is clearly misguided. I suspect that much of this research is not being carried out for patients but as a strategy in the politics of establishing alternative healing initiatives within conventional medical approaches. Therefore we have healing groups promoting their own interests and adopting the methodological approach of randomized clinical trials considered to be suitable for acceptance rather than looking at what is necessary for discovering what is happening. This is not to say that the results of clinical randomized trials are not influential, rather that they are limited in their applicability as far as prayer and healing are to be understood if (a) the patient is expected to be active, (b) there has to be a relationship with the healer, (c) there are no definite endpoints in time, (d) healing can appear as differing phenomena and (e) the prayer has to be non-specific and non-directional (the concept of 'Thy will be done' as an effective form of prayer, following Dossey [1993], ruins a one-tailed statistical test).

Third, healing, like prayer, is not a homogeneous practice and is not susceptible to standardization. Attempts at standardization would no longer make it prayer but superstitious incantation or magical hand-passes.

Lastly, the ability to heal is seen in some traditions as a divine gift; it may not be available to all and even to those that have the gift not available all of the time. Ascertaining who has it, and when, is not easy. Healing is also considered, in some traditions, to be a secondary ability of spiritual development that can be systematically applied, but it is an advanced ability. This again proves to be a difficulty, as presumably there are more practitioners with lower abilities than advanced practitioners that are more reliable in their efficacy. And who in the world of healing practitioners is going to say that they are less advanced? Those who are advanced in such understandings will probably see no need to subject such knowledge to material, worldly proof.

Indeed, we must return to the purpose of proof. We see already that spiritual healing is practised and that medical practitioners refer to such healers. If the grounds of research are for payment or to institute professional practice then maybe the results will be elusive than when the purpose is for the pursuit and improvement of human knowledge. One system of knowledge cannot be predicated on proofs from another system of knowledge.

Conclusion

It would be wrong to permit medicine to use the authority it has gained from scientific and technical proficiency…as a cloak to gain authority over questions that most in society consider moral and religious.

David Smolin (1995, p.995)

When people come to their practitioners they are asking about what will become of them, what will their future be like. Will there be a change? Some practitioners make a prognosis based on the interview that they have had with the patient. Sometimes this will be the dreaded answer to the question: 'How long do I have to live?' But, with each interview, there is the question of when healing will take place – what can be expected in the near future and is there any hope of a cure? The story of what happens is, in part, a clinical history. It is also no less than the narration of destiny, the unfolding of a person's life purpose (Larner 1998). When we talk with the dying, it is this sense of purpose, 'Was it all worth while?', that is a critical moment in coping with the situation. The telling and listening, the *relating* of these stories, is the very stuff of qualitative research.

Narratives are the recounting of what happens in time. They are not simply located in the past but are also about real events that happen now and what expectations there are for the future. The teller of the narrative is an active agent. He or she is not passively experiencing his or her past but performing an identity with another person. That other person as doctor, priest or healer has the moral obligation through the therapeutic contract to listen and engage in the healing relationship. Narratives are told. This performance aspect is what gives a narrative vitality and instructs us, as listeners, to what we must attend (Aldridge 1996). Narratives are not simply private accounts that we relate to ourselves; they have a public function and will vary according to whom is listening and the way in which the listeners are reacting. Qualitative research has incorporated such narratives into its approach to understanding health care (Aldridge 1998; Hall 1998; Strauss and Corbin 1990; van Manen 1998).

Narratives bring a coherence and order to life stories. Stories make sense. Yet the scientific-null hypothesis assumes, at the very core of its reasoning, that there is no such coherence (Larner 1998). Technology strives to domesticate time as chronos, to make time even and predictable. In an earlier book (Aldridge 1996), I wrote of time as kairos, uneven, biological and decisive, in that the moment must be seized. This makes a mockery of fixed outcomes in that the time and logic of healing may have modes elusive to commercialized requirements of health care delivery. Peace of mind may occur but no cure. Forgiveness may take place but no change in survival time. Are we really to throw away such outcomes of peace of mind and forgiveness because they find no immediate material expression? Perhaps it is the very denial of those qualities that provokes the restlessness of people today as they seek an elusive state of health despite the material riches of Western cultures.

No material change may occur in spiritual healing, but the individual transcends his or her immediate situation. Furthermore, there are no personal stories in medical science but group probabilities. This is seriously at odds with the demands of the patient's encounter with his or her doctor, which is personal. People are subjective; they are indeed subjects, and subjects that need to relate a story to another person that understands them. To be treated as objects in a world of social events deprives them of meaning. It is this very lack of meaning that exacerbates suffering.

Becoming sick, being treated, achieving recovery and becoming well are plots in the narrative of life. As such they are a reminder of our mortality. They are an historical relationship – meanings are linked together in time. Stories have a shape, they have purpose and they are bounded in time. Thus, we talk about a case history. It is for this reason that group studies fail to offer an essential understanding of what it is to fall ill and become well. Generalization loses individual intent and time is removed. The individual biographical historicity is lost in favour of the group. Purpose and intent are important in life, and are at the basis of hope. If that purpose is abandoned through hopelessness, then suicide and death are the outcome. In our healing endeavours we need to consider the circumstances in which healing occurs and how those circumstances are enabled. This is not the technological approach of cure but the ecological approach of providing the ground in which healing is achieved, whether it be an organic, psychological, social or spiritual context. Those healing contexts will also be part of a biography; they have an historicity, and this must be included too in our research.

At the heart of much scientific thinking in the medical world is a desire for prediction – to base treatment strategies and outcomes on a group statistic of probability. This is quite rightly explained as the desire to provide the optimum treatment and to eliminate false treatment that harms. Such a statement too is based upon belief, a touching faith in statistical reasoning. Behind this thinking is an assumption that tomorrow will be the same as today, that the future is predicated on the past. What many of our patients hope, and the purpose of our endeavours in both practice and research, is that tomorrow will be new. Qualitative research methods are one way of discovering the new in the way in which we tell our stories together.

CHAPTER 12

The Breath in Healing

Subtlety produces beauty; it is subtlety which is the curl of the Beloved.

Sufi Inayat Khan (1979, p.12)

It may be said that breath is the chain that links body, heart and soul together, and is so important that the body – so loved and cared for, kept in palaces, its slightest cold or cough treated by doctors and medicines – is of no more use and cannot be kept anymore when the breath is gone.

Sufi Inayat Khan (1991, p.71)

'The Breath in Healing' may appear to be a simple title, but like all things concerned with the term 'healing' the concept is complex and fraught with challenges. One of those challenges is that, like the term 'energy', breath is used as both a literal truth and a metaphor. Many healing traditions have used breath as a vehicle for healing but breath itself is more than the commonly understood gaseous compound – it is also used as a powerful metaphor, as in the Christian injunction 'I am the Breath of Life'. To understand breath, we also talk about the process of breathing. Both healing and breathing, then, are dynamic processes.

We have another conceptual problem too with healing; while healing is understood to have occurred, evidence for demonstrating that healing has occurred is dependent upon the observer or the participator, and what actually has done the healing is elusive to demonstration. While we may observe that breathing is taking place, it is an understanding of the quality of breathing that is central to understanding the nature of healing. Such qualitative understandings are only gradually being introduced into health care research (Aldridge 2000b).

When we come to talk about the breath of healing, there is room for confusion. In the latter part of this chapter I will use two specific healing initiatives that are based upon breath as illustration of how breath is used both as a subtle organizing property and as a material manifestation. The first example is the use of breath through singing to intentionally organize the physiological abilities of another person as they recover from coma. Singing is literally the intentional use of breath to heal realized through a particular therapeutic form, which is improvised music therapy. A fundamental property of breathing is that it has rhythm. In musical terms, rhythm has to have the property of intention, otherwise it would be simply cyclic repetition or pulse. The second healing initiative is that of Qigong Yangsheng for the treatment of asthma (Reuther and Aldridge 1998). Breathing is used here also as an intentional activity, this time by the patient to improve his or her own breathing abilities and to heal what is essentially a breathing problem, the material manifestation of air flow. In this latter example, the healer acts as a teacher and guide for the sufferer to influence his or her own breathing.

Breath: The beginning and ending

Life begins and ends with breath. Slight bodily changes are brought about by alteration in the mechanisms of breath. In addition, mental changes are also influenced by breath. Our general condition of well-being is dependent upon the rhythmic cycles of breathing within us. Similarly, emotions change the rhythm of breath, and when we become overexcited then we lose control over the breath. By gaining control of the breath then we gain mastery of mind and body. Not only that, we also establish a connection with the world around us, of which we are part, through the breath. However, such a basic activity as breathing has become transparent to modern day man and taken for granted, until the moment that he becomes sick.

There is a variety of qualities to the breath. It has volume, which we will see later in the asthma study; it needs to be centralized to be certain; the breath must be far-reaching to be strong; it must be rhythmic to achieve balance, which we will see in the music therapy study of coma; and it must have depth to encourage strength. These qualities of breath – volume, focus, reach, balance and strength – can be trained and have ramifications for health. Furthermore, these qualities are also necessary for the efficacy of the healer.

A deeper understanding of breath is concerned with its subtle qualities. Khan (1991) defines how breath shows the nature of man. The person who works with material things and expends greater physical energy has noisy breath, like animals. The breath of a thoughtful person is rhythmic and becomes fine. Even finer breath leads to enhanced perception and to spiritual understanding. In this Sufi sense, breath is 'that vast current running through everything, that current which comes from the Consciousness and goes as far as the external being, the physical world' (p.67). If we also consider the wholistic nature of healing, then it is the breath that links body, heart and soul together. Within this link there are differing levels of refinement and subtlety.

Healing and language, energy and breath

Explanations given for how healing works are various: paraphysical, magnetic, energetic, psychological and social. The main explanatory principle is that there are energies which are transformed by the agency of the healer producing a beneficial influence upon the 'energy field' of the patient. This notion of 'energy field' is the sticking point between orthodox researchers (Jacobs 1989; Wood 1989) and spiritual practitioners in that if such a field exists then it should be possible to measure by physical means. The problem probably lies in the use of the word 'energy', which has a broader interpretation in intentional healing and is likened to organizing principles of vitalism and life force that bring about a harmonizing of the whole person. So too with the concept of breath, where it is both a measurable entity, in terms of composition, volume and flow, but has also organizing properties.

The source of the word 'energy' in the Greek is *ergon*, meaning to work in a physical sense and to be active or possessed by a demon. Work is the meaning used by modern scientists; dynamic activity is the meaning used by healers. If we add the prefix *en*, then we have *energio* – to be in action; in this sense it is used by modern spiritual healers to suggest dynamic forces that are channelled or set in motion by the healer, or the patient. These forces may work directly or they may be forces that organize other forces into patterns. Thus we already have some confusion of levels of influence (see Aldridge 2000a).

Ancient systems of healing were based on the dynamic notion of energy (Leskowitz 1992). Fire energy brings warmth through the principle of motion. Hidden energy, which is air, is the sustaining energy and the activator of fire energy that uses as its vehicle the blood stream, thereby maintaining the chemistry of life and conveying the vital energies of the body. In addition there are three forms of energy distribution: First, through the seven energy centres that serve as points of reception and distribution throughout the physical body; second, through the seven major glands of the endocrine system; third, energy distributed through the nervous system. Restriction or inhibition of the free flow of these energies creates an imbalance or disharmony in the others. Health can be restored by releasing the cause of the blockages, and also through the application of specific musical tones, to restore the flow of energy.

If we look at traditional Indian forms of medicine, Aryuveda and Unani (Greco-Arabian), we have a vitalist epistemology based upon the physician as activator of the seven natural principles which adminster the body (elements, temperaments, humours, members, vital breaths, faculties and functions) (Verma and Keswani 1974). In this sense, after Hippocrates, 'Nature heals; the physician is nature's assistant.' Breath is an important factor in activating the patient. 'Vitality' itself derives from *viva*, 'Let him live.' The breath carries such a living force. 'Breath' and 'spirit' share the same root, in Latin *spirare*, which later becomes *spiritus*, life breathed as the Holy Spirit. Life has the quality of inspiration and is heard in biblical texts as 'I am the Breath of Life'. Similarly the Greek *anemos* and the Latin *anima* are translated as 'wind' and 'breath'. Thus we have the ideas of vitality and animation being achieved through the inspiration of the breath, or pneuma in Unani medicine, which is the conveyor of the spirit and activates particular systems, through its various parts. It is Breath, in the Christian Bible Old Testament, that animates the dry bones with vitality such that they quicken and live. Today, Aryuvedic medicine, yoga and some forms of traditional Chinese medicine still utilize the regulation of breathing as an important factor in healing.

Reaching out on the breath

Benor (1991) has made a detailed study of healing initiatives and offers a definition of healing that succinctly combines most of the modern concepts found in intentional healing. Healing is 'the intentional influence of one or more persons upon a living system without using known physical means of intervention' (p.9). The etymological roots of 'intention' are in the Latin *tendere*, which means a stretching of the mind to become attentive, with expectation. This extended attention of the mind is a dynamic process of shifting awareness to the other as an offer of contact. It is the breath that is the vehicle for this reaching out.

'Influence', from the Latin *influere*, is a 'flowing in'. (Influenza, from the same root, is a malady caused by the flowing in, literally *in-fluence*, of heavenly bodies.) Healing, from this perspective, is the offer of a dynamic process – the stretching of the mind of the healer that flows into the other person on the influential breath.

Conversely, we can speculate about what we project into the world on the out-flowing breath. We understand others, and are ourselves understood, by the way in which we breathe. At its simplest and coarsest, we know when another person is happy, sad or anxious through their breathing. Beyond that, there are levels of subtle understanding inherent in the projected breath. This has ramifications for counselling, therapy and all medical encounters (Aldridge 2000a). We influence others, and are ourselves influenced, by the flow of breath. Perhaps the very basis of medical and therapeutic training might in the future be an emphasis on breathing as the foundation of practice (Aldridge 1989c).

If we return once more to the roots of the everyday words that we use in medicine, then we see that these spiritual and psychological considerations are not strange. 'Patient' is derived from the Latin *pati*, which is to suffer and patiently endure. 'Doctor' is the teacher who discerns from the Latin *docilitas*. 'Therapy' is attentive support from the Greek *therapeutikos*. Therapist and doctor accompany the patient in their suffering along the way, with the responsibility of the healer to reach out to the patient, and the doctor to discern and to teach. Such a stance is not solely concerned with cure; there are also the possibilities of relief from suffering and comfort for the sick. It is in this way that one reaches out to the other in terms of breath. Indeed, we can co-ordinate our breathing with others. This happens when we become intensely empathically involved with another person, and, as we see working with coma patients, that person may be unconscious. Indeed, we discern that attentive therapeutic support by the way others breathe with us.

The same process of empathy can be used intentionally by healers to control breathing and impose calm in a situation, or enliven a situation. Taking the concept of energy mentioned earlier as being possessed by a demon, we can see how healers use the breath to tame the demon in the sufferer. It is this change of consciousness, through control of breathing, that is central to the healing process. We will see this later in the processes of singing in music therapy and in Qigong Yangsheng. Indeed, when I teach meditation to beginners, it is the injunction 'Be aware of your breathing' that is the second step (Aldridge 1987a) after 'Allow your eyes to close'. These two injunctions are concerned with focusing the senses – reducing visual input and concentrating on the breath.

Taking measure

'Medicine', from the Latin root *medicus*, is the practice of measuring illness and injury, and shares its origins with the Latin *metiri*, 'to measure'. This concept of measurement was based on natural cycles, one of which would be the respiratory cycle, and is evident in many healing traditions where pulses are assessed. 'To attend medically', Latin *mederi*, also supports the Latin word *meditari*, from which we have the modern *meditation*. Meditation is literally the measuring of an idea in thought. The task of the healer in this sense is to direct the attention of the patient through the value of suffering to a solution that is beyond the problem itself. In this sense, the healer has the power to change the sign of the patient's suffering from negative to positive, i.e. we are encouraged to see the benefit of suffering in bringing us beyond our present understandings. As the basis of mediation is breathing, then we see how taking measure of our health is a dynamic process dependent upon the qualities of breathing. While we may concern ourselves with quantities of breath, getting enough breath in an asthmatic crisis, it is the subtle aspects of breath that are important for the maintenance and promotion of health.

When we come to consider what is the evidence for healing in the modern world then we must bear these considerations in mind. First, there is an understanding of healing based upon a natural breathing cycle – a cycle that becomes rhythmic when it is intended. Second, the endeavour of healing, through the intentional action of the healer, is to extend the attention of the sufferer beyond a simple cycle to that of a broader perspective. This makes sense systemically, in that we encourage patients to couple with a broader ecology, literally to bring themselves into balance with their environment. This may also be expressed as putting a person's problems into perspective. Whatever explanation we choose to use, it is based on breathing and involves a change of consciousness, and this change of consciousness is basically what is meant by transcendence (Aldridge 2000b).

A change in consciousness perspective adds another dimension to those approaches known as psychotherapies. The vehicle for psychotherapeutic efficacy may be a controlled environment of breathing where transference does take place, but this is a transference of consciousness through breath, not cognition. Indeed, the intentional control of breath is the basis of achieving changes of consciousness in various spiritual traditions. As Grof (1985) suggests, the traditional biographical model used in psychoanalysis is inadequate to describe the broad spectrum of important experiences that became available through breathing.

An illustration that breathing is not simply a material phenomenon can be demonstrated by the fact that athletes are trained to breathe and move strenuously, transporting vast volumes of air through respiration. This control of breath is intended and serves to facilitate their physical bodies. No change in consciousness, however, is intended by such coarse breathing, and none is achieved. Yet we have varying spiritual traditions where an intentional control of the breath achieves changes in consciousness. The key to understanding the breath of healing cannot lie in the exchange of gases. Such exchanges are measurable but simply too coarse to understand changes in consciousness. To understand the influence of breath we must as observers direct our understanding elsewhere. Intention to alter breathing is not the key alone to understanding the breath of healing but the purpose that underlies that intention. Human purposes are not measurable, although the consequences of those purposes may be predicted. But they can be discerned through qualitative research (Aldridge 1993b,c, 1996, 2000a).

Health as performance in a praxis aesthetic

Performed health is dependent upon a variety of negotiated meanings, and how those meanings are transcended. As human beings we continue to develop. Body and self are narrative constructions, stories that are related to intimates at chosen moments. Meanings are linked to actions, and those actions have consequences that are performed. The maintenance and promotion of health, or becoming healthy, is an activity. As such it will be expressed bodily, a praxis aesthetic (Aldridge 2000b). Thus in singing, yoga and Qigong Yangsheng we have bodily practices that are aesthetically pleasing where health is performed.

The social is incorporated, literally 'in the body', and that incorporation is transcended through changes in consciousness, which become themselves incarnate. Through the body we have articulations of distress and health. While health may be concerned with the relief of distress, and can also be performed for its own sake, sickness is a separate phenomenon. It is possible to have a disease but not be distressed. Indeed, it is possible to be dying and not be distressed. When communication fails, we literally 'fall out' with other people, we fall out of relationship. This is evident in the social difficulties that the elderly demented have; they fail to connect to the rhythms of daily life, to other people and within themselves. We lose our consciousness when connections fail, and these are literally organic in the context of dementia, and the implications are far-reaching when our body falls out with our 'self'. Illness occurs when we lose an inherent ecology, and it is breathing that maintains ecology.

When bodily function fails, then we are literally decomposed. Yet as human beings we know that despite our physical failings, something remains within us. There is a self that responds. Despite all that medical science will have to offer us regarding the decomposition of the physical body, it is the composition of the self that we must address in our therapeutic endeavours. In relationship we foster a return to those ecological connections. And it is breath that forms the basis of relationship through rhythm (Aldridge 1996).

Music therapy with coma patients

Intensive care treatment is a highly technological branch of medicine. Even in what may appear to be hopeless cases, it can save lives through the application of this modern technology. However, albeit in the context of undoubted success, intensive care treatment has fallen into disrepute. Patients are seen to suffer from a wide range of problems resulting from insufficient communication, sleep and sensory deprivation and lack of empathy between patient and medical staff. As mentioned earlier, a basis for empathy is a common pattern of breathing. Many activities in an intensive care situation appear to be between the unit staff and the essential machines, i.e. subjects and objects. To a certain extent patients become a part of this object world. They lose that intentionality necessary for life, becoming disoriented in time and space; they lose the rhythm of breathing and consciousness (Aldridge 1989c, 1993a).

A music therapist began working with coma patients in an intensive treatment unit. Five patients, between the ages of 15 and 40 years, and with severe coma (a Glasgow Coma Scale score between 4 and 7), were treated. All the patients had been involved in some sort of accident, had sustained brain damage and most had undergone neurosurgery (Aldridge 1991a).

The form of music therapy used here is based on the principle that we are organized as human beings not in a mechanical way but in a musical form; that is, a harmonic complex of interacting rhythms and melodic contours. To maintain our coherence as beings in the world then we must creatively improvise our identity. Rather than search for a master clock that co-ordinates us chronobiologically, we argue that we are better served by the non-mechanistic concept of musical organization. Music therapy is the medium by which a coherent organization is regained, i.e. linking brain, body and mind. In this perspective the self is more than a corporeal being.

Each music therapy contact lasted between 8 and 12 minutes. The therapist improvised her wordless singing based upon the tempo of the patient's pulse and, more importantly, the patient's breathing pattern. She pitched her singing to a tuning fork. The character of the patient's breathing determined the nature of the singing. The singing was clearly phrased so that when any reaction was seen then the phrase could be repeated.

There is a hierarchy of musical organization from pulse, to metre, to rhythm that becomes itself organized into segments of time as phrasing. Phrasing can be understood by any listener but it is almost impossible to measure. We can see when exactly the notes occur but what organizes them is elusive. As in the process of consciousness, the property of organization is non-material. At the basis of all these activities, starting with pulse, is breath. It is the assessment of intentionality of breath within the pulse, which gives pulse its subtle qualitative dimensions, that is central to some diagnostic traditions.

There were a range of reactions from a change in breathing (it became slower and deeper), fine motor movements, grabbing movements of the hand and turning of the head, and eyes opening to the regaining of consciousness. When the therapist first began to sing there was a slowing down of the heart rate. Then the heart rate rose rapidly and sustained an elevated level until the end of the contact. This may have indicated an attempt at orientation and cognitive processing within the communicational context (Aldridge 1996, 2000b). EEG measurement showed a desynchronization from theta rhythm to alpha rhythm or beta rhythm in former synchronized areas. This effect, indicating arousal and perceptual activity, faded out after the music therapy stopped.

Some of the ward staff were astonished that a patient could respond to such quiet singing. This highlights a difficulty of noisy units such as these. All communication is made above a high level of machine noise. Furthermore, commands to an 'unconscious' patient are made by shouting formal injunctions, i.e. 'Show me your tongue', 'Tell me your name', 'Open your eyes.' Few attempts are made at normal human communication with a patient who cannot speak or with whom staff can have any psychological contact. It is as if these patients were isolated in a landscape of noise, and deprived of human contact.

A benefit of the music therapy was that the staff were made aware of the quality and intensity of the human contact. In the intensive care unit environment of seemingly non-responding patients, dependent upon machines to maintain vital functions and anxiety provoking in terms of possible patient death, then it is all too often a reaction by the carers to withdraw personal contact and interact with the machines. This is further exacerbated by a scientific epistemology which emphasizes the person only as a material being equating mind with brain.

A period of calm was also recognized as having potential benefit for the patient. What some staff failed to realize was that communication is dependent upon rhythm, not upon volume. We might argue that such unconscious patients, struggling to orient themselves in time and space, are further confused by an atmosphere of continuing loud and disorienting random noise. For patients seeking to orient themselves, then, the basic rhythmic context of their own breathing may provide the focus for that orientation – it simply needs a therapist to redirect that attention. This raises the problem of intentionality in human behaviour even when consciousness appears to be absent.

We can speculate that the various body rhythms have become disassociated in such comatose states. The question remains then of how those behaviours can be integrated and where the seat of such integration is. My answer would be that it is breathing that provides the foundation of human communication upon which that coherence of being called health is built. This argument is that used by healers in energy medicine who remind us of energy, like breath, is an organizing property.

Central to the act of breathing, and in terms of healing, breathing together, is the concept of performance in the subjective now (Aldridge 2000a). The co-ordination of human activity that lends itself to the coherence that we experience of being healed is dependent upon a temporal concept. Time is structured and breath is the scaffolding of time in which the present is constructed. The construction in time that we call *now*, when extended, is the basis of cognition. That is how music therapy works; it offers a temporal structure for events that facilitates cognition – rhythm as the basis of consciousness.

At the heart of this temporal coherence is the rhythm of breathing. Through the control of breathing we achieve coherence. Those disorientated in time can become oriented through that non-material activity of breathing, although the material necessity of gaseous exchange is present. This is why some scientific approaches appear to be coarse as they concentrate on the coarse elements of breath, not on the subtle qualities, and why some of us refer to the fact that patterning is what lies behind the explication of the pattern. We shall see later that for asthma patients, an intentional control of breathing is beneficial even at the coarse objective level of improving airway impedance.

Time and space

To act in the world we need the vital co-ordinates of time and space. We exist in the here and now. While we consider chronological time as important for what we do in terms of co-ordination, it is the idea of time as *kairos* that is significant. If chronos is time as measured, kairos is time considered as the right or opportune moment. It contains elements of appropriateness and purpose; that is, intention. Inherent within the term is the concept of decisiveness; there is tension within the moment that calls for a decision. In addition, there is also the expectation that a purpose will be accomplished. Rhythm demands intention. Patients in intensive care are often prisoners of mechanical time. They have not a chronic illness but a kairotic illness (Aldridge 1996). While the various physiological elements may be in place, initiation of those activities to promote coherence cannot take place, acts cannot be brought into being and therefore purposes remain uncompleted. In this way, being in a coma is not something that makes sense, it is something that no longer makes time. Sensory abilities may well be present but they have no context of coherence. While sufferers are *in* time, as chronological events amongst the rest of the world and its myriad of happenings they are no longer *of* time. Mentation for the coma patient is a kairotic process not solely understandable as chronology. De-mentation is the discoupling in kairotic time of physiological events. Achieving consciousness then is becoming in time, and this is facilitated by the intentional breath of the healer. At other levels of consciousness, this may be initiated by the healer or may be initiated by the patient, as we will see below.

Qigong Yangsheng in the management of chronic asthma

Chronic asthma is a common problem in the Western industrialized countries causing a great deal of incapacity. It is also a disease intractable to modern-day treatment initiatives. Essentially the problem is one of extreme difficulty in breathing; there is an impedance of the airways such that breathing is severely restricted and this can lead to death. Any form of therapy that concentrates on improving the capacity to breathe is important. Qigong has the potential to make such an influence on breathing capacity through the activity of mastering breathing itself. Changes in this breathing capacity can be simply measured through an increase in peak expiratory flow rate (PEFR) of the breath.

In a qualitative study by DeVito (1990), adult patients with chronic asthma were asked to recall their feelings associated with sensations of shortness of breath during hospitalization. Several themes emerged that dominated the experience including fear, helplessness and loss of vitality. From this we know that breathing, while being a physical problem, also has ramifications for mental well-being when the core of existence is threatened. My further argument would be that a sense of being healthy, from a holistic perspective, is dependent upon the many subtle layers of breath.

Qigong is an integral part of Chinese medicine. The word 'Qigong' incorporates two concepts. The first is 'Qi', meaning breath, steam, mist, breeze and energy. As we have seen at the beginning of this chapter, definitions are elusive, meanings are subtle. We used the concepts of 'vitality' and 'energy' (Reuther and Aldridge 1998). The definition of terms is complex but that is the challenge of research – to discern complex meanings. It also denotes a component of the qualitative research approach where we concentrate on the meaning of phenomena for both practitioners and patients (Aldridge 2000b; Heath 2000).

A second concept is 'Gong', meaning exercise in the sense of a permanent, diligent and persistent practice. Embodied in this meaning is the idea 'to master a technique'. Thus we have Qigong as a mastery of the vital force or a training in practice of using the life energy.

'Yangsheng' means care of life, so we can readily understand that Qigong Yangsheng will be a therapeutic form of practice designed to care for life energies. We find such definitions in other healing traditions too that focus on breathing and mastery. In this case, the initial training is concerned with a mastery of the coarse breath, although, as in other practices, the influences become more subtle.

The Study

Thirty adult patients, 23 females and 7 males, of varying degrees of asthma severity, were studied as a series of single cases. When we do not know the 'dose-response' of this therapy, nor the conditions necessary for optimal therapeutic efficacy, there is no sense in embarking upon a controlled trial (Aldridge 1991b; Aldridge and Pietroni 1987b).

Peak flow measurement, use of prescribed medication, diary accounts of symptoms (sleeping through the night, coughing, expectoration, dyspnoea and general well-being) and exercise were monitored through the successive phases of treatment, exercise and practice. There was a follow-up period one year after the study had begun such that measurements could be made to avoid seasonal fluctuations.

The 15 expressive forms of Taiji-Qigong developed by Professor Jiao Guorui were taught (Jiao 1995). These exercises can be done standing or sitting and are, therefore, adaptable to the physical strength of the patient. They are easy to learn, may be modified, are versatile and balanced, and may be practised out of sequence. In this educative and experiential approach, a definitive exercise leading to a special effect is of less importance than the positive effect brought about by the harmonious unity of physical movement, mental calm and naturally flowing breathing. The Qigong instructors were all physicians personally trained in this method.

Improvement

To assess the responsiveness of the peak flow measurements, the amplitude of the peak flow rates relative to the highest value was calculated as a percentage (Boulet, Turcotte and Brochu 1994). This percentage is the variability and correlates to the degree of severity of the disease and to the degree of inflammation in the respiratory tract (Higgins *et al.* 1992). In our study, a patient was considered improved when a diminishment of 10 per cent points or more in variability from the first to the fifty-second week was achieved, providing the average of the flow values remained constant or increased and the required medication use remained the same or could be reduced.

Improvement occurred more frequently in the group of exercisers than in the group of non-exercisers ($p < 0.01$ chi square with Yates correction). There were also reductions in hospitalization rates, less sickness leave, diminished antibiotic use and fewer emergency treatment consultations resulting in reduced treatment costs (Reuther 1997). A commitment to continuing exercise, and persistent practice, led to improvement in breathing, and this emphasizes the intentional component of healing; in this case by the practitioner and patient. Objective improvement in breathing ability is dependent upon the patient's commitment to his or her own health.

Improved pulmonary function means, objectively, better breathing and, subjectively, an enhanced feeling of well-being, including fewer experiences of entering the status 'sick'. For me this is a characteristic situation where a disease is considered to be chronic but is indeed kairotic. Chronos fixes the patient within an external time and effectively removes the intentional aspect of breathing and health. Kairos emphasizes the possibility of regaining intentional influence of the breath and making an impact on the disease. Kairos is literally a time of decision – to seize the moment – and this can be applied to breathing.

In this treatment approach, the patient has to take an active part in his or her recovery. He or she is not the recipient of treatment but an active participant. The learning element is an important principle in terms of prevention. We see in this study that motivation is an important factor. Fifty per cent of those engaged in the study failed to continue exercising once the second teaching course was concluded. This reflects the concerns expressed in the literature regarding patient compliance and empowerment (Webber 1990).

Conclusion

Mastery of the breath is vital. It is a foundation of many traditional healing systems and the basis of meditation practice. Breath is influenced by posture and movement, which we see in the Qigong study. The coarse breath is brought under control, and with this a return to the state of health. Central to this activity is the intention of the patient to be healed.

In contrast, we see in the coma study how it is the intention of the healer, reaching out with her own breath, that balances the breath of the patient through rhythm. Through this intended breath we see an improvement in consciousness – the transcendence from one state to another. These are but two simple examples of the breath in healing.

It leads us to conjecture that breathing is a central principle in communication and healing, and forms the basis of many therapeutic disciplines; we would perhaps be advised to encourage our clinicians towards their breath and away from their machines.

Finally, Inayat Khan (1991) reminds us:

> If a person exercises the breath and practises concentration with a scientific idea only, he soon becomes tired. If it is done with the thought of God, with the repetition of the names of God, then – by the thought of the idealized God in whom is all perfection, all beauty, who is Friend to whom we tell our sorrows, all our troubles – a happiness comes, a bliss. (p.70)

Coda

We have seen that breath has qualities and various layers of subtlety. We can discern the effects of the subtleties through scientific methods. However, we can also determine the nature of these subtleties, the phenomena themselves through qualitative research approaches. This will also include understanding breathing and healing as process. The terms we use – 'energy', 'ch'i', 'healing', 'health' – and understandings of the relationships that they have – 'ecology' and 'pattern' – are embedded, and embodied, in our cultures of health care as an anthropology of healing. A time has come where the explication of meanings through qualitative research will enhance the pursuit of scientific research through other methods. Some of the dilemmas concerning the terms 'energy', 'breath' and 'healing' may be resolved through such a discerning approach.

CHAPTER 13

Music Therapy and Neurological Rehabilitation

Recognition and the Performed Body in an Ecological Niche

Traumatic brain injury is a major public health problem and an important challenge for neurological rehabilitation (Mazaux and Richer 1998). Neuro-degenerative diseases are also an enormous public health problem (Brookmeyer *et al.* 1998; Hendrie *et al.* 1995). Interventions that can even modestly offer recovery or relief will have a major public health impact. We see a common core of loss of bodily integrity, failed cognitive competence and the demise of emotional coherence. To this we must add the potential for social isolation that deterioration or injury brings, and isolation is the road to despair. We do not suffer alone; these losses have an impact upon family and social life (Aldridge 1998).

While there are numerous projects aimed at finding medical relief of suffering and the treatment of injury and disease, we are reminded that these problems are also illnesses. Behaviour is influenced. We are challenged as a society that people within our midst are suffering, and it is our responsibility within the delivery of health care to meet that challenge with appropriate responses. A major confrontation for patients is that they awake the deepest fears of a consumer success-oriented society. Decline, physical and mental, is not readily faced within communities that expect youthful appearance, worldly success and physical ability as the outer signs of acceptable personhood (Aldridge 2000b). Any adjuvant therapies that will address these factors of isolation and acceptance will offer a significant part of a modern treatment strategy in neurological rehabilitation. The expressive arts therapies are to be considered as a part of this strategy.

In this chapter I will discuss the difficulties faced by patients in neurological rehabilitation. Essentially we are talking about people confronted by minds and bodies that are failing to perform as previously expected. This situation is for them and their families distressing (Gervasio and Kreutzer 1997). The expectations will be that those persons will be indeed rehabilitated; that they will be brought back to perform their previous habits or, from the medieval root *habilitare*, rendered fit again. Fit is a useful metaphor in this context, as I want to use the word as 'fit' in an ecological sense. Our sensory organization must fit into the ecology of the person and the person in his or her environment (Aldridge 2000b).

How experience is unified and organized is a central question. Behavioural integration is the key to experiential unity that opens the lock of mutual performance necessary for relationship. The experiencing person is not simply a set of brain activities but an embodied mind actively engaged with an environment – the ecology of events and ideas that we call consciousness (Aldridge 2000b). We experience ourselves as active embodied beings intimately connected with the world as we act upon the world. And we too are acted upon. Habit is necessary as it leads to an economy of consciousness, that 'the process of habit formation is a sinking down of knowledge to less conscious and more archaic levels' (Bateson 1978, p.114). We do not always need to know how we perceive, simply what we perceive. In the process of rehabilitation, we must resurrect these habits to achieve the next levels of consciousness, including cognition. Thus the return of gesture, as iconic communication, will be a singular step forward along the road to recovery.

What I will be proposing is that movements are generative of complete sequences of interactions that promote cognition. Perception and action are interwoven as activities. In the network of pre-motor actions, there is a repertoire of possible actions and action must be selected. Attention is necessary to perform an action. Performance focuses attention, thus the emphasis on music therapy as performance; a setting of musical activity that promotes attention from which meaningful, co-ordinated sounds can be performed. In this sense, memory is a state of consciousness brought about by movement and integral to the developmental process.

Performance – movement in a temporal and relational context – will be a central concept at the centre of my thesis. Indeed, as I have written elsewhere, my contention is that we are improvised performed beings; that is, we realize ourselves in the world, mentally, physically and socially, as performances *in* time and *of* time (Aldridge 1991, 1999). What we see in the process of the neuro-rehabilitation is a restriction in performance of movement, of communication, of thinking and, for some, being a whole person. My contention is that music therapy promotes performance and retains residual performance as long as possible.

Memory is crucial to the process of human development, vital in the regaining of cognition and central to our concerns about neuro-degenerative disease. The foundation of memory is the coupling of events in time as an adjunct to bodily action. Through movement we have that tension of consciousness we call memory. Through memory we transcend our abilities beyond behavioural responses to those of an individual identity brought into dialogue. We are active in the world and perform that world. In the development of performance we move from habitual movements to those of choice; this is the development of consciousness and occurs in stages. Indeed, we 're-cognize' the world. Recognition is not simply the act of recognizing others, but 're-cognizing' ourselves in the world with others. Cognition, in this sense, is achieved as an activity through dialogue beyond habit. We may wish to consider 're-cognition' as a subset of rehabilitation. And recognition is a dynamic process of adaptive relationship. We modify ourselves and others, as they in turn mutually modify us and themselves, through interaction. Even in the severely disabled, the possibility of action remains.

The videotaped examples that I will describe are taken from therapy sessions where there has been severe neurological damage, where there is a recognized communication disorder, or from therapy with elderly patients suffering with various dementias. In most of these examples I will be showing performances where communication abilities have been assessed as being severely impaired. Indeed, in many of the examples patients cannot speak. But my contention is that they can, and do, communicate even without speech. Of course, we have the concept of non-verbal communication. What I intend to show are the elements of that communication and the way in which such components prepare the way for verbal communication.

Furthermore, I intend to show that some of the symptoms that we see as of failing performance are, in the context of a performative paradigm, an attempt to achieve communication and an attempt to achieve cognition. The first time that I was alerted to this was in a small study that we completed with developmentally delayed children (Aldridge 1996). After music therapy, all the children scored on the cognitive ability sub-sections of a child development rating scale, whereas some had previously failed to score. On looking through the tests, the statistical interpretation of repeated measures showed an improvement in relationship scores, in hearing and hand–eye co-ordination. Music therapy is about these elements; the therapeutic relationship, within a specific hearing/listening environment, involves the active performance of sounds using integrated movements, which promote development.

Essentially I will be arguing that the basis of human communication is musical. We know that the essential properties of human understanding regarding verbal communication are speech prosodics: tempo, timbre, volume and pitch. This is how we interpret the meaning of what people say to us, particularly in regard to emotional content. At the centre of recovery in rehabilitation is the problem of timing. Timing, I hardly need to add, is a central feature of musical performance (Aldridge 1994).

A problem remains: how do we know that the other person is communicating or attempting to communicate? Again I return to our work with children where the co-ordination of hand and eye movements as gesture, in a listening environment of musical performance, were central to achieving communication. We also know from studies in child development and the study of communication in primates that gesture is a foundation of communicative ability. Gesture as a communicative essential brings, however, a dilemma. While we can see and hear what others do, and this is important for understanding, it is precisely the elements necessary for gesturing that begin to fail in neuro-degenerative diseases or are misplaced after a neurological insult. Timing is lost and movements fail to be co-ordinated, thus communication fails. However, we know from previous studies that music therapy has the potential to promote co-ordination such that communication is achieved (Aldridge 2000a).

Breath, rhythm and consciousness

In an intensive care situation, it appears that patients lose their own agency – the ability to perform intentional acts. That intentionality necessary for life becomes disoriented in time and space; the rhythm of breathing and consciousness is lost. For patients seeking to orient themselves, the basic rhythmic context of their own breathing is the focus for that reorientation. Intentionality in human behaviour may occur even when consciousness appears to be absent, as there are still vital rhythmic processes present.

We can speculate that the various body rhythms have become disassociated in such comatose states. The question remains then of how those behaviours can be integrated and where the seat of such integration is. My answer would be that it is breathing that provides the foundation of human communication, and it is the organization of breathing, as performed in singing, that is the major agent in therapeutic recovery.

Central to the act of breathing, and in terms of healing, breathing together, is the concept of performance in the subjective now. The co-ordination of human activity that lends itself to the coherence that we experience of being healed is dependent upon a temporal concept. Time is structured and breath is the scaffolding of time in which the present is constructed. The construction in time that we call *now*, when extended, is the basis of cognition. That is how music therapy works; it offers a temporal structure for events that facilitates cognition.

At the heart of this temporal coherence is the rhythm of breathing. Through the control of breathing we achieve coherence. Those disorientated in time can become oriented through that non-material activity of breathing, although the material necessity of gaseous exchange is present. This is why some scientific approaches appear to be coarse as they concentrate on the coarse elements of breath, not on the subtle qualities, and why some of us refer to the fact that patterning is what lies behind the explication of the pattern.

Time and space

To act in the world we need the vital co-ordinates of time and space. We exist in the here and now. While we consider chronological time as important for what we do in terms of co-ordination, it is the idea of time as *kairos* that is significant. If chronos is time as measured, kairos is time considered as the right or opportune moment. It contains elements of appropriateness and purpose; that is, intention. Inherent within the term is the concept of decisiveness; there is tension within the moment that calls for a decision. In addition, there is also the expectation that a purpose will be accomplished. Rhythm demands intention.

Patients in rehabilitation are often prisoners of mechanical time. They have not a chronic illness but a kairotic illness. While the various physiological elements may be in place, initiation of those activities to promote coherence cannot take place, acts cannot be brought into being and therefore purposes remain uncompleted. In this way, being in a coma is not something that makes sense, it is something that no longer makes time. Sensory abilities may well be present but they have no context of coherence. While sufferers are *in* time, as chronological events amongst the rest of the world and its myriad of happenings they are no longer *of* time. Mentation for the coma patient is a kairotic process not solely understandable as chronology. De-mentation is the decoupling in kairotic time of physiological events. Achieving consciousness then is becoming in time, and this is facilitated by the intentional breath of the healer. In this way, physiological events and psychological events are woven together into that fabric we know as memory – the warp of which is time.

Maintaining dialogue

Communication is based upon linking behaviours together, our own and those of others. This dialogue, which constitutes a sense of coherence to what we are as 'selves', is narrative in nature. It is personal and social. If this breaks down then we lose a sense of meaning for ourselves, and we lose meaning as a person in a social context. We lose the meaning of what we do and what we do with others. What we do literally makes no sense; this is the process of de-mentation.

The maintenance of meaning on an everyday level demands a sense of coherence between events (Crossley 2000). When disorder happens, then coherence must be rebuilt. Music therapy is one way of establishing a short-term coherence and thereby of re-establishing identity (Aldridge 1989). Meaning is an activity; it demands a temporal structure of connectivity and relationship between events that we call consciousness (Aldridge 2000b). Trauma, whatever its sources, disrupts this coherence and the horizon of time is limited.

A subjective sense of self is dynamic and multifaceted, composed of interactions within the individual and with others (Lysaker and Lysaker 2001). Thus the existence of self is dependent upon a rich context of dialogical interaction. This is what fails in dementia, and it fails progressively. My contention is that we may speak of dialogic-degenerative diseases as much as neuro-degenerative disease. The restricted communicative environments in which people find themselves further compound the stigma of dementia, and indeed of chronic illness. A therapeutic environment will necessarily promote a rich diversity of dialogic possibilities sensitive to a broad range of communicative possibilities – therefore, the range of creative arts therapies including music therapy, art therapy and dance/movement therapy.

Through dialogue we achieve the social. While many authors predicate dialogue on language, my argument is that dialogue is performance such as music. It is common play together that overcomes our differences and promotes plurality. Gurevitch (2000), writing about dialogue, emphasizes that when dialogue breaks down it does so in silence. However, for musical communication, the very core of performance is the tension between sound and silence. So when Gurevitch writes:

> ...the possibility of dialogue as poetics where the plurality of sociality is informed by the breaks of conversation. (p.247)

I would reinterpret this as:

> ...the possibility of dialogue as performance where the plurality of sociality is informed by the pauses of play.

Silence is the basis for the meaning of what becomes evident. What makes sound and silence coherent is a sense of time. When timing fails then we lose coherence. Melody then will become the mutual topic of communication and provide a state of closure for the discourse; it is achieved in the betweenness of the participants and is the manifestation of the social. If language influences the self that we present, then certain linguistic forms will influence the discourse that we use. For our patients with a severely curtailed repertoire of linguistic resources, we are challenged to provide them with a rich communicative repertoire that is musical. An enhanced repertoire of music resources will promote a variety of potential discourses.

What music therapy offers for the patient is a voice from out of this silence. I am using voice in a broad sense here: as utterance, as gesture, as beat on an instrument, as tone. It is through voicing ourselves that we achieve recognition by others and that we 're-cognize' the presence of others. I use 're-cognize' deliberately here as pointing to the achievement of cognition. But we need a site for these voices to perform; these are the dialogues in context. When we limit the sites of these performances then we impoverish the possible dialogues and restrict the ability of patients to achieve their 'selves'. Dialogue is existential and necessary for the achievement of health in the sense of becoming whole (Aldridge 2000b).

Dialogue is not simply given – it has to be achieved and negotiated. And meanings within this dialogue are never forced. We are constantly involved in interpreting the meaning of what others are doing. We do this constantly in clinical practice – first in diagnosis as understanding what the problem is, and then in understanding what is happening through the course of the therapy. These negotiated meanings are fragile, and performance has to be maintained in its mutuality. While we talk of degenerative disease, we must also be aware of the adequacy of our own performative abilities in the context of our therapeutic dialogues such that we are adequate in our performance to meet the needs of others. This performance is based upon what we as practitioners bring to the dialogue as an ability to exist in time: the expressions on our faces, the postures of our bodies, the repertoire of our utterances, the prosodics of speech.

When dialogue fails then we have alienation and despair (Aldridge 1998, 2000b). The maintenance of the self degenerates through isolation; as I mentioned earlier we have the potential for dialogic degenerative disease. Patients may be forced into a silence that they have no possibilities to either transform or structure; they are banished from the social to an isolated and degenerated self.

To resume dialogue, however, is to achieve reciprocal recognition (Gurevitch 2001). We invite communication and require the 'yes' of participation. This is exactly what happens in music therapy – there is an invitation to participate. It is in the performance of both parties that we have the dynamics of interaction. To achieve plurality, we need two voices (Gurevitch 2001).

We have, then, a shift from the self to the other, the act of mutual recognition. Achieving cognition is not simply a personal act. It is social.

Rehabilitation and the family: A communicative context

In addition, we do not live our lives alone, and that means we have to enter into dialogue with others around us. That is what communication is for. Communication is not located in one person alone – we have to establish communicative relationships. Music therapy is a prime example of how, when speech fails, we establish meaningful communication and interpret what the needs of the other are. This is essentially hermeneutic – the interpretation of meaning – and is not restricted to a verbal competence. For those seemingly with damaged capacities, we can retain significant communication such that they can express themselves and such that we can understand each other.

In Gervasio and Kreutzer's (1997) study describing the psychological distress experienced by live-in relatives of people with traumatic brain injury, comparing the distress of spouses with that of other relatives, family caregivers of people felt alienated, isolated, overwhelmed and mentally preoccupied. Spouses experienced more distress than parents. Bos (1997) has suggested coma stimulation as a treatment in which a health care professional or a patient's family member systematically applies stimulation to one or more of the patient's five senses for the purpose of increasing patient responsiveness. Furthering this field of stimulation and responsiveness, but concentrating on auditory stimulation, music, the voices of family members and friends have been used as interventions (Jones *et al.* 1994; Seibert *et al.* 2000). My argument is that music therapy incorporates these elements of relationship, sensory stimulation and appropriate response in a systematic manner based upon the developing communicative needs of the patient as consciousness changes and cognition is achieved (Aldridge 1991b; Aldridge *et al.* 1990). Communication, in this perspective, is not located within the individual but is an interpersonal phenomenon.

Utterance

When the means of producing language is in the process of being lost then we become aware of the restricted means of presenting self. Music therapy is a means of producing communication and it is based on gesture, which is the basis of communication in a variety of species. We know that communication without language is possible in primates (Bond and Corner 2001), for example. An essential feature of gesture is the concept of 'utterance'. We do make sounds outside the range of lexical language. Utterances are linked together in a grammatical form such that meaning is understood. This linking together as grammatical form in time is the basis of song and we are able to understand the general meanings of songs sung in other languages.

Structure, as form, is a way of schematizing experience and this is the way that we learn to think. We achieve cognition through linking together events in time; it is the achievement of memory. We link sounds together into phrases, and this is the basis of musical meaning in that sounds begin to function as music when we discern a structure between the tones. Utterances are a positive sign of the producer attempting to regain cognition, to mentate out of the de-mentation by providing an expressive cue to an underlying temporal dynamic. The task of the other person present, and certainly the music therapist, is to recognize this temporal dynamic and structure a mutual participatory performance.

A quality of utterances, and many gestures, is that they are spontaneously expressive. With demented patients, the challenge of therapy is to move from the spontaneously expressive to the performatively reflexive utterance that is intentional. It is a mutual shared temporal dynamic that offers a structure for spontaneity, which allows repetition within musical form, and thereby focuses attention and the possibility of regulation. As with all acts there is a constitutional aspect – what this event means – and a regulative aspect – what is to be done next as a meaningful response. Thus utterances become articulate.

A fundamental property of mental ability is that it is explicated in verbal and musical expressions, gestures and bodily expressions. As we have seen earlier, understanding is achieved through performance. The body is active in the world and belongs to the world. Illness becomes a restriction of this bodily presence and thus restricts both presence in the world and understanding (Svenaeus 2000). The challenge of music therapy is the challenge that we all face: how to establish the pattern of meaning.

At the heart of this understanding is time. Time is the *how* of events being organized and is the attribution of meaning to change (Tabboni 2001). How we perceive time is multifaceted; it is part of our personality and part of our culture and achieved in our relationships. We have various modes of understanding time, and in neuro-degenerative diseases these are restricted. In Parkinson's disease we have a disruption of time and its expression in emotion (Kremer and Starkstein 2000) and movement (Thaut and McIntosh 1999); in Alzheimer's disease we have a loss of memory and of fluency (Aldridge and Aldridge 1992; Aldridge and Brandt 1991). The phenomenon of 'sundowning' in dementia patients is a physiological change where the time structure that co-ordinates activity and temperature is lost (Volicer *et al.* 2001).

The coupling of the neural system, the musculo-skeletal system and the environment demands a co-ordination of temporal dynamics. There are scale relationships of time dependent upon biological events: muscular, cellular planetary, galactic. Behaviour is temporally structured, and it is in the organization of time that we synchronize our communication. Anticipation of events and co-ordinating responses demands a temporal dynamics based upon attention (Keijzer 1998). Anticipation of events is central to playing rhythm with another person, and we see this in the mutual playing of improvised musical playing where even severely disabled patients have the ability to anticipate events and co-ordinate their behaviour within a context of a flexible temporal dynamic. We are speaking here of musical time that in itself is flexible as performed, not the chronological time of a machine.

Gesture

In therapy we have a performed dialogue. The body is central for interaction. We perform most of our actions in daily life without reflecting on how we do it. Everyday skills are the basis of the knowledge that we need to perform our lives. Knowledge is done. It is based on interaction with others and is the background from which we achieve understanding of what others are doing.

Therefore, the performance possibilities that we offer others will enhance the abilities that they have. Relationship in this sense is not going to be based upon what we say, but what we *do*.

Gesture is a central feature of a communicative setting for the ecology that we call understanding. If there is a breakdown in the background, when relationship fails, then the mutuality of time is lost, events lose their context and we become isolated. We literally fall out with each other, fall out of time and, thereby, fall out of understanding. This is the process of becoming isolated. To repair performance, we have to offer a structure in time. Structured time is precisely what music is in all its myriad of styles and possibilities for performance. For those losing cognition, or struggling to regain cognition, the achievement of musical form is the basis of an enhanced cognitive ability. In coma patients, this is the regaining of levels of consciousness (Aldridge 2000b). Within our varying cultures we have repertoires of performance suitable for promoting understanding; the challenge for us as practitioners is to expand the repertoires of treatment necessary to achieve competent performance for those suffering with neuro-degenerative diseases.

We know that non-verbal behaviours like hand gestures convey important information and are a rich source of unspoken knowledge (Breckinridge Church 1999; Goldin-Meadow 1997, 1999, 2000; Mayberry and Jacques 2000; Mayberry and Nicoladis 2000). They are robust across cultures and are used by people of various ages. Not only do they reflect understanding, they also shape understanding. Like utterances, they are an attempt to regain cognition; they are used to inform the listener of the state of the expresser. We judge intentions by gestures. In children gestures signal that a particular notion is available in the repertoire of understanding but not necessarily accessible to speech. However, for the elderly, we can see that a concept is retained in the repertoire but no longer accessible to speech or conscious reflection. Gestures also allow expressions that do not easily fit into a categorical system but still reflect aspects of the performer's state. This eases the cognitive burden, and for the understanding of emotions allows the performer to achieve emotional expression without prematurely labelling that emotion – in giving the emotion a particular valence.

Setting and performance

How we perceive sounds as music or noise is dependent upon culture. Art productions are a ritualized form of performance, as are some clinical encounters.

Yet the everyday stuff of life is improvised. How we participate in these perfor-mances, and understand what is happening, is a matter of culture. Culture too is performed.

One of those influential cultural aspects will be the setting within which the performance takes place. Thus the setting of the home, the clinic, the day centre or the hospice will be important for the understanding of the perfor-mance.

The nature of this performance too will be dependent upon the engage-ment between the performers, and this is inevitably emotional and sensual (Smith 2000). Emotional relationship is a way of understanding the world and this is absolutely central for the sufferers of neuro-degenerative disease. We have the massive problem of agitation in demented patients, and the confound-ing problem of depression throughout the broad spectrum of disorders. Music therapy, with the cultural aspects of emotion and sensuality related to music, has an important role to play in relieving the suffering of these patients.

Musical performance does not cause feelings but is the embodiment of feelings given form. That is why music therapy is important for demented patients in that it offers a form for interaction. Feelings regain their shape such that they can be initiated, formed and resolved. The idea of emotions achieving closure is important in that it emphasizes performances that are bodily satisfy-ing, if not intellectually satisfying. What cannot be articulated in speech can be expressed through music, primarily because the medium of musical perfor-mance is that of organized perceptions and related actions. The basis of human intimacy is the co-ordination of understanding between self and other. For infant and mother, it begins as a mutual dialogue. Such dialogues also occur for adults, and we simply have to extend our repertoires of caring such that these can be achieved. Music therapy is one form of acceptable, intimate dialogue.

If our bodies are the source of musical performance, then disruptions in kinesis, rhythm and hearing will disturb that performance. The goal of therapy will be to restore the organizational property that binds these sources of perfor-mance together, such that coherence of the whole person can be achieved once more. This binding, organizational property is time experienced as musical form.

Gestures also boost activation levels and are involved in the temporal structure of thinking (Alibali *et al.* 2000, 2001). We see this in the simple beat movements when people listen to music. Even when people are talking on the telephone they gesture. The use of gesture also modulates responses to sensory input. Where agitation is a problem then gesture is an attempt to regulate arousal, either as an over-sensitivity or, as mentioned earlier, to boost activity. Sensory integration, including proprioception, demands an adaptive response if communication is to take place. Integration requires arousal (maintaining alertness), attention (ability to remain focused on a desired stimulus or task), affect (emotional regulation) and action (goal-directed behaviour as praxis in planning behaviour).

For patients in neurological rehabilitation, it is imperative that sensory integration is promoted as soon as possible and that this integration can be practised, maintained and achieved through active musical play. For the active synchrony of neural events then a pattern of strong signals has to be established, and this demands orientation with focused attention, with a conscious discrimination of auditory events (Engel and Singer 2001). Robertson *et al.* (1997) write that insufficient attention to tasks can result in slips of action as automatic, unintended action sequences are triggered inappropriately. Such slips arise in part from deficits in sustained attention, which are particularly likely to happen following frontal lobe and white matter damage in traumatic brain injury.

Mood regulation

'It is not the affect that regulates people rather than people regulating their affect' (Erber and Erber 2000, p.210).

A central feature of our emotional lives is the ability to regulate our emotions (Larsen 2000). Indeed, when such regulation fails, then we take it as a sign that something is going wrong and, in the extreme, we suspect a psychological disturbance. Affective states also influence attention, alter the way in which we perceive the world and influence our social relationships. Emotions are expressive, and we achieve this expression through gesture, postural changes, facial expression and the use of voice. It is not what we say but the way that we say it that indicates our emotional state and intentions. The musical parameters of communication indicate emotional valence.

Emotions are bodily events that have shape and duration. How these events are regulated on a daily basis is also a matter of ecology balancing our personal environment and the social world. Although we consider our emotional life to be personal, it takes little persuasion to convince us that it is our lives with others that has an influence on those emotional reactions. When we fail to interact satisfactorily with others, then a source of emotional regulation may also fail. If we lose attention with both external and internal events then there is loss of feedback and the potential for emotional disregulation. We need to know, for example, the difference between a current state and a desired state. This is a cognitive activity. The linking of emotional events to understand the profile of an emotion is a matter of time. The ability to express emotions is important, but also the facility to inhibit emotions forms the profile of our everyday lives. Choosing the form of an emotion, in terms of expression and inhibition, is necessary for appropriate emotional articulation. In dementia of the Alzheimer's type, agitation is a problem of emotional expression. Being a state of emotional arousal, agitation fails to achieve a satisfactory emotional form, appears to have no potential for inhibition and thus no closure as an emotional form.

Motor mimicry is an essential feature of empathy and understanding the other person (Neumann and Strack 2000). Facial and postural expressions influence emotional expression. Thus the perceptions of another person's behaviour may activate the same action codes within the observer that generate that behaviour. Thus, how we approach the demented is important in the way in which they will respond. Imitation is a feature of musical play and used in improvisation.

We also judge the expressive behaviour of others to know something about ourselves. The vocal expression of emotion embedded in the speaking voice is a powerful indicator of relationship and promotes a response. Expressed emotions promote congruent mood states in the listener; therefore we have to be as careful about how we say what we do as what we say. In music therapy, the use of timbre is central to emotion expression, as it is in the performance of operatic arias.

Cohen-Mansfield (2000) writes of the need to recognize the unmet needs of dementia patients where symptoms may be an attempt to alleviate need (pacing provides stimulation), agitation may be an over-expression of emotional arousal, that symptoms may be an attempt to communicate needs, and that behaviour may represent the outcome of an unmet need (crying from pain).

Children and adolescents who sustain brain injuries may also experience episodic agitation during the course of their recovery where agitation may be the direct effect of the neurological insult itself, as well as the child's response to physical pain and to his or her confusing surroundings. Later during the recovery process, agitation may occur in response to increasing demands made of the child and in response to feelings of loss. Agitation in children is a communication and attempts to provide the child with comfort, support and alternative ways to communicate help. If health care staff and family members understand the underlying factors driving agitation, and recognize it as a transient phase of recovery, then the broader treatment strategy is enhanced (Deaton *et al.* 1995).

Nurses and music therapists have emphasized the benefits of music (Ragneskog and Kihlgren 1997; Thomas *et al.* 1997) or music therapy (Brotons and Pickett-Cooper 1996; Brotons *et al.* 1997; Vink 2000) for the relief of agitation. Such interventions encouraging forms of expression will encourage unmet needs to be resolved.

Time achieves form

My hypothesis is that music offers the patient an alternative form for structuring time that fails in the working memory of the demented and is not yet made manifest in the coma patient. To achieve mentation, cognition and consciousness then we must be brought into movement.

Initially this movement is achieved through the rhythm of breathing and then through gesture and bodily movements in a context of musical improvisation. The co-ordinated time structure for these movements is musical performance, where the rhythmical intentions of the therapist combine with the basic rhythms of the patient. When tones are connected together intentionally, then we have the phenomenon of melody. The extension of melody on the basis of rhythm in time is 'memory'. Once memory is extended further in time, then we have the achievement of consciousness.

Temporal coherence and memory

Music therapy is indicated in neurological rehabilitation because it offers an external sense of temporal coherence that is latent in the patient through the dialogue of relationship.

We know that the nature of communication breakdown, how it is signalled, how it is repaired, and the outcome of the repair process, appears to be disease stage-dependent. Couples in the early and middle stage of neurological disease achieve success in resolving communication breakdowns despite declining cognitive, linguistic and conversation abilities of the individuals with the disease (Orange *et al.* 1998). This has important implications for understanding the influence of the progression of neuro-degenerative diseases on conversational performance and for advancing the development of communication enhancement education and training programmes for spousal caregivers of individuals with such diseases. Similarly, in coma, post-coma recovery and rehabilitation, we will expect to see, and hear, stages of recovery.

Rehabilitation, then, will entail a recovery of that ecological niche which we call 'communication'; this is achieved in the mutuality of performance as dialogue. For sufferers, we are that recovery – we are the context offering them an ecological niche. That is, we are communication and our responsibility lies in developing our own communicative abilities beyond the use of words. As living beings we perform in relationship with our milieu, a milieu that includes others. This ecological milieu is established through a dynamic mutual interaction. We establish communicative forms; these are inherently of time and musical. In this sense, memory is not the recovery of facts but the performance of reality linking events. What we experience as development is a creative act of improvising forms for being in time – this we experience physically as the body but psychologically as consciousness.

Benefits of music therapy

As Cohen-Mansfield (2000) suggests, therapeutic interventions need to be tailored to meet the needs of individual patients and their characteristics. In various social and treatment settings, music therapy can promote dialogue (see Table 13.1). The implication of such dialogues is that the sufferer can maintain, or even recover, an identity that has a broad repertoire of possibilities. When we enter into such dialogues, the caregivers are offered a broader potential of identities. The sufferer is reintegrated within a communicative ecology and this prevents isolation.

Music therapy offers a flexible temporal structure for processing temporal information. If timing is an ability that is failing, then musical form offers an alternative form within which timing can be temporarily recovered and practised. The expression of timing in communication will utilize gestural abilities, including utterance, that spontaneously bind events together and are indicative of performed ability. Gestures are seen within this context as attempts to regain cognition, not solely as failed abilities.

As emotional regulation is a common core problem within these diseases, attempts to positively regulate emotion will have benefits for both sufferers and carers. Emotional arousal is located within a context of attention and action, whereas needs may be unmet, are unable to be expressed or fail to be recognized. The expression of emotion, and similarly the ability to inhibit arousal, will contribute to communicating needs effectively.

Table 13.1 Benefits of music therapy for the neuro-degenerative diseases

- Meets the needs of individual patients and their characteristics
- Promotes dialogue and the maintenance of an identity that has a broad repertoire of possibilities
- Reintegrates the person within a communicative ecology and prevents isolation
- Offers a flexible temporal structure for processing temporal information where timing can be temporarily recovered and practised
- Utilizes gestural abilities, including utterance, binding events together that are indicative of ability, not pathology alone
- Gestures are seen as attempts to regain cognition, not seen as failed abilities
- Regulates emotional arousal in terms of expression and inhibition with implications for sufferers and caregivers
- Need can be expressed by being brought into a communicative form
- Motivates communication and participation without being speech dependent
- Attention, arousal, affect and action embodied in musical form

Communicative abilities are essential. This mutual need is usually achieved through speech. When speech fails, it is important to utilize those properties of human communication that are not speech dependent. Attention, arousal, affect and action all occur in musical performance. Music therapy has the potential to promote communication, stimulate cognitive abilities and alert us to residual communicative abilities.

Gesture and dialogue, then, are important activities for communication. Indeed this embodied activity is communication. To enter into dialogue with the other, we must ourselves embody those common rhythms of consciousness, and this is achieved through music therapy. By playing together, we achieve that understanding necessary for dialogue and thus an embodied hermeneutic.

CHAPTER 14

Guidelines for Clinical Research

There are several stages to preparing a research application. Careful thinking about clinical practice and the allocation of time for research is essential. Methodological decisions must be made before data is collected and this is particularly relevant for statistical interpretations of data.

At the University of Witten Herdecke and Aalborg University there is a preliminary period of the study course where, after submission, there is a process of gradual refinement of the research application that takes place with consultation and supervision. We do not expect that expert clinicians become expert researchers overnight. However, you will find below some considerations that have to be made and are worth thinking about early on in the application process.

There is a wide range of considerations which need to be made before we begin clinical research. Perhaps the most important question to ask is what the specific guidelines for clinical research are within your own institution or the institution where the research is to take place. It is to be hoped that clinicians intending to do research will find sufficient advice to plan a research proposal from the institution where they are working. This will also mean that sufficient advice is given concerning the scientific ethics committee of the institution. One of the keys to successful planning is to ask crucial questions early in the research process. Here, then, are some considerations which a research methodologist would ask of you.

Why are you doing this anyway?

I shall assume that the researcher has already gone through the preliminary stages of having a good idea which appears to be completely original and potentially world shattering when written on the back of an envelope. The next stages of writing the ideas down for colleagues to criticize and making overtures to funding agencies are far more gruelling.

If you wish to do research then it is a continuing struggle to maintain that first flush of excitement against what may seem unreasonable odds and what at times seem to be tiresome practical details. These challenges are the ones which curb our worst excesses and in the end facilitate our research. Research takes a great deal of personal motivation. It is important to find some form of personal and professional support which is supportive but critical. In addition, it is possible to work as a group to support each other, share varying skills and to teach each other about research methods.

How are you going to pay for this research?

It is important to bear in mind that research is greedy for resources. First there is money, which is presumably why you are considering some form of grant funding. Towards the end of this chapter you will find a section about costing.

Do you have the time to do this?

It is essential to plan your own time very carefully as a researcher. Before the research and during the progress of the work, even in preparation, it is important to have time to think about what you are doing. It is also vital to read research literature thoroughly and perhaps with a different approach to the one which is used to scan journals for articles of interest. If you are a clinician who wishes to research concurrent with practice then you may have to consider drastically reducing your clinical practice or consider working with a restricted range of patients. The activity of research thinking and planned reading, while appearing as a luxury to colleagues, may mean a change in attitude to working for the clinician who constantly has to be seen to 'do'. At this stage it is useful to consider how long a period you want to spend on your research project, and then set a target date for the end of that period.

Finally, your immediate family and friends may not quite share your single-minded commitment to advancing the cause of modern scientific endeavour. Apart from research eating into recreation time, those sudden flashes of inspiration of extended thoughts concerning methodological conundrums can occur at weekends or in the evening when you begin to relax. Sometimes spouses do not appreciate the riddle of formulating an algorithm for multiple variables measured over a time series, especially if this occurs over dinner.

Research is a serious activity and cannot be tacked on to other activities. If possible find some specialist advice either from a colleague who has researched in the field you are considering, from a known expert in the field, or from the funding agency you intend to approach. It is at this stage that statistical or methodological advice must be sought, not after data is collected.

For whom are you doing this study?

PURPOSE OF THE ENQUIRY

It is important to state research questions precisely. The questions must be clear and simple. This process of clarifying your own emerging questions so that they can be understood by others is a vital stage for your work, and for finding funds. To a certain extent the purpose of the study will help define the target audience for your work. This will in turn influence the research methods you use.

If the purpose of your work is to satisfy your own curiosity as an individual or group of practitioners then that methodology may be developed in a way which is totally idiosyncratic to your clinical practice. Your work may be seen as the development of a research methodology appropriate for your particular way of working. This could be extended to the arena of your clinical peers to whom you wish to validate a set of hypotheses about your common practice. They may demand that certain restraints are imposed. For example, in working as a research consultant with music therapists their demand of me was to find research methods appropriate to their clinical practice, not to adapt practice to research restrictions.

Those of us who have been through the academic research mill have often been fortunate enough to satisfy our own questions within the guidelines of a particular research discipline. What we may need to develop within complementary medicine is an agency which can offer such impartial supervision and guidance.

Host clinicians when they do research are attempting to convince someone of the validity of their approach – other practitioners, licensing authorities, journal editors, consumers or patients. It is important, then, to be able to see the purpose of what you are doing and why. In the field of complementary practice it is important to state where such practice could be used within a current health care framework, and how such a practice fits in with orthodox practice. In addition it is important to show where the proposed work will improve research expertise, improve current clinical practice or have an educational component.

Once these broad understandings have been considered then it is time to provide more details of the intended study.

Aims of the study

The aims of clinical studies are multifarious. The exploration and generation of hypotheses, the refinement of those hypotheses, the discovery of the optimal use of a therapeutic regimen, the safety of that regimen or the active ingredient in a composite therapy are common aims. Similarly, complementary practitioners often want to make a definitive demonstration of their therapeutic regimen in comparison with another regimen or to demonstrate feasibility or efficacy in a particular setting.

Such clinical trials usually pose two radically different types of problem which demand differing types of solution and different methodological considerations.

The first is an explanatory trial. In this approach we seek information which will give us answers to scientific questions, often at the biological level. Such trials are closer to laboratory conditions and may have no pragmatic consequences. The questions asked in these trials are more concerned with causality and the natural history of disease, the development of medicines and the refinement and application of techniques.

The second type of trial is a comparison of treatments as applied in practice. This is a pragmatic trial. In such a trial treatment conditions would be optimized and our purpose would be to make a decision about which treatment modality to use. In these trials we can incorporate factors other than the biological or psychological. These factors might be concerned with cost, efficacy, ease of use, acceptability by the patient, or possibility for inclusion in general practice. Such trials are related to the context of the treatment approach and provide answers concerned with feasibility, but not necessarily answers that are explanatory; that is, the treatment works but nobody knows why.

Both can be combined, but with extreme caution. In the interest of simplicity it is better to understand what you are attempting and then ask yourself if you are taking on too much. Rather than attempt an overly complex study it may be possible to work as a research group of practitioners satisfying interdependent aims. In this way of working, practitioners can work co-operatively with colleagues developing differing sets of answers which answer a common question.

For example, in the music therapy research mentioned earlier, some therapists concentrated on developing methodologies which showed physiological changes during and after the process of therapy (explanatory trials), others were concerned with clinical outcomes (pragmatic trials), and all were concerned in the theoretical debate, based on experimental observation and clinical expertise about how clinical improvement was effected.

It is in the aims section where you will state your hypotheses to be tested.

Pilot studies

It really is important to make exploratory or pilot studies, not as an easy option. By attempting to try out our ideas in practice we can see the pitfalls and the possibilities of what we are attempting. Some of these pitfalls can be avoided by asking expert opinion beforehand.

Unfortunately the pressure of research sponsors can be for precocious results and evidence that something is being done for their money. Exploratory trials and critical developmental thinking are often sacrificed to such impatience.

Pilot studies are not any easier to construct methodologically than later trials. Definitive studies cannot be generated from poorly thought-out exploratory studies. As much statistical and methodological thinking must go into the pilot studies as the larger study. Data must be carefully evaluated in a series of sequential experiments. These are the platform for the future work.

The question always remains of when to stop piloting and when to begin a definitive study. The main objective in any clinical trial is to find a feasible, effective and tolerable regime which is easy to understand, is easily administered, has an evaluative index which demonstrates the identified clinical change, and has co-operative clinical partners. Once you have such an approach then it is time to try it out. In an application for research funding it is important to link any pilot work to an overall developmental strategy with some clear indication of a future definitive study.

Background to the study

In your preliminary thinking you will have begun to understand the gaps in present knowledge. You will then need to say how your study will begin to fill these gaps and contribute to that knowledge. This understanding is based on your own clinical knowledge, and that of current expertise from other practitioners, but is based predominantly on reviewing the clinical literature.

Reviewing literature can be a research study in itself. It demands a great deal of application to search, collect and read the relevant material. However, it can bring much satisfaction. By reading of other research endeavours over the years we can gain a sense of the community of research practitioners in medicine who, too, have been excited by ideas and attempted to demonstrate those ideas in practice.

There are numerous databases available for searching the literature. These searches are made easier and cheaper by being clear about what categories you wish to search under, in what range of publications, published in which languages and over what period of time. For example, by disease: inflammatory bowel disease; with the following factors: family factors, immunological, historical, epidemiological, psychological; published in English, German and French; during the last five years.

A useful basis is the INFO CD ROM series published by the University of Witten Herdecke that contains music therapy databases as libraries and the online database at http://musictherapyworld.net

A good medical librarian is of invaluable help. These searches usually cost money. A search facility may be available through your professional organization. Once you have the list of papers it is then important to gather those papers together. Some of these papers may be in a local medical or university library. More often than not the papers must be secured through inter-library loans. To do this you will need to make some arrangement with a library. Again, papers cost money and it is important to budget for this. Your professional organization may have a paper ordering service which gathers papers at a reduced cost. These facilities are often slower than doing it yourself, and there is usually a limit to the number of papers you can order.

It is then possible to make an extended search from the reference sections and bibliographies of those collected papers. Then you have to read the papers critically, make notes and write up the conclusions. This is where you find that your writing skills may have become a little rusty.

Literature too can also act as a pilot study of ideas where your work builds upon previous studies. It is always an advantage to contact the authors of studies to ask how they would further their work. In journal papers not everything is revealed about the trial in terms of practical details; that is, it may be an elegant study when reported but difficult to carry out in practice. By looking through the literature with a critical eye it is possible to see exactly what is needed as a next step in your own therapeutic discipline in terms of clinical practice or research methodology. It is also possible to see the mistakes of others and construct a trial that builds upon what has gone before.

Clinical literature is not solely confined to journal articles and books. Some articles quote eminent authors, and they are worth contacting particularly for unpublished material which they may be willing to show you.

If your work is based upon a literature review then it will have an influence upon the statistical methods that you use. Once you know in which direction you expect improvement then this will influence the nature of the statistical test.

Design of the study

In this section you will say what research strategy is to be used. Will you use a laboratory-style explanatory approach or embark upon a survey? Are you using a controlled trial with randomized or matched controls, or are you carrying out a series of related single-case designs? Are you attempting to describe a service within a hospital setting or is this a formal trial of a therapeutic procedure? This is where your methodological musings and debate must leave the heady heights of discussion and appear on paper.

It is important to give a detailed account of the research design you intend to use, and some indication of why you are using that design. In a qualitative approach it is essential to identify which approach is to be used; for example, grounded theory, ethnography, phenomenology, case study design or a construct theory perspective. Each approach will have ramifications for the way in which the data is collected, interpreted and understood.

It is possible to be innovative in clinical trials design. Studies should not conflict with the best practices in the discipline involved: they should be planned so that the many sources of error and bias are avoided; provided that this rigour is sought, they need not conform to the traditional patterns of clinical trials methodology. (See Aldridge 1996.)

Selection of subjects for the study

It is important to describe the class of patients who are to be included in the study. If you are studying a particular disease then it is important to define a sub-class of patients who are suitable for that trial. This will mean giving discrete criteria for patient inclusion and exclusion (e.g. by age, gender, chronicity, previous treatment). Beware of defining this group too narrowly such that they become unrepresentative. The study which accepts a broad spectrum of patients has a generalizability and persuasiveness that is essential to influencing a target audience of practitioners. Although hand-picking patients may be desirable in statistical terms there is a trade off between efficiency and generalizability. If your purpose is to demonstrate the efficacy of your approach with the aim of influencing applicability in general practice then choose carefully over a broad range of patients.

If you are conducting a controlled trial you will have to say what criteria are being used for control selection.

There is also a further sub-class of patients: those who complete the trial, i.e. those you actually gather data about. Withdrawals give rise to serious difficulties, especially if they occur during the treatment regime. People leave trials because they are frightened of what is going on, they may believe that they are not receiving an important life-saving medication, the regime or data collection may be tedious, the medicine may taste nasty or the procedure is painful. Some patients don't see the point of the study after a while and somehow their commitment to research doesn't match that of the researcher. Some patients at follow up are found to have left the area. Some patients die. Some researchers call this process one of 'patient attrition'.

While withdrawals may throw important light on a particular practice and provide useful information it is always better to structure such a possibility into the trial if you believe this is going to happen. A careful pilot study should give some ideas about whether a treatment regime can be sustained or not.

Another important consideration is that of sample size. This is why it is emphasized that statistical thinking is vital at this stage of the study – not after data has been collected.

If groups are to be compared then decisions will have to be made about randomization of subjects to groups, how many patients are needed in those groups to achieve statistical significance, and, more importantly, what is the power of those statistics. It is vital that appropriately sized groups are chosen in clinical trials designs so that clinically meaningful differences are not missed.

For example, if comparing two treatments (X and Y) in a pragmatic approach the researcher will want to know by what margin does one treatment regime surpass the other. This pragmatic approach is concerned with reducing the probability of preferring the inferior treatment (an error of the third kind). Whereas, in an explanatory approach, it is important to avoid concluding that treatments X and Y differ when they are the same (an error of the first kind), or that treatments X and Y are equal when they are not (an error of the second kind).

Choice of data

Perhaps the greatest challenge is to sift out what data to collect. There is a temptation to collect masses and masses of data in some mistaken belief that more data is somehow representative of the whole person. It is important to collect multiple data sets which are indicators of therapeutic influence, but these data have to be analysed at the end of the trial. The challenge then is to define how the criteria which are used for evaluation are related to the treatment intervention, and one with another. The variables measured by the experimenter in this way are the dependent variables.

The panel which assesses your application will want to know why you have chosen particular measures or indices.

In assessing the effects of a treatment regimen we may use several diverse criteria: regression of a tumour, decrease in pain, return to work or mean survival time compared with a given prognosis. Return to work may be an important variable as identified by the patient but it offers no biological information. Regression of tumour size may be biologically important but this may have no effect upon survival.

It is therefore important to develop an instrument for measuring clinical change appropriate to the study. Explanatory studies will seek to find separate criteria. A pragmatic approach will look for a single index which can be used to indicate therapeutic efficacy.

It may be that the aim of the research design itself will concentrate on developing an index. This may be in the form of a questionnaire, or a battery of measures. In constructing such an increment you will be able to use your own expert knowledge, the clinical experience of colleagues, the clinical literature you have reviewed and the experience of patients. It is essential to bear in mind how patient status will change in relationship to the therapeutic application, and that your instrument measures all clinically important treatment effects. (If you take this route beware! Questionnaire design and validation is a project within itself.)

What most of us seek is some sort of gold-standard measure which is both reliable and valid. Reliable in this sense refers to the consistency of a research instrument when applied to a stable population. Valid refers to whether those measures are genuine, i.e. do they measure what you say they are measuring? In addition the measure must be responsive enough to measure a small, but real, difference when one is present.

There are three main types of index which can be developed:

1. The discriminative index which helps to distinguish between individuals or groups where no gold standard exists.

2. The predictive index which is used to classify individuals into predefined categories. This is evident in screening measures which identify specific individuals who will have a target condition or outcome. We see this in prognostic indicators or predictors of mortality.

3. The evaluative index which is used to measure longitudinal change in an individual or group on the given criterion of interest. Such an index can utilize both quantitative and qualitative data and is often used to evaluate functional change.

My aim when advising clients is to find and use at least one index which is well validated in orthodox clinical practice. This helps build a bridge to other research traditions. There are also a number of well-validated and reliable self-report questionnaires. These are very useful if you do not have the resources to interview the subjects of your research yourself.

Data collection

It is necessary to say when the measures will be implemented, who will implement them and design a form for data collection. In planning the collection of data allow time for questionnaires to be filled in. If postal questionnaires are used make an allowance for the follow up of unreturned questionnaires, and be prepared to visit if necessary.

Ideally if data is collected by more than one person then one person must be placed in a position to collate that data. Research is an obsessive activity. Data collection is tedious, but missing data is a calamity.

With the advent of modern computing methods then it is easy to store and manipulate data. Putting data into a database or spreadsheet is relatively straightforward; getting it out again in a meaningful way is not. The statistical decisions which you made earlier, and your understanding of the relationships between sets of data, will be invaluable at this stage. If data is to be stored on a computer remember that someone has to enter that data and it will be necessary to say who will handle the data, and when they will enter the data. Entering large sets of data at the end of a project leads to error. Data sheets can be lost. Human errors from fatigue are common. It may be possible to consider direct entry of data to a computer with some form of data checking routine built in.

It is important to describe how any specialist laboratory tests will be carried out, the nature of those tests and who will carry them out. Specialist testing is expensive and another potential source of error, so it is important to be clear about how valid or necessary such measures are. Some specialist tests can be therapeutic interventions in themselves and it is important to bear this in mind when designing the study and perhaps consider them as control variables. (A control variable is a potential independent variable which is held constant.)

Treatment variables

Treatment variables are the independent variables. They refer to the techniques or the programme of treatment you will use as a clinician. This will probably be the easiest part for you to organize. It is important that you say clearly what you will do, when you will do it and why you are doing it. For complementary practitioners working together it is vital that they achieve some standardization of practice while remaining true to their therapeutic discipline, thereby maintaining their own therapeutic integrity and validity. If your therapeutic discipline contains its own idiosyncratic terms it may be necessary to provide a glossary of terms within the application document.

When a control group is used then it is essential to define how, when and where they will be treated, even if they receive 'no treatment'.

If you are carrying out a clinical trial it will be necessary to incorporate some time when baseline data can be collected before treatment begins. The time when treatment periods begin and end must be planned and recorded. Criteria must be made for when the trial period of treatment is to end, and when a follow-up assessment is to be made.

It is also important to say what will happen to patients discovered to have new needs during the process of the study.

Administration of the study

Analysis of the results

If the data is stored on a computer, and the researchers understand their data, then a statistical package can be used to analyse that data. If statistical advice is sought at the beginning of the trial, and the trial designed according to certain principles, then the appropriate routines will be clear. With the implementation of statistical analysis packages on microcomputers then it is possible to view and analyse the data in a variety of ways. Such retrospective data analysis, sometimes called post hoc hypothesizing, is dangerous. While it may suggest new hypotheses and correlations between data, those relationships may be completely spurious. Analyses of data are only spurs to critical thinking, they cannot replace it.

When considering using a statistical package it may be necessary to enlist the help of a statistician to help interpret the results. Many packages also have a graphics capability which will enable the data to be displayed in forms which are easier to understand than tables of figures.

Timetable of the study

In the process of making the previous decision you will have some idea of how long the study will take. The most common mistake that novice researchers make is to underestimate the amount of time necessary to complete a study. I shall assume that you have contacted the practitioners and referrers to be involved and gained their co-operation.

First you will need to assess how long it will take to recruit the requisite number of patients. If you are recruiting patients with special characteristics through a seemingly co-operative referrer, check the time it will take to recruit a starting sample, assess them and gain their consent. This information will also influence how many patients can be treated in a given period of time. If you are collecting data as well as treating patients then the time you allow for your usual treatment session may be extended.

Second, plot the time it will take for all the subjects of the research to be treated and make a definite date for the trial to end. Ensure that any specialist testing will have been carried out by that date and the results received. Allow for any missing questionnaire data to be followed up.

Third, allow time to analyse the results. Initial data is 'raw data'; it can do nothing by itself – you as researcher must process it. Unlike patients, data is not self-actualizing.

Fourth, consider that the results must be thought about and then written up in some form for publication or as a presentation to your target audience. Because we are practitioners does not always mean that we are writers. If you are writing a joint report then allow time for arguing. A useful tip is to present your work at regular intervals to colleagues, and to the collaborators in your study at the end of the trial. This thinking for a presentation can help your writing, particularly if you record the presentation on audiotape.

Finally, if you are writing and working with colleagues make sure that you have made a decision about who is to be senior author, or at least to have final say on the finished report, and who is to be accredited in the list of authors.

Ethical considerations

If your professional group has a code of ethical consideration for research then it will be necessary to consider them. Mention such a code of practice in your research application. If you are working with an institution then there will be an ethical committee which will need to see your research submission. Your sponsors will want to satisfy themselves that you have obtained approval for your intended research from an ethical committee. While your sponsors may be flexible in their approach, local ethical committees may not be quite as well educated. The onus is on the clinician/researcher to consult with them and explain what he or she intends to do.

As soon as data is collected, and particularly if it is stored on a computer, then that data must be protected and made confidential. Similarly, if the research is to be written as a report which can potentially be published then arrangements must be made to maintain confidentiality and this must be stated in the application.

The consent of patients and co-operating practitioners must also be obtained. Be clear how you are to obtain this consent, and what information you will give to the patient in the trial. The rights of the patient to refuse to participate in, or withdraw from, the trial must be observed.

It is essential that any possible risks to the patient are made clear and harmful consequences removed. If an unorthodox practice is to be used then be prepared for what seem to be obstructive and awkward questions. As practitioners we take for granted what we do. Our normal decisions and practices can sometimes be misunderstood or misinterpreted.

For example, a news programme which juxtaposes concern about the spread of AIDS and highlights the use of needles by addicts, coupled with the debate about complementary medical practice, notably acupuncture, can indirectly raise issues about risks to the patient from the use of needles. If you are about to embark on an acupuncture trial, and are attempting to recruit patients from referrers who are only marginally convinced about co-operating, then such news can have negative consequences.

Any statements about insurance for professional indemnity and the limit of that indemnity can be included here.

Costing of the project

As mentioned earlier, research is greedy for resources and particularly for money. In a research submission you will need to justify your needs and also satisfy your potential sponsors that the request is valid. Ask for enough. Do not underestimate your requirements. Find out what is the minimum or maximum trial budget that they will consider. Some research councils will not consider small-scale trials as the administration costs alone are too expensive.

The principal considerations are:

Staffing costs:

1. the salary of the investigator(s) and the hidden pension and insurance costs over a given period of time. Allow for annual increments.

2. secretarial costs

3. specialist consultancy services for data handling, statistical advice and analysis and research supervision

4. specialist consultancy services for patient assessment.

Treatment costs: any tests will need to be costed, particularly when carried out by an external agency, and the cost of treatments or medicines will need to be considered.

Handling charges: most sponsors will support an institution rather than an individual. Such institutions will often charge a handling cost as a percentage of the funds received.

Administrative costs: there will be accommodation charges, telephone bills, stationery needs, printing requirements, postage and overheads.

Travel costs: visits to expert informants, visits to follow-up patients.

Hardware costs: any specialist equipment that must be rented or bought.

Computing costs: it may be necessary to purchase software for computing or to have that software adapted or written for your trial. If you have access to a computer centre then that centre may charge for such support.

Library services: searching for references in the literature, collecting literature and photocopying literature is costly.

Sometimes it is necessary to break these costs down into yearly requirements.

Personnel

For the main personnel working on the project it is important to include curricula vitae, and their appropriate clinical and academic qualifications. Some sponsors require you to nominate a key person to oversee the work. If you are using an external supervisor then his or her qualifications will need to be included.

Research experience can be included in this section. A lack of experience should not preclude the clinician from a research grant, providing the sponsor is satisfied that there is adequate research supervision. With the dwindling resources available for research through academic institutions we are in danger of seriously damaging our research tradition in England. However, by taking research out of the academic environment we have a chance to promote research training for clinicians within the context of their own practice. This approach is not bound by traditional thinking and should enliven our scientific medical culture.

Submitting the research

Send the completed design with a covering letter. It may be that you can submit your design for a preliminary review before a formal submission to a full committee. Be prepared to revise and negotiate a little. Most big committees meet only once or twice a year so it is important to find the final date for submission.

Conclusion

If you can incorporate all these considerations then the research itself should be easy. Applying for funds is the worst part. It takes a lot of work and organization with no guarantee of results.

Remember that research takes time: personal time, reading time, thinking time, and time away from your routine practice. It is prudent to negotiate such changes with your friends, colleagues and family.

Be clear about the intended audience for your research.

Research is expensive. It may be worthwhile investing in preliminary research planning which would include a brief review of the literature and statistical or methodological advice.

At the University of Witten Herdecke and Aalborg University we have research facilities that offer methodological advice, research supervision and consultation, and library and literature support.

It is worthwhile to spend some time in visiting institutions where research is taking place and talking to researchers and their supervisors. Most of us involved in supervising want to promote research and to bring candidates forward for doctoral studies. That may mean initially helping people to try out small studies.

Being a researcher requires a certain attitude of questioning. This is sometimes difficult for the expert practitioner who must then put his or her own practice into question. I often hear practitioners who have quasi-research questions. This is evident in that they state a question and then provide an answer from the literature before the question itself has been investigated. Research can be an anxiety-provoking business, as essentially it obliges us to say that we do not know. To enter into the research process then, we must know enough to know that we do not know and have the courage to admit it. At the end, we know a little more about how little we know.

Timetable of research events	
Aims of the study	• Have a good idea, decide to research, negotiate possible changes. • Try the ideas out on friends and colleagues. • Derive hypotheses or generate questions for qualitative research. • Identify target audience for the research results (patients, payers, professionals). • Identify sponsors.
Pilot study?	• Look at the literature for examples of good practice or influential study. • Ask about ethical committee guidelines. • Try out techniques and method of data collection. • Gain statistical and methodological advice.
Review literature	• Make a careful study of the relevant literature.
Design study	• Sample size, choice of patients, what type of clinical trial, identify the dependent and treatment variables. • For a qualitative study identify the appropriate methodological strategy to answer your questions. Develop a focus. • Gain statistical and methodological advice. • Identify and secure research supervision or consultation (this may be a peer group).
Administration of the study	• Identify who will collect the data, say how the data will be collected and stored. • Arrange for data to be transcribed and organize either triangulation studies or expert groups for qualitative research.
Ethical committee	• Submit research plan early. • Revise.
Submit proposal	• Arrange for the payment of costs and access to a research budget.
Do trial	
Analyse results	• Ask the statistician or the methodologist. • For a qualitative study this may mean repeating the process several times.
Write up	• Get advice from colleagues. • Relate your findings to current and new literature. • Present your work regularly if you can – it helps to focus and consolidate your findings. • Consult editors and be prepared to revise your paper.

References

Aasgaard, T. (1994) 'Music Therapy at the End of Life – and at the Funeral.' *Nordisk Tidsskrift for Musikkterapi 3*, 2, 86–88.

Aasgaard, T. (1999) 'Music Therapy as Milieu in the Hospice and Paediatric Oncology Ward.' In D. Aldridge (ed) *Music Therapy and Palliative Care*. London: Jessica Kingsley Publishers.

Aasgaard, T. (2001) 'An Ecology of Love: Aspects of music therapy in the pediatric oncology department.' *Journal of Palliative Care 17*, 3, 177–181.

Abrams, A. (2001) 'Music, Cancer, and Immunity.' *Clinical Journal of Oncology Nursing 5*, 5, 222–224.

Albrecht, G. (1994) 'Subjective Health Assessment.' In C. Jenkinson (ed) *Measuring Health and Medical Outcomes*. London: UCL Press.

Aldridge, D. (1984a) 'Suicidal behaviour and family interaction.' *Journal of Family Therapy 6*, 309–322.

Aldridge, D. (1986) 'Licence to Heal.' *Crucible*, April–June, 58–66.

Aldridge, D. (1987a) *One Body: a guide to healing in the Church*. London: SPCK.

Aldridge, D. (1987b) 'A Community Approach to Cancer in Families.' *Journal of Maternal and Child Health 12*, 182–185.

Aldridge, D. (1987c) 'Families, Cancer and Dying.' *Family Practice 4*, 212–218.

Aldridge, D. (1987d) 'A Team Approach to Terminal Care: Personal implications for patients and practitioners.' *Journal of the Royal College of General Practitioners 37*, 364.

Aldridge, D. (1988a) 'Single Case Research Designs.' *Complementary Medical Research 3*, 37–46.

Aldridge, D. (1988b) 'Families, Cancer and Dying.' *Journal of the Institute of Religion and Medicine 3*, 312–322.

Aldridge, D. (1988c) 'Goal Setting: The patient's assessment of outcome and recognition of therapeutic change.' *Complementary Medical Research 3*, 89–97.

Aldridge, D. (1989a) 'Europe Looks at Complementary Medicine.' *British Medical Journal 299*, 1121–1122.

Aldridge, D. (1989b) 'A Phenomenological Comparison of the Organization of Music and the Self.' *Arts in Psychotherapy 16*, 91–97.

Aldridge, D. (1989c) 'Music, Communication and Medicine.' *Journal of the Royal Society of Medicine 82*, 743–745.

Aldridge, D. (1990a) 'Making and Taking Health Care Decisions.' *Journal of the Royal Society of Medicine 83*, 720–723.

Aldridge, D. (1990b) 'The Delivery of Health Care Alternatives.' *Journal of the Royal Society of Medicine 83*, 345–346.

Aldridge, D. (1990c) 'The Development of a Research Strategy for Music Therapists in a Hospital Setting.' *The Arts in Psychotherapy 17*, 231–237.

Aldridge, D. (1991a) 'Aesthetics and the Individual in the Practice of Medical Research: A discussion paper.' *Journal of the Royal Society of Medicine 84*, 147–150.

Aldridge, D. (1991b) 'Creativity and consciousness: Music therapy in intensive care.' *Arts in Psychotherapy 18*, 4, 359–362.

Aldridge, D. (1991c) 'Healing and Medicine.' *Journal of the Royal Society of Medicine 84*, 516–518.

Aldridge, D. (1991d) 'Single Case Designs for the Clinician.' *Journal of the Royal Society of Medicine 84*, 249–252.

Aldridge, D. (1991e) 'Single Case Designs – an extended bibliography.' *Complementary Medical Research 5*, 2, 99–109.

Aldridge, D. (1991f) 'Spirituality, Healing and Medicine.' *Journal of British General Practice 41*, 425–427.

Aldridge, D. (1992a) 'The Needs of Individual Patients in Clinical Research.' *Advances 8*, 58–65.

Aldridge, D. (1992b) 'Of Ethics and Education: Strategies for curriculum development.' *Journal of the Royal Society of Medicine 85*, 594–597.

Aldridge, D. (1993a) 'Alzheimer's Disease and Music: Assessment and therapy.' *Journal of the Royal Society of Medicine 86*, 93–95.

Aldridge, D. (1993b) 'The Music of the Body: Music therapy in medical settings.' *Advances 9*, 1, 17–35.

Aldridge, D. (1993c) 'Observational Methods: A search for methods in an ecosystemic research paradigm.' In G. Lewith and D. Aldridge (eds) *Clinical research methodology for complementary therapies.* London: Hodder and Stoughton.

Aldridge, D. (1994) 'Unconventional Medicine in Europe.' *Advances 10*, 52–60.

Aldridge, D. (1995) 'Spirituality, Hope and Music Therapy in Palliative Care.' *The Arts in Psychotherapy 22*, 2, 103–109.

Aldridge, D. (1996) *Music Therapy Research and Practice in Medicine: From out of the silence.* London: Jessica Kingsley Publishers.

Aldridge, D. (1998) *Suicide: The Tragedy of Hopelessness.* London: Jessica Kingsley Publishers.

Aldridge, D. (1999) *Music Therapy in Palliative Care: New voices.* London: Jessica Kingsley Publishers.

Aldridge, D. (2000a) *Spirituality, Healing and Medicine: Return to the silence.* London: Jessica Kingsley Publishers.

Aldridge, D. (2000b) *Kairos IV: Beiträge zur Musiktherapie in der Medizin.* Bern: Hans Huber.

Aldridge, D. (2000c) *Music Therapy in Dementia Care.* London: Jessica Kingsley Publishers.

Aldridge, D. (2002) 'Philosophical speculations on two therapeutic applications of breath.' *Subtle Energies and Energy Medicine 12*, 2, 107–124.

Aldridge, D. and Brandt, G. (1991) 'Music therapy and Alzheimer's disease.' *Journal of British Music Therapy 5*, 2, 28–63.

Aldridge, D. and Dallos, R. (1986) 'Distinguishing Families where Suicidal Behavior is Present from Families where Suicidal Behavior is Absent.' *Journal of Family Therapy 8*, 243–252.

Aldridge, D., Gustorff, D. and Hannich, H.J. (1990) 'Where Am I? Music therapy applied to coma patients.' [Editorial] *Journal of the Royal Society of Medicine 83*, 6, 345–346.

Aldridge, D. and Pietroni, P. (1987a) 'Research Trials in General Practice: Towards a focus on clinical practice.' *Family Practice 4*, 311–315.

Aldridge, D. and Pietroni, P. (1987b) 'The Clinical Assessment of Acupuncture for Asthma Therapy.' *Journal of the Royal Society of Medicine 80*, 222–224.

Aldridge, D. and Rossiter, J. (1983) 'A Strategic Approach to Suicidal Behaviour.' *Journal of Systemic and Strategic Therapies 2*, 4, 49–62.

Aldridge, D. and Rossiter, J. (1984a) 'A Strategic Assessment of Deliberate Self Harm.' *Journal of Family Therapy 6*, 119–132.

Aldridge, D. and Rossiter, J. (1984b) 'A strategic assessment of deliberate self harm.' *Journal of Family Therapy 6*, 119–132.

Aldridge, D. and Rossiter, J. (1985) 'Difficult Patients, Intractable Symptoms and Spontaneous Recovery in Suicidal Behaviour.' *Journal of Systemic and Strategic Therapies 14*, 66–76.

Aldridge, G. (1996) '"A Walk through Paris": The development of melodic expression in music therapy with a breast-cancer patient.' *Arts in Psychotherapy 23*, 207–223.

Alibali, M., Heath, D. and Myers, H. (2001) 'Effects of visibilty between speaker and listener on gesture production: Some gestures are meant to be seen.' *Journal of Memory and Language 44*, 169–188.

Alibali, M., Kita, S. and Young, A. (2000) 'Gesture and the process of speech production: We think, therefore we gesture.' *Language and Cognitive Processes 15*, 6, 593–613.

Allen, M. (1983) 'Activity Generated Endorphins: A review of their role in sports science.' *Canadian Journal of Applied Sport Science 8*, 3, 115–133.

Amies, D. (1979) 'Music Therapy in Palliative Care.' *Canadian Medical Association Journal 120*, 11, 1327–1328.

Andersen, J. (1995) *Lifestyles, Consumption and Alternative Therapies.* Troense, Denmark: Odense University Press.

Andersen, M. and Lobel, M. (1995) 'Predictors of Health Self-Appraisal: What's involved in feeling healthy?' *Basic and Applied Social Psychology 16*, 121–136.

Arai, F., Osako, M., Shimoaraiso, Y., Sakamoto, T., Miyashita, T., Yamanouchi, H., Kadokura, K., Yoshida, K., Dozono, F., Mamitsuka, K. and Dozono, H. (1999) [Home Hospice Care at a Clinic.] *Gan To Kagaku Ryoho 26*, Suppl 2, 269–272.

Armstrong, D. (1995) 'The Rise of Surveillance Medicine.' *Sociology of Health and Illness 17*, 393–404.

Arnold, A.G., Lane, D.J. and Zapata, E. (1983) 'Acute Severe Asthma: Factors that influence hospital referral by the general practitioner and self referral by the patient.' *British Journal of Diseases of the Chest 77*, 51–59.

Ashby, J. and Lenhart, R. (1994) 'Prayer as a coping strategy for chronic pain patients.' *Rehabilitation Psychology 39, 3*, 205–208.

Ayer, A. (1982) *Philosophy in the Twentieth Century.* London: Weidenfeld and Nicholson.

Aylwin, S.M., Durand, M.A. and Wilson, K. (1985) 'Thinking symptoms and the common cold.' Paper presented to the Psychological Society of Ireland Annual Conference, Ennis, November.

Bailey, L.M. (1983) 'The Effects of Live Music Versus Tape-recorded Music on Hospitalised Cancer Patients.' *Music Therapy 3, 1*, 17–28.

Bailey, L.M. (1984) 'The Use of Songs with Cancer Patients and their Families.' *Music Therapy 4, 1*, 5–17.

Bailey, S. (1997) 'The Arts in Spiritual Care.' *Seminars on Oncology Nursing 13, 4*, 242–247.

Barlow, D.H. and Hersen, M. (1984) *Single Case Experimental Designs: Strategies for studying behaviour change.* New York: Pergamon Press.

Barrera, M., Rykov, M. and Doyle, S. (2002) 'The Effects of Interactive Music Therapy on Hospitalized Children with Cancer: A pilot study.' *Psycho-Oncology 11*, 379–388.

Bartlett, D., Kaufman, D. and Smeltekop, R. (1993) 'The Effects of Music Listening and Perceived Sensory Experiences on the Immune System as Measured by Interleukin-1 and Cortisol.' *Journal of Music Therapy 30, 4*, 194–209.

Bateson, G. (1973) *Steps to an Ecology of Mind.* Glasgow: Fontana.

Bateson, G. (1978) 'Afterword.' In J. Brockman (ed) *About Bateson.* London: Wildwood House.

Bateson, G. (1979) *Mind and Nature.* Glasgow: Fontana.

Bateson, M.C. (1972) *Our Own Metaphor.* New York: Alfred Knopf.

Bearon, L. and Koenig, H. (1990) 'Religious cognitions and use of prayer in health and illness.' *Gerontologist 30* (2), 249–253.

Bechler-Karsch, A. (1993) 'The Therapeutic Use of Music.' *Online Journal of Knowledge Synthesis for Nursing 1, 4*, U1–U21.

Beck, S. (1991) 'The Therapeutic Use of Music for Cancer-related Pain: A crossover study.' *Oncology Nursing Forum 18, 8*, 1327–1337.

Belcher, A., Dettmore, D. and Holzemer, S. (1989) 'Spirituality and sense of well-being in persons with AIDS.' *Holistic Nursing Practice 3, 4*, 16–25.

Bellamy, M. and Willard, P. (1993) 'Music Therapy: An Integral Component of the Oncology Experience.' *International Journal of Arts Medicine 2, 1*, 14–19.

Bemporad, J. (1996) 'Self-Starvation Through the Ages: Reflections on the pre-history of anorexia nervosa.' *International Journal of Eating Disorders 19, 3*, 217–237.

Benor, D. (1990) Survey of spiritual healing. *Complementary Medical Research 4, 3*, 9-33.

Benor, D. (1991) 'Spiritual Healing in Clinical Practice.' *Nursing Times 87, 44*, 35–37.

Benor, D. (1992) *Healing research. Volume 1.* München: Helix Editions.

Berger, D. and Nolte, D. (1977) 'Acupuncture in Bronchial Asthma: Bodyplethysmographic measurements of acute bronchospamolytic effects.' *Comparative Medicine East and West 5, 3/4*, 265–269.

Bergmark, K. (1998) 'The Links and Alcoholics Anonymous: Two "A.A" movements in Sweden.' In I. Eisenbach-Stagl and P. Rosenqvist (eds) *Diversity in unity: Studies of Alcoholics Anonymous in eight societies.* pp.75–89. Helsinki: Nordic Council for Alcohol and Drug Research.

Biddle, S. (1995) 'Exercise and Social Health.' *Research Quarterly for Exercise and Sport 66*, 292–297.

Black, H. (1999) 'Poverty and Prayer: Spiritual narratives of elderly African-American women.' *Review of Religious Research 40, 4*, 359–372.

Blumer, H. (1962) 'Society as Symbolic Interaction.' In A.M. Rose (ed) *Human Behaviour and Social Processes.* London: Routledge and Kegan Paul.

Bodner, G., Topilsky, M. and Greif, J. (1983) 'Pneumothorax as a Complication of Acupuncture in the Treatment of Bronchial Asthma.' *Annals of Allergy 51*, 401–403.

Bonadonna, G. and Valaguassa, P. (1992) 'Treating early breast cancer.' [Letter] *The Lancet 339*, 675.

Bond, J. and Corner, L. (2001) 'Researching dementia: Are there unique methodological challenges for health services resarch.' *Ageing and Society 21*, 95–116.

Bonny, H. and Pahnke, W. (1972) 'The Use of Music in Psychedelic (LSD) Psychotherapy.' *Journal of Music Therapy 9*, 2, 64–87.

Borman, P. and Dixon, D. (1998) 'Spirituality and the 12 steps of substance abuse recovery.' *Journal of Psychology and Theology 26*, 3, 287–291.

Bos, S. (1997) 'Coma stimulation.' *Online Journal of Knowledge Synthesis for Nursing 4*, 1, U3–U14.

Boulet, L.P., Turcotte, H. and Brochu, A. (1994) 'Persistence of Airway Obstruction and Hyperresponsiveness in Subjects with Asthma Remission.' *Chest 105*, 1024–1031.

Bourdieu, P. (1993) *The field of cultural production*. New York: Columbia University Press.

Boutell, K. and Bozett, F. (1990) 'Nurses' assessment of patients' spirituality: continuing education implications.' *Journal of Continuing Education in Nursing 21*, 4, 172–176.

Brandenburg, S. (1988) 'Getting Closer to Anna: Music Therapy with a Multiply-handicapped Child with Cancer.' *Musiktherapeutische Umschau 9*, 297–312.

Breckinridge Church, R. (1999) 'Using gesture and speech to capture transitions in learning.' *Cognitive Development 14*, 2, 313–342.

Brewster Smith, M. (1994) 'Selfhood at risk: post-modern perils and the perils of postmodernism.' American Psychologist 49, 405–411.

Brock, D. (1991) 'The Idea of Shared Decision Making between Physicians and Patients.' *Kennedy Institute of Ethics Journal 1*, 1, 28–47.

Brodsky, W. (1989) 'Music Therapy as an Intervention for Children with Cancer in Isolation Rooms.' First International Paediatric Oncology Nursing Meeting (1987, Jerusalem, Israel). *Music Therapy 8*, 1, 17–34.

Brookmeyer, R., Gray, S. and Kawas, C. (1998) 'Projections of Alzheimer's disease in the United States and the public health impact of delaying disease onset.' *American Journal of Public Health 88*, 9, 1337–1342.

Brotons, M. and Pickett-Cooper, P. (1996) 'The effects of music therapy intervention on agitation behaviors of Alzheimer's disease patients.' *Journal of Music Therapy 33*, 1, 2–18.

Brotons, M., Koger, S. and Pickett-Cooper, P. (1997) 'Music and dementias: A review of literature.' *Journal of Music Therapy 34*, 4, 204–245.

Brown, C. (1995) 'Is spiritual healing a valid and effective therapy?' *Journal of the Royal Society of Medicine 88*, 12, 722.

Brown, C. and Sheldon, M. (1989) 'Spiritual healing in general practice (letter).' *Journal of the Royal College of General Practitioners 39*, 328, 476–477.

Brown, G.W., Harris, T.O. and Peto, J. (1973) Life Events and Psychiatric Disorders. Part 2: Nature of the causal link. *Psychological Medicine 3*, 159–176.

Browner, C. (1998) 'Varieties of reasoning in medical anthropology.' *Medical Anthropology Quarterly 12*, 3, 356–362.

Bruscia, K. (1991) 'Embracing Life with AIDS: Psychotherapy through guided imagery and music.' In K. Bruscia (ed) *Case studies in Music Therapy*. Phoenixville, PA: Barcelona Publishers.

Bruscia, K. (1995) 'Images in AIDS.' In C. Lee (ed) *Lonely Waters*. Oxford: Sobell Publications.

Bunt, L., Burns, S. and Turton, P. (2000) 'Variations on a Theme: The evolution of a music therapy research programme at the Bristol Cancer Help Centre. *British Journal of Music Therapy 14*, 2, 62–69.

Burkhardt, M. (1989) 'Spirituality: an analysis of the concept.' *Holistic Nursing Practitioner 3*, 3, 69–77.

Burkhardt, R. and Kienle, G. (1980) 'Controlled Clinical Trials and Drug Regulations.' *Controlled Clinical Trials 1*, 151–164.

Burkhardt, R. and Kienle, G. (1983) 'Basic Problems in Controlled Trials.' *Journal of Medical Ethics 9*, 80–84.

Burns, D. (2001) 'The Effect of the Bonny Method of Guided Imagery and Music on the Mood and Life Quality of Cancer Patients. *Journal of Music Therapy 38*, 1, 51–65.

Burns, S., Harbuz, M., Hucklebridge, F. and Bunt, L. (2000) 'A Pilot Study into the Therapeutic Effects of Music Therapy with Cancer Patients.' *Psycho-Oncology 9*, 5, 177.

Burns, S., Harbuz, M., Hucklebridge, F. and Bunt, L. (2001) 'A Pilot Study into the Therapeutic Effects of Music Therapy at a Cancer Help Center.' *Alternative Therapies in Health and Medicine 7*, 1, 48–56.

Buxton, M., Smith, D. and Seymour, R. (1987) 'Spirituality and other points of resistance to the 12-step recovery process.' *Journal of Psychoactive Drugs 19*, 3, 275–286.

Byrd, R. (1988) 'Positive therapeutic effects of intercessory prayer in a coronary care unit population.' *Southern Medical Journal 81*, 7, 826–829.

Cai, G., Qiao, Y., Li, P., Jiao, L. and Lu, L. (2001) 'Music Therapy in Treatment of Cancer Patients.' *Chinese Mental Health Journal 15*, 3, 179–181.

Camp, P. (1996) 'Having Faith: Experiencing coronary artery bypass grafting.' *Journal of Cardiovascular Nursing 10*, 3, 55–64.

Camprubi Duocastella, A. (1999) 'Effect of Music on Children with Cancer.' *Revista De Enfermeria 22*, 4, 293–298.

Carney, D. (1992) 'Biology of Small-Cell Lung Cancer.' *The Lancet 339*, 843–846.

Carney, S. and Mitchell, K. (1987) 'An Evaluation of Student Satisfaction with Professional Skills Teaching in an Integrated Medical School.' *Medical Teacher 9*, 2, 179–182.

Carroll, S. (1993) 'Spirituality and purpose in life in alcoholism recovery.' *Journal of Studies on Alcohol 54*, 3, 297–301.

Carson, V. and Green, H. (1992) 'Spiritual well-being: a predictor of hardiness in patients with acquired immunodeficiency syndrome.' *Journal of Professional Nursing 8*, 4, 209–220.

Cassell, E. (1991) *The Nature of Suffering and the Goals of Medicine.* New York: Oxford University Press.

Chandler, C., Holden, J. and Kolander, C. (1992) 'Counseling for spiritual wellness: theory and practice.' *Journal of Counseling and Development 71*, 168–175.

Chang, B., Noonan, A. and Tennstedt, S. (1998) 'The role of religion/spirituality in coping with caregiving for disabled elders.' *Gerontologist 38*, 4, 463–470.

Charmaz, K. (1995) 'The Body, Identity, and Self: Adapting to impairment.' *The Sociological Quarterly 36*, 657–680.

Chatters, L. and Taylor, R. (1989) 'Age differences in religious participation among black adults.' *Journal of Gerontology 44(5)*, S183–189.

Christensen, P.A., Laurensen, L.C., Taudorf, E., Sorensen, S.C. and Weeke, B. (1984) 'Acupuncture and Bronchial Asthma.' *Allergy 39*, 5, 379–385.

Cioffi, D. (1996) 'Making Public the Private: Possible effects of expressing somatic experience.' *Psychology and Health 11*, 203–222.

Cioppa, F.J. (1976) 'Clinical Evaluation of Acupuncture in 129 Patients.' *Diseases of the Nervous System 37*, 11, 639–643.

Clark, A. and Fallowfield, L. (1986) 'Quality of Life Measurements in Patients with Malignant Disease: A review.' *Journal of the Royal Society of Medicine 79*, 165–169.

Clark, J. and Dawson, L. (1996) 'Personal religiousness and ethical judgements: An empirical analysis.' *Journal of Business Ethics 15*, 3, 359–372.

Classen, D., Scott Evans, R., Pestonik, S., Horn, S., Menlove, R. and Burke, J. (1992) 'The Timing of Prophylactic Administration of Antibiotics and the Risk of Surgical Wound Infection.' *The New England Journal of Medicine 326*, 281–286.

Cohen-Mansfield, J. (2000) 'Use of patient characteristics to determine non-pharmacologic interventions for behavioral and psychological symptoms of dementia.' *International Psychogeriatrics 12*, Suppl 1, 373–380.

Coles, C.R. (1987) 'The Actual Effects of Examinations on Medical Student Learning.' *Assessment and Evaluation in Higher Education 12*, 3, 209–219.

Coles, C.R. (1990) 'Elaborated Learning in Undergraduate Medical Education.' *Medical Education 24*, 14–22.

Collipp, P. (1969) 'The efficacy of prayer: a triple blind study.' *Medical Times 97*, 201–204.

Conrad, N. (1985) 'Spiritual support for the dying.' *Nursing Clinics of North America 20*, 2, 415–426.

Cook, J. (1986) 'Music as an Intervention in the Oncology Setting.' *Cancer Nursing 9*, 1, 23–28.

Cooke, M. (1992) 'Supporting health care workers in the treatment of HIV-infected patients.' *Primary Care 19*, 1, 245–256.

Coyle, N. (1987) 'A Model of Continuity of Care for Cancer Patients with Chronic Pain.' *Medical Clinics of North America 71*, 2, 259–270.

Crane, J., Pearce, N., Beasley, R. and Burgess, C. (1992) 'Worldwide Worsening Wheezing – Is the cure the cause?' [Letter] *The Lancet 339*, 814.

Crossley, M. (2000) 'Narrative psychology, trauma and the study of self/identity.' *Theory and Psychology* *10,* 4, 527–546.

Crossley, N. (1995) 'Body Techniques, Agency and Intercorporeality: On Goffman's relations in public.' *Sociology 29,* 133–149.

Cunningham, M., Monson, B. and Bookbinder, M. (1997) 'Introducing a Music Program in the Perioperative Area.' *AORN Journal 66,* 4, 674, 676–682.

Cupitt, D. (1997) *After God. The future of religion.* New York: Basic Books.

Cushman, D. and Whiting, G. (1972) 'An Approach to Communication Theory: Towards consensus on rules.' *The Journal of Communication 22,* 217–238.

Cvitkovic, E. (1992) *New Anticancer Agents in Current Clinical Development.* Athens.

Dalai Lama (1999) *The Path of Tranquillity.* New York: Viking.

Daveson, B. and Kennelly, J. (2000) 'Music Therapy in Palliative Care for Hospitalized Children and Adolescents.' *Journal of Palliative Care 16,* 1, 35–38.

Deaton, A., Metzger, S. and Wheeler, A. (1995) 'Agitation in pediatric brain injury: A useful communication or a hurdle to overcome?' *Neurorehabilitation 5,* 4, 317–321.

Decker, L. (1993) 'The role of trauma in spiritual development.' *Journal of Humanistic Psychology 33,* 4, 33–46.

Declaration of Helsinki (1975) *Recommendations Guiding Doctors in Biomedical Research.* Tokyo, Japan:

De Marchais, J. (1990) 'Involvement of Teachers as Problem-based Learning Tutors in the New Sherbrooke Programme.' *Annals of Community-Oriented Education 3,* 1, 35–54.

de Vries, K. (2001) 'Enhancing Creativity to Improve Palliative Care: The role of an experiental self-care workshop.' *International Journal of Palliative Nursing 7,* 10, 505–511.

DeVito, A.J. (1990) 'Dyspnea During Hospitalizations for Acute Phase of Illness as Recalled by Patients with Chronic Obstructive Pulmonary Disease.' *Heart Lung 19,* 2, 186–191.

Dias, P.L., Subraniam, S. and Lionel, N.D. (1982) 'Effects of Acupuncture in Bronchial Asthma; A Preliminary Communication.' *Royal Society of Medicine 75,* 245–248.

Dickinson, R. (1995) 'Two Cultures – One Voice? Problems in broadcaster/health educator co-operation.' *Health Education Research 10,* 421–430.

Dixon, M. (1998) 'Does 'healing' benefit patients with chronic symptoms? A quasi-randomized trial in general practice.' *Journal of the Royal Society of Medicine 91,* 183–188.

Dohrenwend, B.S. and Dohrenwend, B.P. (1974) *Stressful Life Events: Their Nature and Effects.* New York: John Wiley and Sons.

Donnelly, W.J., Spyykerboer, J.E. and Thong, Y.H. (1985) 'Are Patients Who Use Alternative Medicine Dissatisfied with Orthodox Medicine?' *Medical Journal of Australia 142,* 10, 539–541.

DoRozario, L. (1997) 'Spirituality in the Lives of People with Disability and Chronic Illness: A creative paradigm of wholeness and reconstitution.' *Disability Rehabilitation 19,* 10, 427–434.

Dossey, B. (1999) 'Barbara Dossey on holistic nursing, Florence Nightingale, and healing rituals.' *Alternative Therapies 5,* 1, 79–86.

Dossey, L. (1993) *Healing words: The power of prayer and the practice of medicine.* New York: Harper Collins.

Doyle, D. (1992) 'Have we looked beyond the physical and psychosocial?' *Journal of Pain Symptom Management 7,* 5, 302–311.

Dreyfus, H. (1987) 'Foucault's Critique of Psychiatric Medicine.' *The Journal of Medicine and Philosophy 12,* 311–333.

Duckro, P. and Magaletta, P. (1994) 'The effect of prayer on physical health: Experimental evidence.' *Journal of Religion and Health 33,* 3, 211–219.

Dudley, H.A.F. (1983) 'The Controlled Clinical Trial and the Advance of Reliable Knowledge: An outsider looks in.' *British Medical Journal 287,* 957–996.

Dun, B. (1999) 'Creativity and Communication Aspects of Music Therapy in a Children's Hospital.' In D. Aldridge (ed) Music *Therapy in Palliative Care.* London: Jessica Kingsley Publishers.

Duocastella, A. (1999) 'The Effects of Music on Children with Neoplasia.' *Revista Rol de Enfermeria 22,* 4, 293–295, 297–298.

Editorial (1983) 'Ethics, Philosophy and Clinical Trials.' *Journal of Medical Ethics 9,* 59–60.

Eisenbach-Stagl, I. (1998) 'How to live a sober life in a wet society: Alcoholics Anonymous in Austria.' In I. Eisenbach-Stagl and P. Rosenqvist (eds) *Diversity in unity. Studies of Alcoholics Anonymous in eight societies.* pp.131–147. Helsinki: Nordic Council for Alcohol and Drug Research.

Emke, I. (1996) 'Methodology and Methodolatry: Creativity and the impoverishment of the imagination in sociology.' *Canadian Journal of Sociology 21*, 1, 77–90.

Engel, A. and Singer, W. (2001) 'Temporal binding and the neural correlates of sensory awareness.' *Trends in Cognitive Sciences 5*, 1, 16–25.

Engel, G. (1977) 'The Need for a New Medical Model: A challenge for biomedicine.' *Science 196*, 129–136.

Erber, R. and Erber, M. (2000) 'Mysteries of mood regulation, Part II: The case of the happy thermostat.' *Psychological Inquiry 11*, 3, 210–213.

Evans, R., Barer, M. and Marmor, T. (1994) *Why are Some People Healthy and Others Not?* New York: Aldine de Gruyter.

Fagen, T.S. (1982) 'Music Therapy in the Treatment of Anxiety and Fear in Terminal Pediatric Patients.' *Music Therapy 2*, 1, 13–23.

Farquhar, J. (1994) 'Eating Chinese Medicine.' *Cultural Anthropology 9*, 471–497.

Ferrell, B., Grant, M., Funk, B., OtisGreen, S. and Garcia, N. (1998) 'Quality of life in breast cancer Part II: Psychological and spiritual well-being.' *Cancer Nursing 21*, 1, 1–9.

Ferrell, B., Rhiner, M. and Rivera, L. (1993) 'Empowering patients to Control Pain.' *Current Issues in Cancer Nursing Practice Updates 2*, 4, 1–9.

Finlay-Jones, R. and Brown, G.W. (1981) 'Types of Stressful Life Events and the Onset of Anxiety and Depressive Disorders.' *Psychological Medicine 11*, 803–815.

Fischer, S. and Johnson, P. (1999) 'Therapeutic Touch: A viable link in midwifery.' *Journal of Nurse-Midwifery 44*, 3, 300–309.

Fitzgerald, C., Eelstein, M. and Mansel, R. (1992) 'Treating Early Breast Cancer.' [Letter] *The Lancet 339*, 676.

Flaskerud, J. and Rush, C. (1989) 'AIDS and traditional health beliefs and practices of black women.' *Nursing Research 38*, 4, 210–215.

Foley, K. (1986) 'The Treatment of Pain in the Patient with Cancer.' *Ca: A Cancer Journal for Clinicians 36*, 4, 194–215.

Foley, L., Wagner, J. and Waskel, S. (1998) 'Spirituality in the lives of older women. *Journal of Women & Aging' 10*, 2, 85–91.

Foucault, M. (1989) *The Birth of the Clinic: An Archaeology of Medical Perception.* London: Routledge.

Foxglove, T. (1999) 'Music Therapy for People with Life-Limiting Illness.' *Nursing Times 95*, 18, 52–54.

Frager, G. (1997) 'Palliative Care and Terminal Care of Children.' *Child and Adolescent Psychiatric Clinics of North America 6*, 4, 889.

Frank, J. (1985) 'The Effects of Music Therapy and Guided Visual Imagery on Chemotherapy Induced Nausea and Vomiting.' *Oncology Nursing Forum 12*, 5, 47–52.

Fransella, F. and Frost, K. (1977) *On Being a Woman: A review of research on how women see themselves.* London: Tavistock.

Freeling, P. (1985) 'Health Outcomes in Primary Care: An approach to problems.' *Family Practice 2*, 177–181.

Frego, R. (1995) 'Music Movement Therapy for People with AIDS: The use of music movement therapy as a form of palliative care for people with AIDS.' *International Journal of Arts Medicine 4*, 2, 21–25.

Freireich, E. (1981) 'Informed Consent Versus Randomization. In S. Salmon and S. Jones (eds) *Adjuvant Therapy III.* New York: Grune and Stratton.

Freireich, E. (1990) 'Is there any Mileage Left in the Randomized Clinical Trial?' *Cancer Investigation 8*, 231–232.

Froehlich, M. A. (1996) 'Music Therapy with the Terminally Ill Child. In M. A. Froehlich (ed) *Music Therapy with Hospitalized Children.* Cherry Hill, NJ: Jeffrey Books.

Fuller, J.A. (1974) 'Acupuncture.' *Medical Journal of Australia 2*, 9, 340–341.

Furnham, A. (1994) 'Explaining Health and Illness: Lay perceptions on current and future health, the causes of illness and the nature of recovery.' *Social Science and Medicine 39*, 715–725.

Furnham, A. and Boughton, J. (1995) 'Eating Behaviour and Body Dissatisfaction Among Dieters, Aerobic Exercisers and a Control Group.' *European Eating Disorders Review 3*, 35–45.

Furnham, A., Titman, P. and Sleeman, E. (1994) 'Perception of Female Body Shapes as a Function of Exercise.' *Journal of Social Behavior and Personality 9*, 335–352.

Gallagher, L. and Steele, A. (2001) 'Developing and Using a Computerized Database for Music Therapy in Palliative Medicine.' *Journal of Palliative Care 17*, 3, 147–154.

Gallagher, L., Houston, M., Abdullah, O. and Walsh, D. (1998) 'Music Therapy with Cancer Patients and their Families.' *Journal of Palliative Care 14*, 3, 129–131.

Gallagher, L.M., Huston, M.J., Nelson, K.A., Walsh, D. and Steele, A.L. (2001) 'Music Therapy in Palliative Medicine.' *Supportive Care in Cancer 9*, 3, 156–161.

Ganz, P. (1992) 'Treatment Options for Breast Cancer – beyond survival.' *The New England Journal of Medicine 326*, 1147–1149.

Ganzevoort, R. (1998) 'Religious coping considered, part one: An integrated approach.' *Journal of Psychology and Theology 26*, 3, 260–275.

Garrett, C. (1997) Recovery from Anorexia Nervosa: A sociological perspective. *International Journal of Eating Disorders 21*, 3, 261–272.

Garrett, G. (1991) 'A natural way to go? Death and bereavement in old age.' *Professional Nurse 6*, 12, 744–746.

Geertz, C. (1957) Ritual and social change. American Anthropologist 59, 32–54.

Gergen, K. (1991) *The Saturated Self: Dilemmas of Identity in Contemporary Life*. New York: Basic Books.

Gervasio, A. and Kreutzer, J. (1997) 'Kinship and family members' psychological distress after traumatic brain injury: A large sample study.' *Journal of Head Trauma Rehabilitation 12*, 3, 14–26.

Gillon, R. (1986) 'On Sickness and Health.' *British Medical Journal 292*, 318–320.

Glaser, B. and Strauss, A. (1967) *The Discovery of Grounded Theory: Strategies for Qualitative Research*. Chicago: Aldine Pub. Co.

Gold, J. (1986) 'Quality of Life Measurements in Patients with Malignant Disease.' *Journal of the Royal Society of Medicine 79*, 622.

Gold, R. (1995) 'Why we Need to Rethink AIDS Education for Gay Men.' *AIDS Care 7*, S11–19.

Goldin-Meadow, S. (1997) 'When gestures and words speak differently.' *Current Directions in Psychological Science 5*, 138–143.

Goldin-Meadow, S. (1999) 'The role of gesture in communication and thinking.' *Trends in Cognitive Sciences 3*, 11, 419–429.

Goldin-Meadow, S. (2000) 'Beyond words: The importance of gesture to researchers and learners.' *Child Development 71*, 1, 231–239.

Goodare, H. (1992) 'Adjuvant Treatment in Breast Cancer.' [Letter] *The Lancet 339*, 424.

Gordon, K. (1986) 'The Multi-state Kalman Filter in Medical Monitoring.' *Computing Methods and Programs in Biomedicine 23*, 147–154.

Gorham, M. (1989) 'Spirituality and problem solving with seniors.' *Perspectives. 13*, 3, 13–16.

Grasser, C. and Craft, B. (1984) 'The patient's approach to wellness.' *Nursing Clinics of North America 19*, 2, 207–218.

Green, L., Fullilove, M. and Fullilove, R. (1998) 'Stories of spiritual awakening - The nature of spirituality in recovery.' *Journal of Substance Abuse Treatment 15*, 4, 325–331.

Gregg, I. (1985) 'The Quality of Asthma in General Practice – A challenge for the future.' *Family Practice 2*, 94–100.

Greisinger, A., Lorimor, R., Aday, L., Winn, R. and Baile, W. (1997) 'Terminally ill cancer patients. Their most important concerns.' *Cancer Practice 5*, 3, 147–154.

Griessmeier, B. (1990) 'Is it me or isn't it?' *Musiktherapeutische Umschau 11*, 37–56.

Griessmeier, B. (1995) 'Music Therapy on a Children's Cancer Ward.' *European Journal of Cancer 31A*, 1341.

Griessmeier, B. (2001) 'Between Heaven and Hell – Children's Emotional Perception of Stemcell Transplantation.' *Klinische Padiatrie 213*, 4, 255–257.

Griessmeier, B. and Bossinger, W. (1994) *Musiktherapie mit Krebskranken Kindern*. Stuttgart: Gustav Fischer Verlag.

Griffith, E. (1983) 'The Significance of Ritual in a Church-based Healing Model.' *American Journal of Psychiatry 140*, 5, 568–572.

Grof, S. (1985) 'Modern Consciousness Research and Human Survival.' Ninth Conference of the International Transpersonal Association (1985, Kyoto, Japan). ReVISION 8, 1, 27–39.

Grohmann, W. (1987) *Klee*. London: Thames and Hudson.

Group, E.B.C.T.C. (1992) 'Systemic Treatment of Early Breast Cancer by Hormonal, Cytotoxic, or Immune Therapy.' *The Lancet 339*, 1–15, 71–85.

Gu, E. (1996) 'The Irrationalistic View of Aesthetic Freedom and the Philosophical Sources of Social Discontent of Liu Xiaobo.' *Issues in Study, 1*, 89–119.

Gurevitch, Z. (2000) 'Plurality in dialogue: a comment on Bakhtin.' *Sociology 34, 2*, 243–263.

Gurevitch, Z. (2001) 'Dialectical dialogue. the struggle for speech, repressive silence, and the shift to multiplicity.' *British Journal of Sociology 52, 1*, 87–104.

Guillemin, R., Vargo, T. and Rossier, J. (1977) 'Beta Endorphin and Adrenicorticotrophin are Secreted Concomitantly by the Pituitary Gland.' *Science 197*, 1367.

Gutierrez, A., Lemoine, N. and Sikora, K. (1992) 'Gene therapy for cancer.' *The Lancet 339*, 715–721.

Gutterman, L. (1990) 'A day treatment program for persons with AIDS'. *American Journal of Occupational Therapy 44, 3*, 234–237.

Guyatt, G., Satchett, D., Taylor, D., Chong, J., Roberts, R. and Pugsley, S. (1986) 'Determining Optimal Therapy Randomized Trials in Individual Patients.' *New England Journal of Medicine 314*, 889–892.

Haley, J. (1980) *Leaving Home.* New York: McGraw Hill.

Hall, B. (1998) 'Patterns of Spirituality in Persons with Advanced HIV Disease.' *Research in Nursing and Health 21, 2*, 143–153.

Hamilton, M., Waddington, P., Gregory, S. and Walker, A. (1995) 'Eat, Drink and Be Saved: The spiritual significance of alternative diets.' *Social Compass 42*, 497–511.

Hansen, H. (1992) 'Management of Small-cell Cancer of the Lung.' *The Lancet 339*, 846–849.

Hanser, S. (1985) 'Music Therapy and Stress Reduction Research.' *Journal of Music Therapy 22, 4*, 193–206.

Harcourt, L. (1988) 'Music for Health.' *New Zealand Nursing Journal 81, 1*, 24–26.

Harré, R. and Secord, P. (1971) *The Explanation of Social Behaviour.* London: Basil Blackwell.

Harré, R. and Secord, P. (1973) *The Explanation of Social Behaviour.* Totowa, New Jersey: Littlefield and Adams.

Harrington, V., Lackey, N. and Gates, M. (1996) 'Needs of caregivers of clinic and hospice cancer patients.' *Cancer Nursing 19, 2*, 118–125.

Hart, J. (1984) 'Where is General Practice Going?' *New Doctor 33*, 8–10.

Hartley, N. (1999) 'Music Therapist's Personal Reflections on Working with those who are Living with HIV/AIDS.' In D. Aldridge (ed) *Music Therapy in Palliative Care: New Voices.* London: Jessica Kingsley Publishers.

Hartley, N. (2001) 'On a Personal Note: A music therapist's reflections on working with those who are living with a terminal illness.' *Journal of Palliative Care 17, 3*, 135–141.

Hartley, P. (1996) 'Does Health Education Promote Eating Disorders?' *European Eating Disorders Review 4, 1*, 3–11.

Hayhoe, S. (1982) 'Effects of Acupuncture in Bronchial Asthma.' [Letter] *Journal of the Royal Society of Medicine 75*, 11, 917.

Heath, P. (2000) 'The PK Zone: A phenomenological study.' *The Journal of Parapsychology 64*, 53–72.

Helman, C. (1986) 'The Consultation in Context.' *Holistic Medicine 1*, 37–41.

Hendrie, H. (1998) 'Epidemiology of dementia and Alzheimer's disease.' *American Journal of Geriatric Psychiatry 6, 2*, S3–S18.

Heron, J. (1984) 'Critique of Conventional Research Methodology.' *Complementary Medicinal Research 1*, 12–22.

Heyde, W. and von Langsdorff, S. (1983) 'Rehabilitation of Cancer Patients including Creative Therapies.' *Rehabilitation 22, 1*, 25–27.

Higgins, B.G., Britton, J.R., Chinn, S., Cooper, S., Burney, P.G.J. and Tattersfield, A.E. (1992) 'Comparison of Bronchial Reactivity and Peak Expiratory Flow Variability Measurements for Epidemiologic Studies.' *American Review of Respiratory Diseases, 145*, 588–593.

Higginson, I., Hearn, J., Myers, K. and Naysmith, A. (2000) 'Palliative Day Care: What do services do?' *Palliative Medicine 14, 4*, 277–286.

Highfield, M. (1992) 'Spiritual health of oncology patients: Nurse and patient perspectives.' *Cancer Nursing 15, 1*, 1–8.

Hileman, J., Lackey, N. and Hassanein, R. (1992) 'Identifying the needs of home caregivers of patients with cancer.' *Oncololigal Nurse Forum 19, 5*, 771–777.

Hilliard, R. (2001) 'The Use of Music Therapy in Meeting the Multidimensional Needs of Hospice Patients and Families.' *Journal of Palliative Care 17*, 3, 161–166.

Hirsch, S. and Meckes, D. (2000) 'Treatment of the Whole Person: Incorporating emergent perspectives in collaborative medicine, empowerment, and music therapy.' *Journal of Psychosocial Oncology 18*, 2, 65–77.

Hoffman, L. (1981) *Foundations of Family Therapy: A Conceptual Framework of Systems Change.* New York: Basic Books.

Hoffmann, P. (1998) 'Musik ist ein Gespräch von Seele zu Seele': Musiktherapie mit Schwerkranken und Sterbenden.' In D. Aldridge (ed) *Kairos II: Beiträge zur Musiktherapie in der Medizin.* Bern: Hans Huber.

Hogan, B. (1999) 'Music Therapy at the End of Life: Searching for the rite of passage.' In D. Aldridge (ed) *Music Therapy in Palliative Care: New voices.* London: Jessica Kingsley Publishers.

Holt, J., Houg, B. and Romano, J. (1999) 'Spiritual wellness for clients with HIV/AIDS: Review of counselling issues.' *Journal of Counselling and Development 77*, Spring, 160–170.

Hossri, C. (1976) 'The Treatment of Asthma in Children through Acupuncture Massage.' *Journal of the American Society of Psychosomatic and Dental Medicine 23*, 1, 3–16.

Howie, J. (1984) 'Research in General Practice: Pursuit of knowledge or defence of wisdom.' *British Medical Journal 289*, 1770–1772.

Hsu, L. (2000) 'Spirit (Shen), Styles of Knowing, and Authority in Contemporary Chinese Medicine.' *Culture, Medicine and Psychiatry 24*, 197–229.

Idler, E. (1995) 'Religion, health and the nonphysical senses of self.' *Social Forces 74*, 22, 683–704.

Jackson, D. (1965) 'Family Rules: Marital Quid Pro Quo.' *Archives of General Psychiatry 12*, 589–594.

Jackson, M. (1996) 'Music Therapy for Living: A case study on a woman with terminal breast cancer.' *Journal of Palliative Care 12*, 3, 69.

Jacobs, S. (1989) 'A Philosophy of Energy.' *Holistic Medicine 4*, 95–111.

Jacobsen, A. (1993) 'Non-Pharmacological Methods in Patients with Gynecological Cancer: Pain, anxiety, uneasiness, physical tension, nausea and vomiting.' *Journal of Cancer Care 2*, 2, 104–106.

Jenkins, R.A. (1995) 'Religion and HIV: Implications for research and intervention.' *Journal of Social Issues 51*, 2, 131–144.

Jiao, G. (1995) *Die 15 Ausdrucksformen des Taiji-Qigong.* Uelzen: Medizinisch Literarische Verlagsgesellschaft.

Jochims, S. (1981) 'Music Therapy in Cancer Aftercare.' *Musiktherapeutische Umschau 2*, 127–133.

Johnson, M. (1998) 'Being Mentally Ill: A phenomenological inquiry.' *Archives of Psychiatric Nursing 12*, 4, 195–201.

Johnson, N., Boyle, C. and Heller, R. (1995) 'Leisure-time Physical Activity and Other Health Behaviours: Are they needed?' *Australian Journal of Public Health 19*, 69–75.

Johnston, K. and Rohaly-Davis, J. (1996) 'An Introduction to Music Therapy: Helping the Oncology Patient in the ICU.' *Critical Care Nursing Quarterly 18*, 4, 54–60.

Jones, R., Hux, K., Morton-Anderson, K. and Knepper, L. (1994)' Auditory stimulation effect on a comatose survivor of traumatic brain injury.' *Archives of Physical Medicine and Rehabilitation 75*, 2, 164–171.

Joseph, M. (1998) 'The effect of strong religious beliefs on coping with stress.' *Stress Medicine 14*, 219–224.

Joslin, C. (1992) 'The Patient's View of Breast Cancer Trials.' [letter] *The Lancet 339*, 314.

Joyce, C. and Welldon, R. (1965) 'The efficacy of prayer: a double-blind clinical trial.' *Journal of Chronic Diseases 18*, 367–377.

Jung, C.G. (1959) *The Archetypes and the Collective Unconscious.* London: Routledge and Kegan Paul.

Jung, C.G. (1961) *Modern Man in Search of a Soul.* London: Routledge and Kegan Paul.

Kaczorowski, J. (1989) 'Spiritual well-being and anxiety in adults diagnosed with cancer.' *Hospital Journal 5*, 3-4, 105–116.

Kaplan, H. (1992) 'Adjuvant Treatment in Breast Cancer.' [Letter] *The Lancet 339*, 424.

Kaplan, M., Marks, G. and Mertens, S. (1997) 'Distress and coping among women with HIV infection: Preliminary findings from a multiethnic sample.' *American Journal of Orthopsychiatry 67*, 1, 80–91.

Karambadzakis, D. and Muthesius, D. (1997) 'Bewältigung lebensbedrohlicher Krankheiten am Beispiel einer ambulanten Musiktherapie mit einer Krebspatientin.' *Musictherapeutische Umschau, 4*, 297–307.

Keijzer, F. (1998) 'Doing without representations which specify what to do.' *Philosophical Psychology 11*, 3, 269–302.

Kelly, M. and Field, D. (1996) 'Medical Sociology, Chronic Illness and the Body.' *Sociology of Health and Illness 18*, 241–257.

Kendler, K.S., Gardner, C.O. and Prescott, C.A. (1997) 'Religion, psychopathology, and substance use and abuse: A multimeasure, genetic-epidemiologic study.' *American Journal of Psychiatry 154, 3*, 322–329.

Kerkvliet, G. (1990) 'Music Therapy may Help Control Cancer Pain.' *Journal of the National Cancer Institute 82*, 5, 350–352.

Khan, I. (1974) *The Development of Spiritual Healing*. Claremont, CA: Hunter House.

Khan, I. (1979) *The bowl of Saki*. Geneva: Sufi Publishing Co. Ltd.

Khan, I. (1991) *Sufi Teachings: The Art of Being*. Shaftesbury: Element Books.

Khushf, G. (1996) 'Post-modern Reflections on the Ethics of Naming.' In J.L. Peset and D. Gracia (eds) *The Ethics of Diagnosis*. New York: Kluwe.

King, D., Sobal, J., Haggerty, J., Dent, M. and Patton, D. (1992) 'Experiences and attitudes about faith healing among family physicians.' *Journal of Family Practice 35*, 2, 158–162.

King, M. and Dein, S. (1998) 'The spiritual variable in psychiatric research.' *Psychological Medicine 28*, 1259–1262.

King, M., Speck, P. and Thomas, A. (1999) 'The effect of spiritual outcome from illness.' *Social Science and Medicine 48*, 1291–1299.

King, M.B. (1997) 'Psychiatry and religion, context, consensus and controversies, by D. Bhugra.' *British Journal of Psychiatry 170*, 93–94.

Kirkwood, W. and Brown, D. (1995) 'Public Communication about the Causes of Disease: The Rhetoric of Responsibility.' *Journal of Communication 45*, 55–76.

Kirmayer, L. (1994) 'Symptom Attribution in Cultural Perspective.' *Canadian Journal of Psychiatry 39*, 584–595.

Kleinman, A. (1973) 'Medicine's Symbolic Reality. On a central problem in the philosophy of medicine.' *Inquiry 16*, 206–213.

Kleinman, A. and Sung, L.H. (1979) 'Why do Indigenous Practitioners Successfully Heal?' *Social Science and Medicine 13*, 7–26.

Knight, W. and Rickard, N. (2001) 'Relaxing Music Prevents Stress-induced Increases in Subjective Anxiety, Systolic Blood Pressure and Heart Rate in Healthy Males and Females.' *Journal of Music Therapy 38*, 4, 254–272.

Koenig, H., Bearon, L. and Dayringer, R. (1989) 'Physician perspectives on the role of religion in the physician,older patient relationship.' *Journal of Family Practice 28*, 4, 441–448.

Koenig, H., Hays, J., George, L., Blazer, D., Larson, D. and Landerman, L. (1997) 'Modeling the cross-sectional relationships between religion, physical health, social support, and depressive symptoms.' *American Journal of Geriatric Psychiatry 5*, 2, 131–144.

Kotarba, J. and Hurt, D. (1995) 'An Ethnography of an AIDS Hospice: Toward a theory of organizational pastiche.' *Symbolic Interaction 18*, 4, 413–438.

Kreitman, N., Smith, P. and Eng-Seong, T. (1969) 'Attempted Suicide in Social Networks.' *British Journal of Preventive Social Medicine 23*, 116–123.

Kremer, J. and Starkstein, S. (2000) 'Affective disorders in Parkinson's disease.' *International Review of Psychiatry 12*.

Kuhn, C. (1988) 'A spiritual inventory of the medically ill patient.' *Psychiatric Medicine 6*, 2, 87–100.

Kurland, D. (1976) 'Treatment of Headache Pain with Auto-acupressure.' *Diseases of the Nervous System 37*, 3, 127–129.

Labun, E. (1988) 'Spiritual care: an element in nursing care planning.' *Journal of Advanced Nursing 13*, 3, 314–320.

Lane, D. (1994) 'Effects of Music Therapy on Immune Function of Hospitalized Patients.' *Quality of Life – A Nursing Challenge 3*, 74–80.

Lapierre, L. (1994) 'A model for describing spirituality.' *Journal of Religion and Health 33*, 2, 153–161.

Larner, G. (1998) 'Through a Glass Darkly.' *Theory and Psychology 8*, 4, 549–572.

Larsen, R. (2000) 'Towards a science of mood regulation.' *Psychological Inquiry 11*, 3, 129–141.

Lawton, J. (1998) 'Contemporary Hospice Care: The sequestration of the unbounded body and "dirty dying".' *Sociology of Health and Illness 20*, 2, 121–143.

Le Shan, L. (1991) 'Can Randomized Studies of Psychosocial Interventions for Cancer Harm the Control Groups?' *Advances 8*, 80–87.

Leach, E. (1957) *Culture and Communication: The Logic by which Symbols are Connected.* London: Cambridge University Press.

Lee, C. (1995) *Lonely Waters.* Oxford: Sobell House.

Leskowitz, E. (1992) 'Life Energy and Western Medicine: A reappraisal.' *Advances 8,* 1, 63–67.

Lesser, J., Anderson, N. and Koniak-Griffin, D. (1998) '"Sometimes you don't feel ready to be an adult or a mom": The experience of adolescent pregnancy.' *Journal of Child and Adolescent Psychiatric Nursing 11,* 1, 7–16.

Lewinsohn, R. (1998) 'Medical Theories, Science, and the Practice of Medicine.' *Social Science and Medicine 46,* 10, 1261–1270.

Lewis, J. (1995) 'Genre and Embodiment: From Brazilian Capoeira to the ethnology of human movement.' *Cultural Anthropology 10,* 221–243.

Lewis, M., Curtis, M. and Lundy, K. (1995) '"He Calls Me his Angel of Mercy": The experience of caring for elderly parents in the home.' *Holistic Nursing Practice 9,* 4, 54–65.

Lewith, G. and Machin, D. (1983) 'On the Evaluation of the Clinical Effects of Acupuncture.' *Pain 16,* 111–127.

Little, M., Jordens, C., Paul, K., Montgomery, K. and Philipson, B. (1998) 'Liminality: A major category of the experience of cancer illness.' *Social Science and Medicine 47,* 10, 1485–1494.

Loewy, J. (1997) *Music Therapy and Paediatric Pain.* Cherry Hill, NJ: Jeffrey Books.

Long, A. (1997) 'Nursing: A spiritual perspective.' *Nursing Ethics 4,* 6, 496–510.

Louis, T., Lavori, P., Bailar, J. and Polansky, M. (1984) 'Cross-over and Self-controlled Trials in Clinical Research.' *New England Journal of Medicine 310,* 24–31.

Love, R., Mazess, R., Barden, H., Epstein, S., Newcomb, P., Jordan, C., Carbone, P. and DeMets, D. (1992) 'Effects of Tamoxifen on Bone Mineral Density in Postmenopausal Women with Breast Cancer.' *The New England Journal of Medicine 326,* 852–856.

Lowis, M.J. and Hughes, J. (1997) 'A comparison of the effects of sacred and secular music on elderly people.' *Journal of Psychology 131,* 1, 45–55.

Lukoff, D., Lu, F. and Turner, R. (1995) 'Cultural considerations in the assessment and treatme nt of religious and spiritual problems.' *Psychiatric Clinics of North America 18,* 3, 467–485.

Lukoff, D., Provenzano, R., Lu, F and Turner, R. (1999) 'Religious and spiritual case reports on medline: A systematic analysis of records from 1980 to 1996.' *Alternative Therapies 5,* 1, 64–70.

Lynch, P. (1995) 'Adolescent Smoking – An alternative perspective using personal construct theory.' *Health Education Research 10,* 187–198.

Lysaker, P. and Lysaker, J. (2001) 'Psychosis and the Disintegration of Dialogical Self-structure: Problems Posed by Schizophrenia for the Maintenance of Dialogue.' *British Journal of Medical Psychology 74,* 23–33.

MacDonald, H. (1996) 'Mastering Uncertainty: mothering the child with asthma.' *Pediatric Nursing 22,* 1, 55–59.

MacLean, B. (1993) 'Music Debate Continues.' [Letter] *Journal of Gerontology Nursing 19,* 2, 5–6.

Madanes, C. (1981) *Strategic Family Therapy.* San Francisco: Jossey Bass.

Madigan, R. and Munro, M. (1996) '"House Beautiful": Style and consumption in the home.' *Sociology 30,* 41–57.

Magaletta, P. and Duckro, P. (1996) 'Prayer in the medical encounter.' *Journal of Religion and Health 35,* 3, 203–209.

Magill, L. (2001) 'The Use of Music Therapy to Address the Suffering in Advanced Cancer Pain.' *Journal of Palliative Care 17,* 3, 1567–1572.

Magill, L. (2002) 'Music Therapy and Spirituality.' *Music Therapy Today (online),* December, http://www.musictherapyworld.net

Magill, L., Chung, M. and Kennedy, F. (2000) 'Music Therapy in Palliative Care: Regaining control.' *Journal of Palliative Care 16,* 3, 92.

Magill Levreault, L. (1993) 'Music Therapy in Pain and Symptom Management.' *Journal of Palliative Care 9,* 4, 42–48.

Mandel, S. (1993) 'The Role of the Music Therapist on the Hospice/Palliative Care Team.' *Journal of Palliative Care 9,* 4, 37–39.

Mango, C. (1992) 'Emma: Art Therapy Illustrating Personal and Universal Images of Loss.' *Omega Journal of Death and Dying 25,* 4, 259–269.

Mankowski, E. and Rappaport, J. (2000) 'Narrative Concepts and Analysis in Spiritually-based Communities.' *Journal of Community Psychology 28*, 5, 479–493.

Marcus, P. (1982) 'Effects of Acupuncture in Bronchial Asthma.' [Letter] *Journal of the Royal Society of Medicine 75*, 8, 670.

Markides, K. (1983) 'Aging, religiosity, and adjustment: a longitudinal analysis.' *Journal of Gerontology 38*, 5, 621–625.

Marr, J. (1999) 'GIM at the End of Life: Case Studies in Palliative Care.' *Journal of the Association for Music and Imagery 6*, 34–54.

Marsham, R. (1990) 'Sufi orders.' In I. Shah (eds) *Sufi thought and action*. pp.112–122. London: Octagon Press.

Martin, E. (1996) 'The Society of Flows and the Flows of Culture.' *Critique of Anthropology 16*, 1, 49–56.

Mathew, R., Georgi, J., Wilson, W. and Mathew, V. (1996) 'A retrospective study of the concept of spirituality as understood by recovering individuals.' *Journal of Substance Abuse Treatment 13*, 1, 67–73.

Mayberry, R. and Jacques, J. (2000) 'Gesture production during stuttered speech: insights into the nature of gesture-speech integration.' In D. McNeill (eds) *Language and Gesture*. pp.199–214. Cambridge: Cambridge University Press.

Mazaux, J.M. and Richer, E. (1998) 'Rehabilitation after traumatic brain injury in adults.' *Disability and Rehabilitation 20*, 12, 435–447.

McCarthy, K. (1984) 'Early alcoholism treatment: the Emmanuel Movement and Richard Peabody.' *Journal for the Study of Alcohol 45(1)*, 59–74.

McCauley, K. (1996) 'Music Therapy with Pediatric AIDS Patients.' In M.A. Froehlich (ed) *Music Therapy with Hospitalized Children*. Cherry Hill, NJ: Jeffrey Books.

McCullough, M. (1995) 'Prayer and health: Conceptual issues, research view, and rseearch agenda.' *Journal of Psychology and Theology 25*, 1, 15–29.

McMillan, S. and Weitzner, M. (1998) 'Quality of life in cancer patients – Use of a revised hospice index.' *Cancer Practice 6*, 5, 282–288.

McRobbie, A. (1996) 'All the World's a Stage, Screen or Magazine: When culture is the logic of late capitalism.' *Media, Culture and Society 18*, 335–342.

Mechanic, D. (1968) *Medical Sociology*. New York: The Free Press.

Mechanic, D. (1974) 'Social Structure and Personal Adaptation: Some neglected dimensions.' In G.V. Coelho, D. Hamburg and J.E. Adams (eds) *Coping and Adaptation*. New York: Basic Books.

Mechanic, D. (1986) 'The Concept of Illness Behaviour: Culture, situation and personal disposition.' *Psychological Medicine 16*, 1–7.

Meillier, L., Lund, A. and Kok, G. (1996) 'Reactions to Health Education among Men.' *Health Education Research 11*, 107–115.

Merton, T. (1996) *A Search for Solitude: Pursuing the Monk's True Life*. L. Cunningham. New York: Harper Collins.

Milburn, K. (1996) 'The Importance of lay Theorising for Health Promotion Research and Practice.' *Health Promotion International 11*, 41–46.

Miller, R. (1998) 'Epistemology and Psychotherapy Data: The unspeakable, unbearable, horrible truth.' *Clinical Psychology: Science and Practice 5*, 2, 242–250.

Miller, W. (1998) 'Researching the spiritual dimensions of alcohol and other drug problems.' *Addiction 93*, 7, 979–990.

Millman, B. (1977) 'Acupuncture: Context and critique.' *Annual Review of Medicine 28*, 223–234.

Montelpare, W. and Kanters, M. (1994) 'Symptom Reporting, Perceived Health and Leisure Pursuits.' *Health Values 18*, 34–40.

Mramor, K. (2001) 'Music Therapy with Persons who are Indigent and Terminally Ill.' *Journal of Palliative Care 17*, 3, 182–187.

Munro, S. (1984) *Music Therapy in Palliative/Hospice Care*. Saint Louis, MO: MMB.

Munro, S. and Mount, B. (1978) 'Music Therapy in Palliative Care.' *Canadian Medical Association Journal 119*, 9, 1029–1034.

Murrant, G., Rykov, M., Amonite, D. and Loynd, M. (2000) 'Creativity and Self-care for Caregivers.' *Journal of Palliative Care 16*, 2, 44–49.

Nagai Jacobson, M. and Burkhardt, M. (1989) 'Spirituality: cornerstone of holistic nursing practice.' *Holistic Nursing Practitioner 3*, 3, 18–26.

Nakagami, Y. (1997) [Hospice Program and Palliative Medicine.] *Gan To Kagaku Ryoho 24*, 7, 792–799.

Narayanasamy, A. (1999) 'A review of spirituality as applied to nursing.' *International Journal of Nursing Studies 36*, 117–125.

Nattinger, A., Gottlieb, M., Veum, J., Yahnke, D. and Goodwin, J. (1992) 'Geographic Variation in the Use of Breast-conserving Treatment for Breast Cancer.' *New England Journal of Medicine 326*, 1102–1107.

Neugebauer, L. (1999) 'Music Therapy with HIV and AIDS Patients.' In D. Aldridge (ed) *Music Therapy in Palliative Care: New voices.* London: Jessica Kingsley Publishers.

Neumann, R. and Strack, F. (2000) '"Mood contagion". The automatic transfer of mood between persons.' *Journal of Personality and Social Psychology 79*, 2, 211–223.

NFSH (1999) *National Federation of Spiritual Healers Code of Conduct.* The Director, NFSH: Sunbury on Thames, Middlesex TW16 6RG, England.

Nguyen, M., Otis, J. and Potvin, L. (1996) 'Determinants of Intention to Adopt a Low-fat Diet in Men 30 to 60 Years Old: Implications for health promotion.' *American Journal of Health Promotion 10*, 201–207.

Nicholson, K. (2001) 'Weaving a Circle: A relaxation program using imagery and music.' *Journal of Palliative Care 17*, 3, 173–176.

O'Brien, T. (1992) 'Global Surveillance of Antibiotic Resistance.' *The Lancet 326*, 339–340.

O'Callaghan, C. (1996a) 'Lyrical Themes in Songs Written by Palliative Care Patients.' *Journal of Music Therapy 33*, 2, 74–92.

O'Callaghan, C.C. (1996b) 'Pain, Music Creativity and Music Therapy in Palliative Care.' *American Journal of Hospice and Palliative Care 13*, 2, 43–49.

O'Callaghan, C. (2001) 'Bringing Music to Life: A study of music therapy and palliative care experiences in a cancer hospital.' *Journal of Palliative Care 17*, 3, 155–160.

O'Kelly, J. (2002) 'Music Therapy in Palliative Care: Current perspectives. *International Journal of Palliative Nursing 8*, 3, 131–136.

Olofsson, A. (1995) 'The Value of Integrating Music Therapy and Expressive Art Therapy in Working with Cancer Patients.' In C. Lee (eds) *Lonely Waters: Proceedings of the International Conference of Music Therapy in Palliative Care.* Oxford: Sobell House Publications.

Orange, J., VanGennep, K., Miller, L. and Johnson, A. (1998) 'Resolution of communication breakdown in dementia of the Alzheimer's type: A longitudinal study.' *Journal of Applied Communication Research 26*, 1, 120–138.

Park, K. (1998) 'The religious construction of sanctuary provision in two congregations.' *Sociological Spectrum 18*, 393–421.

Parsons, T. (1951) *The Social System.* New York: The Free Press.

Patel, V., Gwanzura, F., Simunyu, E., Lloyd, K. and Mann, A. (1995) 'The Phenomenology and Explanatory Models of Common Mental Disorder: A study in primary care in Harare, Zimbabwe.' *Psychological Medicine 25*, 6, 1191–1199.

Pearce, W.B. and Cronen, V.E. (1980) *'Communication, Action and Meaning': The Creation of Social Realities.* New York: Praeger Scientific.

Penzer, V. (1985) 'Acupressure in Dental Practice: Magic at the tips of your fingers.' *Journal of the Massachusetts Dental Society 34*, 2, 71–75.

Peteet, J. (1993) 'A closer look at the role of a spiritual approach in addictions treatment.' *Journal of Substance Abuse Treatment 10*, 3, 263–267.

Peteet, J., Stomper, P., Ross, D., Cotton, V., Truesdell, P. and Moczynski, W. (1992) 'Emotional support for patients with cancer who are undergoing CT: semistructured interviews of patients at a cancer institute'. *Radiology 182*, 1, 99–102.

Petterson, M. (2001) 'Music for Healing: The creative arts program at the Ireland Cancer Center.' *Alternative Therapies in Health and Medicine 7*, 1, 88–89.

Pfaff, V., Smith, K. and Gowan, D. (1989) 'The Effects of Music-assisted Relaxation on the Distress of Pediatric Cancer Patients Undergoing Bone Marrow Aspirations.' *Children's Health Care 18*, 4, 232–236.

Pietroni, P. (1984) 'Holistic Medicine: New map, old territory.' *The British Journal of Holistic Medicine 1*, 3–13.

Pietroni, P. (1986) *Holistic living.* London: Dent.

Pietroni, P. and Aldridge, D. (1987) 'Summary of Discussion on BMA Report.' *Holistic Medicine 2*, 95–102.

Pinell, P. (1996) 'Modern Medicine and the Civilising Process.' *Sociology of Health and Illness 18*, 1–16.

Popay, J. and Williams, G. (1996) 'Public Health Research and Lay Knowledge.' *Social Science and Medicine 42*, 5, 759–768.

Porchet-Munro, S. (1988) 'Music Therapy in Support of Cancer Patients.' *Recent Results Cancer Research 108*, 289–294.

Porchet-Munro, S. (1993) 'Music Therapy Perspectives in Palliative Care Education.' *Journal of Palliative Care 9*, 4, 39–42.

Porter, R. (1986) 'Psychotherapy Research: Physiological measures and intrapsychic events.' *Journal of the Royal Society of Medicine 76*, 257–261.

Potts, R. (1996) 'Spirituality and the Experience of Cancer in an African-American Community: Implications for psychosocial oncology.' *Journal of Psychosocial Oncology 14*, 1, 1–19.

Powles, T. and Smith, I. (1992) 'Adjuvant Treatment in Breast Cancer.' [letter] *The Lancet. 339*, 423.

Pringle, M. (1984) 'A Minority Interest: Why?' *British Medical Journal 289*, 163–164.

Prywes, M. (1983) 'The Beer Sheva Experience: Integration of medical care and medical education.' *Israel Journal of Medical Sciences 19*, 775–779.

Pullman, D. (2002) 'Human Dignity and the Ethics and Aesthetics of Pain and Suffering.' *Theoretical Medicine 23*, 75–94.

Rabinow, P. (1986) *The Foucault Reader.* London: Penguin.

Radley, A. and Billig, M. (1996) 'Accounts of Health and Illness: Dilemmas and representations.' *Sociology of Health and Illness 18*, 220–240.

Ragneskog, H. and Kihlgren, M. (1997) 'Music and other strategies to improve the care of agitated patients with dementia – Interviews with experienced staff.' *Scandanavian Journal of Caring Sciences 11*, 3, 176–182.

Rasmussen, S. (1996) 'Matters of Taste: Food, eating, and reflections on "The Body Politic" in Tuareg society.' *Journal of Anthropological Research 52*, 61–83.

Reason, P. and Rowan, J. (1981) *Human Inquiry.* Chichester: John Wiley.

Rebuck, A. (1985) 'The Outpatient Management of Asthma.' *Annals of Allergy 55*, 3, 507–510.

Reed, P. (1987) 'Spirituality and well-being in terminally ill hospitalized adults.' *Research in Nursing and Health 10*, 5, 335–344.

Reizenstein, P. (1992) 'Treating Early Breast Cancer.' [Letter] *The Lancet 339*, 676.

Reuther, I. (1997) Qigong Yangsheng als komplementäre Therapie bei Asthma: eine Pilotstudie. Doctoral dissertation, University of Witten Herdecke.

Reuther, I. and Aldridge, D. (1998) 'Qigong Yangsheng as a Complementary Therapy in the Management of Asthma: A single case approach.' *The Journal of Alternative and Complementary Medicine 4*, 2, 173–183.

Ribble, D. (1989) 'Psychosocial support groups for people with HIV infection and AIDS.' *Holistic Nursing Practice 3*, 4, 52–62.

Richards, T. and Folkman, S. (1997) 'Spiritual aspects of loss at the time of a partner's death from AIDS.' *Death Studies 21*, 6, 527–552.

Richardson, A. (1992) 'Studies Exploring Self-care for the Person Coping with Cancer Treatment: A review.' *International Journal of Nursing Studies 29*, 2, 191–204.

Rier, D. (2000) 'The Missing Voice of the Critically Ill: A medical sociologist's first-person account.' *Sociology, Health and Illness 22*, 1, 68–93.

Robb, S. (2000) 'The Effect of Therapeutic Music Interventions on the Behavior of Hospitalized Children in Isolation: Developing a contextual support model of music therapy.' *Journal of Music Therapy 37*, 118–146.

Robertson, I., Manly, T., Andrade, J., Baddeley, B. and Yiend, J. (1997) '"Oops!": Performance correlates of everyday attentional failures in traumatic brain injured and normal subjects.' *Neuropsychologia 35*, 6, 747–758.

Roche, J. (1989) 'Spirituality and the ALS patient.' *Rehabilitation Nurse 14*, 3, 139–141.

Rose, A. (1984) 'Chronic Illness in General Practice.' *Family Practice 1*, 162–167.

Rosenthal, R., Wang, K. and Norman, P. (1975) 'All that is Asthma Does not Wheeze.' *New England Journal of Medicine 292*, 7, 372.

Rosner, F. (1975) 'The efficacy of prayer: scientific versus religious evidence.' *Journal of Religion and Health 14*, 294–298.

Rostom, A. and Gershuny, A. (1992) 'Adjuvant Treatment in Breast Cancer.' [Letter] *The Lancet 339*, 424.

Rukholm, E., Bailey, P., Coutu-Wakulczyk, G. and Bailey, W. (1991) 'Needs and anxiety levels in relatives of intensive care unit patients.' *Journal of Advanced Nursing 16*, 8, 920–928.

Rustoen, T. and Hanestad, B. (1998) 'Nursing intervention to increase hope in cancer patients.' *Journal of Clinical Nursing 7*, 1, 19–27.

Rykov, M. (2001) 'Facing the Music: Speculations on the dark side of the moon.' *Journal of Palliative Care 17*, 3, 133–134.

Rykov, M. and Salmon, D. (1998) 'Bibliography for Music Therapy in Palliative Care, 1963–1997.' *American Journal of Hospice and Palliative Care 15*, 3, 174–180.

Rykov, M. and Salmon, D. (2001) 'Moments Musicaux.' *Journal of Palliative Care 17*, 3, 133–134.

Salmon, D. (1993) 'Music and Emotion in Palliative Care.' *Journal of Palliative Care 9*, 4, 48–52.

Salmon, D. (2001) 'Music Therapy as a Psychospiritual Process in Palliative Care.' *Journal of Palliative Care 17*, 3, 142–146.

Sander Wint, S., Eshelman, D., Steele, J. and Guzzetta, C. (2002) 'Effects of Distraction using Virtual Reality Glasses during Lumbar Punctures in Adolescents with Cancer.' *Oncology Nursing Forum 29*, 1, 8–15.

Sands, R. (1990) 'Ethnographic Research: A qualitative research approach to study of the interdisciplinary team.' *Social Work Health Care 15*, 1, 115–129.

Santiago-Irizarry,V. (1996) 'Culture as Cure.' *Cultural Anthropology 11*, 1, 3–24.

Saudia, T., Kinney, M., Brown, K. and Young, W. (1991) 'Health locus of control and helpfulness of prayer.' *Heart Lung 20*, 1, 60–65.

Savage, L. and Canody, C. (1999) 'Life with a Left Ventricular Assist Device: The patient's perspective.' *American Journal of Critical Care 8*, 5, 340–343.

Schroeder-Sheker, T. (1994) 'Music for the Dying: A personal account of the new field of music thanatology – history, theories, and clinical narratives.' *Holistic Nursing Practice 12*, 1, 83–99.

Schwab, J.J. and Schwab, M.E. (1978) *Sociocultural Roots of Mental Illness.* New York: Plenum Medical Book Company.

Schwalbe, M. (1993) 'Goffman Against Postmodernism: Emotion and the reality of the self.' *Symbolic Interaction 16*, 333–350.

Seibert, P., Fee, L., Basom, J. and Zimmerman, C. (2000) 'Music and the brain: The impact of music on an oboist's fight for recovery.' *Brain Injury 14*, 3, 295–302.

Shah, I. (1969) *Wisdom of the idiots.* London: Octagon Press.

Shah, I. (1983) *Learning how to learn.* London: Octagon Press.

Shah, I. (1990) *Sufi thought and action.* London: Octagon Press.

Shah, I. (1991) *World Tales.* London: Octagon Press.

Shao, J. and Ding, Y. (1985) 'Clinical Observation of 111 Cases of Asthma Treated by Acupuncture and Moxibustion.' *Journal of Traditional Chinese Medicine 5*, 1, 23–25.

Shatin, L. (1980) 'Music Therapy in Palliative Care.' *Canadian Medical Association Journal 122*, 878.

Sheldon, J. (1998) 'Using Music to Soothe your Clients.' *Nursing 28*, 12, 6-8 Home Health: 64hh8.

Small, C. (1998) *Musicking. The meanings of performing and listening.* Hanover, USA: Wesleyan University Press.

Smith, S. (2000) 'Performing the (sound)world.' *Environment and Planning D: Society and Space 18*, 615–637.

Smithells, R., Sheppard, S., Schorah, C., Seller, M., Nevin, N., Harris, R., Read, A. and Fielding, D. (1980) 'Possible Prevention of Neural-tube Defects by Periconceptional Vitamin Supplements.' *The Lancet 1*, 339–340.

Smolin, D. (1995) 'Praying for Baby Rena: Religious liberty, medical futility, and miracles.' *Seton Hall Law Review 25*, 3, 960–996.

Soeken, K. and Carson, V. (1987) 'Responding to the spiritual needs of the chronically ill.' *Nursing Clinics of North America 22(3)*, 603–611.

Solfin, J. (1984) 'Mental healing.' In S. Krippner (eds) *Advances in Parapsychological Research.* 31–63. Jefferson,N.C: McFarland and Co.

Sommer, A. (1992) 'Vitamin A Deficiency and Childhood Mortality.' *The Lancet, 339*, 864.

Sowell, R. and Misener, T. (1997) 'Decisions to have a baby by HIV-infected women.' *Western Journal of Nursing Research 19*, 1, 56–70.

Spencer, J., Davidson, H. and White, V. (1997) 'Helping Clients Develop Hopes for the Future.' *American Journal of Occupational Therapy 51*, 3, 191–198.

Spickard, J. (1994) 'Body, Nature and Culture in Spiritual Healing.' in Johannessen, H., Olesen, S., Anderson, J. *Studies in Alternative Therapy 2*, 65-81. Odense: Odense University Press.

Spitzer, W.O., Dobson, A.J., Hall, J., Chesterman, E., Levi, J., Shepherd, R., Battista, R.N. and Catchlove, B.R. (1981) 'Measuring the Quality of Life of Cancer Patients.' *Journal of Chronic Diseases 34*, 585–597.

Standley, J. (1995) 'Music as a Therapeutic Intervention in Medical and Dental Settings.' In R. West (ed) *Art and Science of Music Therapy.* Chur: Harwood Academic Publishers.

Stephens, R.J., Hopwood, P., Girling, D.J. and Machin, D. (1997) 'Randomized trials with quality of life endpoints: Are doctors' ratings of patients' physical symptoms interchangeable with patients' self-ratings?' *Quality of Life Research 6*, 3, 225–236.

Starrett, G. (1995) 'The Hexis of Interpretation: Islam and the body in the Egyptian popular school.' *American Ethnologist 22*, 953–969.

Steidle-Röder, M. (1993) 'Possibilities and Limitations of Music Therapy with a Cancer Patient: "I couldn't live without music."' *Musiktherapeutische Umschau 14*, 2, 142–157.

Stein, H. (1988) 'Uncomfortable Knowledge: An ethnographic clinical training model.' *Family Systems Medicine 6*, 1, 117–126.

Stevens, M., Dalla Pozza, L., Cavalletto, B., Cooper, M. and Kilham, H. (1994) 'Pain and Symptom Control in Paediatric Palliative Care.' *Cancer Surveys 31*, 21, 211–231.

Stokols, D., Allen, J. and Bellingham, R. (1996) 'The Social Ecology of Health Promotion: Implications for research and practice.' *American Journal of Health Promotion 10*, 4, 247–251.

Storr, A. (1992) *Music and the mind.* New York: The Free Press.

Strauss, A. and Corbin, J. (1990) *Basics of Qualitative Research: Grounded Theory Procedures and Techniques.* Newbury Park, CA: Sage.

Stravynski, A. and O'Connor, K. (1995) 'Understanding and Managing Abnormal Behavior: The need for a clinical science.' *The Journal of Psychology 129*, 605–620.

Suarez, M., Raffaelli, M. and OLeary, A. (1996) 'Use of folk healing practices by HIV-infected Hispanics living in the United States.' *AIDS Care 8*, 6, 683–690.

Sukkar, M. (1986) 'Curriculum Development: A strategy for change.' *Medical Education 20*, 4, 301–306.

Sutton, T. and Murphy, S. (1989) 'Stressors and patterns of coping in renal transplant patients.' *Nursing Research 38*, 1, 46–49.

Svenaeus, F. (2000) 'Hermeneutics of clinical practice: The question of textuality.' *Theoretical Medicine and Bioethics 21*, 2, 171–189.

Tabboni, S. (2001) 'The idea of social time in Norbert Elias.' *Time and Society 10*, 1, 5–27.

Takishima, T., Moe, S., Tamura, G., Ishihara, T. and Watanabe, K. (1982) 'The Bronchodilating Effect of Acupuncture in Patients with Acute Asthma.' *Annals of Allergy 48*,144–149.

Tashkin, D.P., Bresler, D.E., Kroenig, R.J., Kerschner, H., Katz, R.L. and Coulson, A. (1977) 'Comparison of Real and Simulated Acupuncture and Isoprotenerol in Metacholine-induced Asthma.' *Annals of Allergy 39*, 6, 379–387.

Tashkin, D.P., Kroenig, R.J., Bresler, D.E., Simmons, M., Coulson, A.H. and Kerschnar, H. (1985) 'A Control Trial of Real and Simulated Acupuncture in the Management of Chronic Asthma.' *Journal of Allergy and Clinical Immunology 76*, 6, 855–864.

Taylor, R. and Chatters, L. (1991) 'Nonorganizational religious participation among elderly black adults.' *Journal of Gerontology 46*, 2.

Thaut, M. and McIntosh, G. (1999) 'Music therapy in mobility training with the elderly: a review of current research.' *Care Management Journal 1*, 1, 71–74.

The Lancet (1992a) 'Adjuvant Systemic Treatment for Early Breast Cancer.' [Editorial] *The Lancet 339*, 27.

The Lancet (1992b) 'Chemoprophylaxis for Infective Endocarditis: Faith, hope and charity challenged.' [Editorial] *The Lancet 339*, 525–526.

The Lancet (1992c) 'Warm Heart Surgery.' [Editorial] *The Lancet 339*, 841.

Thomas, D., Heitman, R. and Alexander, T. (1997) 'The effects of music on bathing cooperation for residents with dementia.' *Journal of Music Therapy 34*, 4, 246–259.

Thornton, H. 1992. 'Breast Cancer Trials: A patient's viewpoint.' *The Lancet 339*, 44–45.

Tinsley, H. and Eldredge, B. (1995) 'Psychological Benefits of Leisure Participation: A taxonomy of leisure activities based on their need-gratifying properties.' *Journal of Counselling Psychology 42*, 123–132.

Tobia, D., Shamos, E., Harper, D., Walch, S and Currie, J. (1999) 'The Benefits of Group Music at the 1996 Music Weekend for Women with Cancer.' *Journal of Cancer Education 14*, 2, 115–119.

Tosteson, D. (1990) 'New Pathways in General Medical Education.' *The New England Journal of Medicine 322*, 4, 234–238.

Tournier, P. (1981) *Creative suffering.* London: SCM Press.

Touw-Otten, F. and Spreeuwenberg, C. (1985) 'Multi-disciplinary Research Between Natural and Social Sciences in General Medical Practice.' *Family Practice 2*, 42–45.

Træen, B. (1995) 'Life Style Patterns Among Urban Café Guests in Norway.' *Addiction Research 3*, 123–134.

Trethewey, A. (1997) 'Resistance, Identity, and Empowerment: A postmodern feminist analysis of clients in a human service organization.' *Communication Monograph 64*, 4, 281–301.

Tröhler, U. (1988) 'The History of Therapeutic Evaluation.' In J. Watt *Talking Health.* London: Royal Society of Medicine.

Tsouyopoulos, N. (1984) 'German Philosophy and the Rise of Modern Clinical Medicine.' *Theoretical Medicine 5*, 345–347.

Turnbull, J. (1989) 'What is Normative Versus Criterion-referenced Assessment?' *Medical Teacher 11*, 2, 145–150.

Turner, T. (1995) 'Social Body and Embodied Subject: Bodiliness, subjectivity, and sociality among the Kayapo.' *Cultural Anthropologist 10*, 143–170.

Underwood, P., Gray, D. and Winkler, R. (1985) 'Cutting Open Newton's Apple to Find the Cause of Gravity: A reply to Julian Tudor Hart on the future of general practice.' *British Medical Journal 291*, 1322–1324.

Urba, W. and Longo, D. (1992) 'Hodgkin's Disease.' *The New England Journal of Medicine 326*, 678–687.

Vågerö, D. (1994) 'Equity and Efficiency in Health Reform. A European view.' *Social Science and Medicine 39*, 1203–1210.

VandeCreek, L., Rogers, E. and Lester, J. (1999) Use of alternative therapies among breast cancer out patients compared with the general population. *Alternative Therapies 5*, 1, 71–76.

van der Geest, S. (1994) 'Christ as a Pharmacist: Medical symbols in German devotion.' *Social Science and Medicine 39*, 727–732.

van Manen, M. (1998) 'Modalities of Body Experience in Illness and Health.' *Qualitative Health Research 8*, 1, 7–24.

Varela, F. (1979) *Principles of Biological Autonomy.* New York: North Holland Press.

Verma, R. and Keswani, N. (1974) 'The Physiological Concepts of Unani Medicine.' In N. Keswani (ed) *The Science of Medicine and Physiological Concepts in Ancient and Medieval India.* New Dehli: All-India Institute of Medical Sciences.

Vickers, A. and Cassileth, B. (2001) 'Unconventional Therapies for Cancer and Cancer-related Symptoms.' *Lancet Oncology 2*, 4, 226–232.

Vink, A. (2000) 'The problem of agitation in elderly people and the potential benefit of music therapy.' In D. Aldridge (eds) *Music therapy in dementia care.* 102–118. London: Jessica Kingsley Publishers.

Volicer, L., Harper, D., Manning, B., Goldstein, R. and Satlin, A. (2001) 'Sundowning and circadian rhythms in Alzheimer's disease.' *American Journal of Psychiatry 158*, 5, 704–711.

Voss, R., Douville, V., Little Soldier, A. and Twiss, G. (1999) 'Tribal and Shamanic-based Social Work Practice: A Lakota perspective.' *Social Work 44*, 3, 228–241.

Walden, E. (2001) 'The Effects of Group Music Therapy on Mood States and Concentration in Adult Oncology Patients.' *Journal of Music Therapy 38*, 3, 212–238.

Wallulis, J. (1994) 'The Complexity of Bodily Feeling.' *Human Studies 37*, 373–380.

Warde, A. (1994) 'Consumption, Identity-Formation and Uncertainty.' *Sociology 28*, 877–898.

Warner-Robbins, C. and Christiana, N. (1989) 'The spiritual needs of persons with AIDS.' *Family and Community Health 12*, 2, 43–51.

Warren, R. (1992) 'The Patient's View of Breast Cancer Trials.' [Letter] *The Lancet 339*, 315.

Watt, D. and Verma, .S (1998) 'Wellness Programs: A review of the evidence.' *Canadian Medical Association Journal 158*, 2, 224–230.

Watts, G. (1992) 'Treating Early Breast Cancer.' [Letter] *The Lancet 339*, 675–676.

Watzlawick, P. (1984) *The Invented Reality.* New York: W.W. Norton and Co.

Weaver, T. (1985) 'Acupressure: An overview of theory and application.' *Nurse Practitioner 10*, 8, 38–42.

Webber, G. (1990) 'Patient Education: A review of the issues.' *Medical Care 28*, 11, 1089–1103.

Weber, S. (1999) 'Music: A means of comfort.' In D. Aldridge (ed) *Music therapy in palliative care: New voices.* London: Jessica Kingsley Publishers.

Weber, S., Nuessler, V. and Wilmanns, W. (1997) 'A Pilot Study on the Influence of Receptive Music Listening on Cancer Patients During Chemotherapy.' *International Journal of Arts Medicine 5*, 2, 27–35.

Weinstein, M. (1974) 'Allocation of Subjects in Medical Experiments.' *New England Journal of Medicine 291*, 1278–1285.

Wenglert, L. and Rosén, A-S. (1995) 'Optimism, Self-esteem, Mood and Subjective Health.' *Personal and Individual Difference 18*, 653–661.

West, T.M. (1994) 'Psychological issues in hospice music therapy. Special Issue: Psychiatric music therapy.' *Music Therapy Perspectives 12*, 2, 117–124.

WHO (1988) 'The Edinburgh Declaration.' *Medical Education 22*, 481.

WHO (1990) 'Cancer Pain Relief and Palliative Care.' In Committee (ed) *WHO Technical Report Series 804.* Geneva: World Health Organization.

WHO (1998) *Cancer Pain Relief and Palliative Care in Children.* Geneva: World Health Organization.

Wilkin, D. (1986) 'Outcomes Research in General Practice.' *Journal of the Royal College of General Practitioners, Jan*, 4–5.

Wirth, D. (1995) 'The significance of belief and expectancy within the spiritual healing encounter.' *Social Science and Medicine 41*, 2, 249–260.

Wirth, D., Chang, R., Eidelman, W. and Paxton, J. (1996) 'Haematological indicators of complementary healing intervention.' *Complementary Therapies in Medicine 4*, 14–20.

Wirth, D. and Cram, J. (1997) 'Multisite surface electromyography and complementary healing intervention: A comparative analysis.' *The Journal of Alternative and Complementary Medicine 3*, 4, 493–502.

Wirth, D., Richardson, J. and Eidelman, W. (1996) 'Wound healing and complementary therapies: A review.' *The Journal of Alternative and Complementary Medicine 2*, 4, 493–502.

Wood, C. (1989) 'The Physical Nature of Energy in the Human Organism.' *Holistic Medicine 4*, 63–66.

Xie, Z., Wang, G., Yin, Z., Liao, S., Lin, J., Yu, Z. and Liu, G. (2001) 'Effect of Music Therapy and Inner Image Relaxation on Quality of Life in Cancer Patients Receiving Chemotherapy.' *Chinese Mental Health Journal 15*, 3, 176–178.

Yu, D. and Lee, S. (1976) 'Effect of Acupuncture on Bronchial Asthma.' *Clinical Science and Molecular Medicine 51*, 503–509.

Zaza, C., Sellick, S., Willan, A., Reyno, L. and Browman, G. (1999) 'Health Care Professionals' Familiarity with Non-pharmacological Strategies for Managing Cancer Pain.' *Psychooncology 8*, 2, 99–111.

Zborowski, M. (1952) 'Cultural Components in Responses to Pain.' *Journal of Social Issues 4*, 16–30.

Zigmond, D. (1987) 'Three types of encounter in the healing arts: Dialogue, dialectic, and didacticism.' *Holistic Medicine 2*, 69–81.

Zimmerman, L., Pozehl, B., Duncan, K. and Schmitz, R. (1989) 'Effects of music in patients who had chronic cancer pain.' *Western Journal of Nursing Research 11*, 3, 298–309.

Zola, I. (1966) 'Culture and symptoms: an analysis of patients' presenting complaints.' *American Sociological Review 31*, 615–629

Subject index

Aalborg University 180, 195
abandonment 89
abortion 54
academia and medical research 8–10
academic strategy 56
acupuncture 12, 27, 49–50
    clinical assessment of, for
        asthma 49–53
    clinical evaluations 51–2
    discussion on 52–3
    massage 52
administrative costs 193
aesthetics
    and individual in practice of
        medical research 61–72
    and medicine 15, 16, 34
African-Americans, cancer
    experiences of 138
AIDS see HIV/AIDS
alcoholism 115
allergies 20
alternative medicine 10, 13, 39, 41
amnesia 90
analgesics 30
anthropology, medical 18
antibiotics 77
anxiety 89
anxiolytic effect of music 97
Apollonian mode of knowing 48
artificial nutrition 54
arts
    and medicine 14, 61
    and science 70
art therapy 61
    criticisms of research 64
    trials 67
Aryuvedic medicine
assessment of competence 58
asthma 12, 50–1, 81
    chronic, Qigong Yangsheng
        for managing 159–60
    measuring improvement
        161–2
    study 160–2
    clinical assessment of
        acupuncture for 49–53
    clinical evaluations 51–2
    clinically controlled trials
        of asthma 51
    therapy 51
Australia 99

beginning and endings 22
bereavement 93, 97
Beveridge Report 15
'Blind Ones and the Matter of the
    Elephant, The' 118–19
body work 37
breast cancer 76, 79, 81, 98
breath
    beginning and ending 150–52
    energy and 151–2

in healing 149–62
reaching out ion 152–3
rhythm and consciousness
    166–7
Bristol Cancer Help Centre 100
British Medical Association 13, 15
Byrd's study on healing effect of
    prayer 122–3

Canada 96
cancer 9, 78, 107
    chronic pain and music 99
    in families, community
        approach to 84–95
    holistic treatment 17
    music therapy and 96–106
        case vignette 103–5
        pain management and
            hospice care 97–101
        psychosocial interventions 73
        and relief and comfort 91
        studies 75, 98
caregivers need care 126–7
changes in personal and family
    coping 88
charismatic ideology
    medicines as 38–40
    and praxis aesthetic 33–48
chemoprophylaxis 77
chemotherapy 99
ch'i 49
children
    acupuncture massage for
        asthma relief 52
    with cancer 101
Chinese medicine 42, 110, 152, 160
Chinese political thinking 36
cholesterol and coronary disease 36
Christianity 85, 110, 117, 122, 152
chronic bronchial asthma see asthma
chronic complaints and recalcitrance
    124–5
chronic disease 54, 76
chthonian mode of knowing 48
Church 9, 10, 117
    community 92
    and lay healing 10
cigarette smoking, young people and
    46
circadian rhythms 49
clinical assessment of acupuncture
    for asthma 49–53
clinical research
    guidelines 180–96
        admininistration of study
            190–1
        analysis of results
            190–1
        timetable of study 191
    aims of study 183–4
    background to study
        184–6
    costing of project 193–4
    design of study 186–90
        choice of data 188–9
        data   collection
            189–90

selection of subjects
    186–7
treatment variables
    190
do you have time to do
    this? 181–2
ethical considerations 192
for whom are you doing
    this study? 182
how are you going to pay
    for this research? 181
personnel 194
pilot studies 186
purpose of enquiry 182
submitting research 194
timetable of research
    events 196
why are you doing this
    anyway? 180–1
individual patient and limits of
    randomized controlled
    trials 73–83
    vs clinical validity 74–5
clinical trials 14
    of asthma 51
    controlled, challenges to
        orthodoxy of 77–8
    transcendental understanding
        of 107–19
coherent self, suffering and loss of
    116–17
cold, catching
    in context of marriage and
        family 20
    objectification of 19
    politics of 23
    process of 22
coma patients 15
    music therapy with 156–8
comfort and relief 90–2
coming into being 71
communication 170–1
community
    approach to cancer in families
        84–95
    first contact 85–6
    health 38
competence, assessment of 58
complementary medicine 10
computing costs 193
confusion 90
consciousness 71
    rhythm and breath 166–7
constitutive rules 23–4, 27, 29
contract learning 57
controlled clinical trials, challenges
    to orthodoxy of 77–8
co-ordination of support 93–4
coping, changes in personal and
    family 88
costing of project 193–4
criterion-referenced testing 58
critical junctures 87
Crypt Project 11, 12–13
cultural context
    of clinical care 31
    of definition of health 40–4
culture and symptoms 24